AN INCREDIBLE JOURNEY

FROM A MUD

John L Shabaya

Rosalind,

Glad our paths crossed between Ely & Addenbrooke's. Thanks for showing interest in my story. Enjoy

John Shabaya

10th May 2023

AN INCREDIBLE JOURNEY

ISBN 978-1-71668-821-8
2020
HEARING OTHERS' VOICES
Balestier Press
Singapore and London
www.balestier.com

Foreword. Edwin Panford-Quainoo 9

Acknowledgements 13

Preface 14

Charter One: The Beginning 19

Chapter Two: Realisation 24

Chapter Three: Growing Up in Kenya: Early Years 31

Chapter Four : Colonial Kenya 41

Chapter Five: Fond Childhood Memories 47

Chapter Six: Beloved Illiterate Parents 58

Chapter Seven: Post Independent Kenya 70

Chapter Eight: Family Impact 74

Chapter Nine: Passion for Education 80

Chapter Ten: Which School 93

Chapter Eleven: The Greatest Blunder 102

Chapter Twelve: The Day of Reckoning. 111

Chapter Thirteen: What next. 119

Chapter Fourteen: On My Own, Where Next? 130

Chapter Fifteen: The Rock Bottom. 142

Chapter Sixteen: Greater Promotion. 153

Chapter Seventeen: The Higher Call. 158

Chapter Eighteen: What Did I Study? 169

Chapter Nineteen: At Limuru 176

Chapter Twenty: In the High Grounds. 188

Chapter Twenty-One: The Urban Jungle. 200

Chapter Twenty-Two: Look Elsewhere 205

Chapter Twenty-Three: The Cambridge Attraction. 212

Chapter Twenty-Four: Why Cambridge? 219
Chapter Twenty-Five: Money To Cambridge 225
Chapter Twenty-Six: At Cambridge 233
Chapter Twenty-Seven: Does Teaching Matter? 240
Chapter Twenty-Eight: The Pedagogy 247
Chapter Twenty-Nine: Teaching in England. 256
Chapter Thirty: Anecdotes 263
Chapter Thirty-One: What Are My Interests? 278
Chapter Thirty-Two: Taxi 288

Chapter Thirty-Three: Not Tired. 299
Chapter Thirty-Four: Atsinafa Education Centre 303
Chapter Thirty-Five: A Pastor and A Preacher. 316
Chapter Thirty-Six: Lost and Found 323
Chapter Thirty-Seven: Where I Have Been 328
Chapter Thirty-Eight: Different Paths, Separate Ways 341
Chapter Thirty-Nine: The End 347

More things you might like. 353
Questions for discussion, reflection or action 354
"Hearing Others' Voices" 356
Join us! 360

DEDICATION

In loving memory of my mother,
Atsinafa Muhadia Shabaya
and
My dear Auntie Ezina Sambili

Foreword

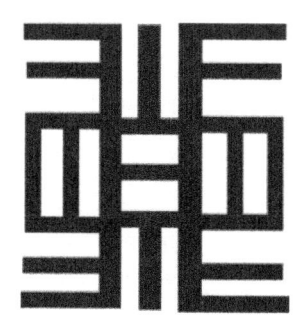

Nea onnim no sua a, ohu (Ghanian)

"He who does not know can know from learning"

Every life is bound to have people with whom the crossing of paths has such profound influence. For me, John Shabaya, 'Uncle John' as I would fondly call him, or Dad when I am speaking to his daughters, has been one of those extraordinary, unique people.

In our culture, everyone older, an elder, is either an Uncle, Auntie, Mum or Dad. You do so to convey respect and humility. My initial contact with 'Uncle John' was in the early 90s when I first moved to Cambridge from Ghana. Back then I was closer to his younger brother, Patrick Shabaya. Due to our friendship, I would see 'Uncle John' on a regular basis and share stories.

Each time spent in his company, was like another layer of the 'onion,' peeled and revealed. I have always been in awe of what he has achieved, the richness, the diversity of the life he has lived and continues to live.

I absolutely love the fascinating stories, and the real moments of triumph. So, you can imagine my joy when he informed me, he was writing about his life story. That day was certainly a day to celebrate, because, finally the stories that I and so many others have heard, as you will find out when you read this book, were irrevocably being written to be treasured eternally.

Of course, there are also moments where the stories were not all of celebrations, but I guess that is life and certainly adds to the richness of it all. 'Uncle John' has been a great source of encouragement when needed most. He has been a mentor, a proof-reader to a lot of the documents I have written.

With his teaching background, 'Uncle John' always has this ability of getting you to understand and look at things in the most profound way. That, I imagine has come from his personal experiences of the peaks and troughs of life.

The taxi business was without a doubt a big part of his more recent life. I recall the day he told me he had driven The Malala Family and he had been in their home, the way he said it with such calmness whereas I, on the other hand, was just ecstatic! Hearing these stories made me more excited to hear the next instalment whenever we spoke over the phone or met face-to-face.

As you read this story you will realise, like I have, that he has a certain tenacity that is undeniably admirable and if you spend time in his company long enough, you will come to acknowledge that this tenacity is certainly infectious! I have really learnt a lot from him, and I deeply appreciate our time together and the conversations we have had over the years.

I want to welcome you to an incredible life story: "An Incredible Journey."

Edwin Panford-Quainoo MRPharmS PFPH CPhOGH Fellow

ACKNOWLEDGEMENTS

Special thanks to Berin and Daniel Krenek for being friends with exceedingly great generosity, particularly for lending me a laptop, to write this story. Thanks too to Rehema my daughter and Edwin for the last-minute rescue with a refurbished laptop, that has seen the completion of this book.

My sincere thanks to my daughters: Rose Shabaya, Rehema Shabaya and Sagina Koloko, who have walked along and beside me, sometimes ahead of me and encouraged me to write and complete this story.

Thanks too to my sons: Wycliffe Lisamula, Mike-Jo Wafula and Sean-Jo Shabaya, nick-named Jo-Jo, especially for their moral support, vital for sharing this story.

Finally, to my dear wife, Everlyne Shabaya, for her encouragement, and my friend Judith Wyss, to all those not mentioned, who walked beside me, to each one of you:

THANK YOU SO MUCH! ASANTE SANA! URIO MUNO!

JOHN L SHABAYA 2020

Preface

We are living in the digital era, the time when almost and everything happens instantly. There is significant reliance on technology, more virtual connections and relationships. We have digital books, content and dominance of social media with great impact on people's well-being.

Unbelievably, currently, even now, I constantly encounter some people, particularly young people who have no dreams at all, no passion for anything to pursue or intend to pursue instantly, incidentally, by the way or even gradually.

Bless you if you are one of those with a passion. Bless you even more if you are already committed to pursuing your passion.

Some people are simply waiting for some fortune to drop from somewhere, without any effort. A few folks are only daydreaming that one day, they will wake up and suddenly everything will be alright.

Moreover, some people are simply disillusioned with life and cannot just be bothered. Others find resilience and determination rather difficult. There are those who are, the 'I will do it,' without a set time, goals and concrete attempts to do it or towards doing it.

You may be one of them. You may be feeling as if you are at the crossroads, the intersection of your life. Your journey is at a halt. You may be wondering what to do next, what to do with yourself and your life. Maybe you do not know which path to take or even curve for your life.

If so, this book is for you. You will hear about another person's story, dilemma and passion. Hopefully, you will discover your own passion, commit yourself to your passion. I hope you will discover; it is not a must to be famous. Just endeavour to do your best, be honest with yourself and be successful at your passion or with your passion. But if you are already famous or become famous later, so be it, rejoice and celebrate.

For now, focus onto the path of pursuing your passion, rather than just sitting there and waiting for the instant success. Of course, for many people, instant success is rare and is not the only route or avenue to success or to one's destiny. Therefore, endeavour to discover your passion and follow it relentlessly. With your passion at hand, the will power inside you will kick in, you will normally be fired towards your destiny.

This book and its series, will help you to listen to others, hear others' voices, sift through and take at heart that which you can learn from, that which can inspire and encourage you. Most of all believe also in yourself. Then, pursue your passion, live out your own story.

We all stand in 'owe' of some sort, on our journey through life. So, have something you strongly believe in and have a passion for or, whatever it may be. That will underpin your pursuits and determination. That will fuel your impetus so that you certainly make it, amidst the ups and downs of life.

My passion was education, amidst other things. I committed and focused my energies on it. I have never ever regretted. The first huddle was to discover my passion or even create one, if necessary, as you will find out in my story.

The Incredible Journey is therefore a story about my passion, how I discovered my path, seized opportunities and even created opportunities, en route my destiny. How and where I got the strength and determination to carry on relentlessly and I am still carrying on. As my Portuguese speaking friends used to say, '*Aluta continua,*' the struggle continues.

My story reflects, outlines my struggles and joy. It celebrates how I discovered the will power inside me. It sketches how I subsequently walked on my pilgrimage, shoulder high, amidst several obstacles and challenges, how I walked on my life's journey towards my destiny.

I hope my story will be of some inspiration to you. However, if you already have a passion, a path you have already taken, for you, it will be an affirmation. Whatever it will be for you, let it be.

Aged 15 years, in 1966, a new chapter began in my life, on my Incredible Journey. I migrated from the village to Nairobi, after my failure of the basic Primary School Exams in Kenya.

Chapter One: The Beginning

                    Here I am
From rags to fine garbs.
From a mud hut to Cambridge.
From shacks to Cambridge
From Humble Beginnings
To an Incredible Journey.
This is the story of my life.

Hear the voice of a village boy.
Born of very deprived, poor parents.
Born of illiterate parents,
But I dreamed big dreams.
Hear my voice.
I loved, Wanted,
And longed to travel the world.
I failed my Primary School Exams,
Meant to catapult learners
to a great and bright future.
Meant to launch me,
into a pre-eminent and brilliant future.
Therefore Doomed!

I Constantly heard voices of failure.

The community around me,
My Primary School teachers,
kept telling me:
'You are a failure!
Do not dream young man!
Dreams don't always come true.'

They reiterated,
'Just like your father,
You will never make it!
You have failed to get your KEY
The key to life,
The opener of the future for learners
The opener of your dreams.

Your dreams are over.
Do not dream again!
Do not dream any-more!
You have no hope.
Your future is doomed.'
But I never, never, ever gave up.
I continued to dream,
To dream against all odds.
Here I am
A Cambridge University graduate, UK.
A High School teacher, UK.

Head of a Department,
A Subject Leader, UK.

Taught for over 19 years in UK.
I have been a clergy,
I have been an Officer,
Kenya Defence Forces,
Up to the rank of Major.
Travelled extensively,
All over the world.
Retired from teaching, UK,
But not tired.
Never really stopped
Working and volunteering.
I am a Charity Worker.
Founder Room2Excel
An Educational Charity.
Founder & Director:
Atsinafa Education Centre,
Western Kenya,
A legacy to my illiterate mother.
A Translator and Proof-reader.
A Cab, a Taxi Driver.
I endeavour to give back,
To the community.

Read and hear the voice of
Hope and determination.
Hear the voice of encouragement.
Read my dare to dream,
And dare to try story.

Read and hear:
How one can emerge:
From subsequent ashes,
From dust,
From failure to success.
From a remote village,
In Kenya to Cambridge, UK
From an illiterate home,
From a mud hut,
To Cambridge University.
How one can get the money,
To study at Cambridge University.

I am the boy,
Born in Ishanji Village,
Born in Western Kenya
Grew up in a mud hut.
And ended up in Cambridge University.
Yes, I am
JOHN LISAMULA SHABAYA.

23

An Incredible Journey,
Is the Story of My Life!

Chapter Two: Realisation

This book reflects my pilgrimage, a shared human experience. For me, I believe Life is a journey; each one of us is inevitably travelling along and is on a journey through life. This book epitomises some glimpses of shared life's experiences, life's pilgrimage, the journey that resonates with many other people's experiences, my experiences, your experiences.

Mostly this book focuses more on my journey to Cambridge, a realisation and a synopsis of unstoppable journey amidst immense obstacles, that made it, 'An Incredible Journey,' and worthwhile. Hence, there is a lot that may resonate with other people's experience, your own experience, my experience. If not, there is a lot to read; especially that which inspired me, inspires me still. I hope my experience, the shared human experience will help with the reflection on what inspires, or what one wants and chooses to inspire one's own life, your life, my life.

This book celebrates, and rightly so, what I could and can remember along this journey, my Incredible Journey. The contents of this is what was and has been the impetus, the driving force in my life and how I have gone through it all.

The book highlights the fact that, there are significant, shared struggles, experiences, etc., within the human existence. It also rightly, implicitly, sometimes, explicitly celebrates life. It shows, perhaps there is a plausibly prototype life, that may motivate others not to give up, when it gets **tough**, but endeavour to hold on, explore and discover the opportune time and potential opportunities.

'Where does one get inspiration, the inspiration to keep going.......? As for me, I got my greatest inspiration from my both deceased mother and grandmother. I spent a lot of time with these two ladies.

A lot of my precious time was spent with my grandmothers, but more so with grandma Shamola Sambili, my father's mother. Whenever my mother visited dad in Nairobi, Kenya, during term time, school time, I was left under the care of my grandma Shamola. I bonded with Grandma Shamola Sambili a great deal, that I named my first daughter after her.

Grandma Shamola (literally the crawling one), had a lot of gentle stamina and determination, often, coupled with very encouraging words of wisdom. Having fended for her own children, she aged gracefully. Even though she lived in my grandfather's shadow, in difficult times, she stood out. She was always a pillar and a shoulder to lean on. Whenever I was in trouble, particularly in times of great decision making, or when sinking in the troubled waters of life, grandma Shamola Sambili was there for me.

Accordingly, in her old age, she had grown into a wise lady, with a lot of wisdom and with surpassing encouragement. Of course, she had seen it all. As a young girl, and into her adult life, she had seen two world wars: WW1: 1914-1918 and WW2: 1939-1945. She also saw Kenya become a British Colony in 1920. Moreover, she had experienced and lived through several draughts, crop failure and hunger spells.

Grandma Shamola Sambili, had seen her husband's, my granddad's business, collapse in her face. She had witnessed several epidemics, that took lives of some of her beloved children. Indeed, she had seen it all and amazingly survived. As such, nothing could really shock her, or even shake her 'to the borne'. For that matter, she inspired many. She particularly, inspired me greatly, especially on my fateful day in 1966.

Who could compare themselves with Grandma Shamola Sambili? She even lost one of her own eyes, just in-front of her face. It just popped from its socket and that was it. Gracefully, she tried putting it back in the socket, but it was too late. It was gone. She became one eyed grandma and survived for over one hundred years, a century plus.

Her life really started, in what I would call her retirement, when her husband, my granddad died in 1965. From that time, she displayed a lot of determination, never seen before in her, and even never known to exist in her. The shadow she had lived under, was suddenly taken away, gone for good, gone forever. Henceforth, she was on her own. She grieved extensively, as if the whole world, her world had ended.

One day, she woke up, walked up towards grandpa's tombstone, went to grandpa's graveside, looked at the shoot, the new bud on the *mukumu tree* – the sycamore tree, traditionally planted by and on male elders' graveside, symbolising hope. For her, on that day, it was indeed a symbol of hope.

She just exclaimed, '*Gadushi yaho*,' literally, 'that's enough,' in other words, 'enough is enough.' From that moment and thereafter, her face beamed with hope and joy. She became a bold and unmovable self-reliant lady, self-driven, with a lot of business acumen, astuteness and shrewdness. She embarked on what I would call mini entrepreneurship.

Henceforth, she started selling bananas, all the way, from Ishanji Village, Kakamega County, Western Kenya to Eldoret in the Rift Valley Province, now Uasin Gishu County. Moreover, she contributed significantly to charity, through her local church and so forth. She was committed to whatever she put her hands on, always doing the best she could. Grandma Shamola has therefore been an indispensable inspiration in my life and now in my own retirement.

Three generations: my grandmother Shamola Sambili with her great granddaughter, her namesake, my eldest daughter Rose in Ishanji Village, Western Kenya at my grandmother's homestead with her banana plantation in the background in dry season.

One of my earlier greatest interests and dreams, was to be a journalist, a writer or an author. I loved telling stories, inherited from my grandmas and my parents, inspired by African oral tradition. I had hoped to collect some of my childhood stories, to share with kids through the local papers and magazines and later publish into a book. Therefore, the writing of my story is a dream come true, a realised ambition. Even though this is not a fictional story, it is a story, a real story, The Story of My Life.

The writing of my story has also been a long-term request by many with whom I happened to encounter and share my story, in most cases, just briefly, when travelling or just going about with my 'business.' I have turned the quest down severally. However, the final impetus and gentle push has been really by Prof Ruth Finnegan, who has become a dear friend. Without Prof Ruth Finnegan, the writing of this book, would not have been realised.

I also vividly recall, picking up The Vice-Chancellor of Cambridge University who was also a very Senior Officer at MRC. I do not know what MRC acronym really stands for. It could be Medical Research Council, or Medical Research Centre.

This encounter, to be specific, was approximately ten years ago, it was on 05 November 2010. We had a remarkably interesting conversation that I found inspirational. He kept asking me perceptive questions, particularly, about my life.

Finally, he asked me, 'What did you do before you became a Taxi Driver?' He continued to prod, 'Have you done any other job before, other than being a Taxi Driver? I wondered, and asked him politely, 'Sir, why are you asking, me such searching questions.' He replied, 'you speak and behave like 'an extra-ordinary' Taxi Driver.'

He further insisted, 'at least, tell me where you were educated.' Knowing who he was, with the pride of my achievements then, pride almost took over the best part of me. For once, I felt almost like regretting being a Part-time Taxi Driver, one year to my retirement from teaching.

In view of this and feeling rather ashamed, I did not want to 'let the cat out of the bag.' I hesitated to answer the question. However, as he sounded, genuine, sensitive to my feelings, and the agony I was going through, attempting to withhold my answer, it became more difficult for me to hesitate anymore, but to answer the question. I picked up courage and decided to 'let the cat out of the bag.'

'I am actually a graduate of Fitzwilliam College, Cambridge University and a secondary school teacher.' Taxiing and cabbing is my hobby,' I answered confidently. With no condemnation, he reciprocated with his own personal story.

His story was very fascinating, engrossing that I wished I could remember it verbatim. However, I can only remember that he came from a humble background, born of immigrant parents. Through his parents' hard work, his own hard work as well and various scholarships, he was catapulted to fame, and has been promoted to a variety of higher offices, including becoming the Vice-Chancellor of Cambridge University.

I graphically and vividly, recall his final and last words to me. Again, without condemning me for being a graduate, and driving a taxi/cab, he beckoned me: 'Write your story, it will be a good read. It will be an encouragement to many young people and grownups a like.'

Here it is, may it just do that; be an encouragement to many.

Chapter Three: Growing Up in Kenya: Early Years

Caretaker at Lavington United Church, Nairobi, Kenya, aged 19 years.

I am often asked, 'how was it like growing up in Kenya? Some of the people I encounter, especially the younger generation also enquire: 'do you have any recollection of your early years?'

The ensuing story is my recollections, mainly from my mother, father and my extended family.

On one dry sunny Wednesday, in the month of December, not even in a hut, but in a banana plantation, in a tiny rural Village, a long-awaited baby boy was born to incredibly grateful parents. On that day, there was great joy in Ishanji Village, a village in Western Kenya, near the border of Kenya and Uganda, close to Lake Victoria, a village not far from Latitude zero degrees - 0° : The great Equator, the imaginary line that divides the world almost into two halves: the North and South.

I was the long, awaited baby boy, born circa12 December 1951. I was named *Yohana* (Kiswahili for John), a variant of a Greek name *Ιωαννης Ioannes (Joannes)* with Hebrew etymology, meaning God is gracious or God has shown favour. My mother, being illiterate and excited, probably, distorted the local language or assumed *Yohana* and *Yahana* were synonyms. Of course, the two words are phonetically awfully close. '*Yahana*' literally means, He has given, God has bestowed or given graciously. My mum also reckons that my birth was foretold, by her church's prophet (foreseer), Isaya Kituyi. Even the name Yohana, my name John, was from the respective Prophet Isaya's prophetic dream and mouth.

My mother reckons that, before I was born, she had been without a child for a long time. In fact, in Luhya and most African cultures then, the birth of a child was the seal of a couple's marriage. Therefore, prior to my birth, mum and dad's marital status was incomplete and unsealed.

In fact, in most African cultures in those days, no child, meant no marriage! In addition, my mother told me that our Idakho clan, Maragoli clan, and Luhya tribe's culture then, stipulated that if a couple is married for over two years without a child, their marriage became null and void.

Therefore, in accordance with the Luhya culture and traditions of the time, if I had not been born then, born sooner than later, promptly born at the time and by the time I was born, my mother would have been divorced. According to my Mum, such a divorce would have been devastating. She loved my Dad and consequently, my Dad also loved her dearly.

However, my mother would have been affected more than my father. Divorce carried an eternal stigma for a woman, especially if one was divorced for being barren. The Idakho-Luhya culture dictated that a barren woman goes back to her parents.

My mother had already witnessed and empathised with that stigma. Ezina Sambili, her eldest sister had encountered a painful and devastating divorce for being barren. The ensuing divorce almost sunk her into a serious depression and alcohol dependence. Going back to her people, with the stigma of that magnitude: Being barren and divorced, would have been an exceedingly difficult journey for my mother to make. As a matter of fact, it would not have been a walk with ardours, great enthusiasm, but rather an arduous walk.

Consequently, I was born in the days when Luhya culture and most African cultures, marriage was mainly, to produce children. The African culture focused more on marriage as a guarantee of the survival and continuation of the clan, the community and the tribe at large, rather than romantic love between a couple. Most marriages were therefore arranged marriages, including my parents' marriage.

As a matter of fact, in Africa, the community was vital. There was no life outside the community. To be, was to be in the community and with the community. To be, was to belong to the community. Therefore, in accordance with the African philosophy, 'I am because we are.' The greatest and the most loathed punishment then, was to be ostracised from the community, your community.

You were properly initiated into the community from childhood. One endeavoured to stay within the expectations of the community, observing the various traditions, statutes, etc. You never attempted to go against the embedded oral statutes and culture, lest you be excommunicated, ostracised and thereafter, exterminated. Being excommunicated and ostracised from the community was greatly feared by all. It was an eternal death sentence.

Contrastingly, my father had more pressure. He was pressurised more by his family and community at large, to have a child. This was more so, because his elder brother, Uncle Thomas Lisimba had misfortunes. His wife had several miscarriages and premature deaths of most of their children.

Furthermore, my father's follower, Uncle Heyi Wa Malaya was not married then and had been conscripted into the British Army. My grandparents feared for my uncle's life while overseas, fighting for the British Empire. My father was hence, much more pressurised to have children of his own, to ensure the survival of the clan and continuity of the family tree, should my uncle, while fighting for the British Empire, Die in Action (DIA).

Thus, despite the inevitable infertility or barrenness for some people, young couples like my parents, were expected to be productive and multiply, no matter what.

Their off springs would warranty the sustainability of the clan, the tribe and the community.

The kids also provided the required labour, vital for the survival of the community, in the hostile environment from many aspects. That was the culture of generations preceding and surrounding my birth. Surprisingly, this is still a significant part of African philosophy and traditional culture, for many in Kenya, other African cultures and countries.

Being born circa 1951, within the decade that marked and sealed the end of World War Two (WW2), my uncle and many other young African men from my village, had been conscripted in the Kings African Rifles, to fight for the British Empire in World War Two. They had just returned from war, fighting in countries far and wide. They had fought for the British Empire and conquered.

My uncle and comrades, all had stories to tell. They often joked, 'the sun never sets in the British Empire.' Of course, the British Empire extended all over, and spanned the world: From East to West, a cross the entire globe, and even North to South. Britannia influenced and ruled most of the world.

Additionally, they also reminisced over stories of places where they had been, places far away and different from our village. They recounted what they had seen, their encounters, their travels and adventures, etc.

My uncle had seen so many high and snow peaked mountains, higher than our nearby hills, our Kimingini Hill, facing our village, across Yala River, located on the edge of Idakho, Isukha, and Tiriki Locations' triangle, in Kakamega County. The other nearest massive hills were the Great Nandi Escarpments, in the Luhya, Kalenjini and

Luo tribes' triangle, where Kakamega, Kisumu and Nandi Counties converge.

My uncle and his comrades had fond memories of the places they had been to. My uncle never ceased talking about these places, whenever he could. These places were populated with people of different cultures, colour and languages. Whenever he had an opportunity, he always reiterated to me that indeed there were other human beings, existing beyond our horizon! Some were so short; others were tall, slender built, while others were light skinned with 'woollen' hair, etc.

I longed for the day I will grow up, the day I will be able to travel outside my village, to confirm the stories of my uncle. I wanted to travel far, to see places far and wide. I wanted to meet people of these different cultures and backgrounds. I wanted to be wise. As Americans would say, I wanted to be 'smart' and learn languages different from mine.

As I continued to grow in stature, I dreamed of a day, I will encounter and learn from a 'different world,' a world beyond my village, yet inhabited by human beings. I wanted to confirm the existence of countries near and far. I wanted to confirm that my uncle's stories were not just made up bedtime stories, or just folklore, but real-life stories.

Naturally, my uncle and his comrades talked about the world beyond our village, being enormous. They acknowledged there were many, many more other places that they had never been to or seen, but just heard about.

I dreamed of joining the army, to experience what my uncle had encountered; see what my uncle and his comrades had seen, while in the army. I wanted to visit places my uncles and his comrades had been to, and visit other places they had talked about, but never seen, or ever been to. I wanted to find out if such places really existed. Those were my childhood dreams, probably my 'daydreams' as a child, in a mud hut in Western Kenya.

I can vividly remember my mother telling me, 'my son, stop daydreaming, there is no more World War Two (WW 2)'. She ingeminated: 'There is no more conscription into the British Army.' She reiterated, 'now, there is only Kenya Emergency (1952-1960): The Mau Mau Uprising.

In accordance with my mother, Mau Mau was the bloodiest post World War Two (WW2) encounter of Africans and the British. My mother never referred to it as war. For her, it was just a conflict between the British and Kenyans, the Mau Mau freedom fighters. For her, it was *'majensi'* – emergency declared by the British, to root out, the so-called Mau Mau Rebellion or Mau Mau Revolt.'

In view of this, my mother often reminded me, 'nowadays, coming from a village like ours, my son, the only way you can travel and see the world is through education.' She had heard of and known of a man from Vokoli Village in the neighbouring Maragoli Location, Vihiga County, who had pursued education.

Through education, Adagala went overseas and thus travelled far and wide. In fact, there was a saying in my mother's home Chamakanga Village: *Adagala, nu mulala kuvaduka ivulaya*, Adagala, is among the few (the ones) who have been overseas.

Growing up in Kenya in the 1950's and 1960's, was a scary and exciting time simultaneously. My mother often referred to my birth as the beginning of 'An Incredible Journey,' both for herself and for myself.

When I was born, I did not enjoy the luxuries of the essential maternity ward or hospital. In my home area, and most villages in Kenya, there were no hospitals, not even a makeshift Maternity Hospital in the vicinity. Most hospitals were European Missionary Hospitals, many miles far away at Mission Stations, like Kaimosi Mission Hospital, Friends Mission, Vihiga County; St Elizabeth Mukumu Mission Hospital, Roman Catholic Mission, Kakamega County; and Mwihila Mission Hospital, Church of God Mission, Kakamega County.

I was born and grew up in an era of exceedingly high death rate of women at birth and incredibly high child mortality in Kenya and Africa. For mothers and infants, it was an era of 'survival of the fittest' at birth, and then throughout motherhood and childhood.

My mother reckons that during my birth, she was just helped by the village traditional midwives, untrained medically. This was a common experience and practice in villages, with extremely high risks of health, safety hazards and even some great blunders.

Tetanus and many other tropical diseases like malaria were rampant. My mother used to tell me that my umbilical cord, was cut off by a very crude object. The crude object was usually used by several traditional midwives, on several other babies, who had preceded me at birth in Ishanji Village and the neighbouring villages.

It is indeed a miracle that I was not infected at birth. Even if I were infected, who knows? I was not tested or monitored by any medical team then. There were no Antenatal and Postnatal clinics. There were no vaccinations or immunisations as such. Comparatively, this is a more recent development or requirement in

Kenya. According to my mother, by the time I was born, there were none in my village or in the vicinity.

To have grown into an adult, I must have been born with great resilience. Most first-born babies of my time never made it beyond a few months after birth. Their demise just propped up the growing numbers, statistics and graphs of infant mortality in Kenya and Africa.

Indeed, there were a lot of wailing mothers for their dying babies in my village. Less baby survivors were a big threat for the continuation and survival of the tribe and the community. This therefore hit or touched the very core of the African existence. Children's survival into adulthood, was incredibly significant in the African context, philosophy and the core of its existence.

When I was born, my father was not anywhere near to be seen or even nearby. Even if he was nearby, the culture forbade him and all men to witness labour pangs and childbirth, or for that matter, delivery of a baby. That was a women's matter, especially elderly ladies business.

When I was born, my father had left the village. He was far away in Nairobi, the big city, now the capital city of Kenya, working as unskilled labourer fending for his family. Therefore, I began my 'Incredible Journey', without, the joy of being held in my dear father's arms. I there empathise with children born during 2020, corona virus pandemic (COVID-19) lock-down, with government stipulations of keeping social distance, no close contact, cuddles and hugs.

My father was entitled to two weeks leave or holiday per annum, which he rarely took. As his wages were meagre, in most cases, he forfeited his holiday or leave. He exchanged his holiday or leave in lieu of pay. This enabled my Father to earn at least two weeks double pay in a year to make ends meet and to support his family back home, in Western Kenya.

Chapter Four: Colonial Kenya

Subsistent farming, signs of progress and bright future for our family.

I was born at a time when European Explorers and the Christian Missionaries had perforated the hinterland of Kenya; followed by the White Settlers, Colonial Administrators, and Commercial Asians. As such, I am often asked: 'How was it like growing up in Colonial Kenya?'

By 1901, the railway line from Mombasa on the Indian Ocean, had passed Nairobi, Nakuru, transposed the so called 'White Highlands,' crossed the Rift Valley and reached Kisumu on Lake Victoria, on the Equator, Latitude 0°. This was indeed the hinterland of East Africa. It opened the interior for various 'invaders.'

On the religious front, the East African Revival (*Tukundereza* – Luganda language: Praise the Lord Group), a Christian Movement, was at its peak a cross the East African region: Kenya, Uganda and Tanganyika, now known as Tanzania. There was en masse conversion of upcountry Africans to Christianity and Western civilisation, with a significant onslaught of African culture. Islam was also deep rooting itself in the mainland Kenya. Likewise, other Asians had come with their religions like Hinduism, Buddhism and Sikhism, to name but a few, but with almost no African converts.

Likewise, on the commercial front, Asian commercial conquest of the interior of Kenya was gaining momentum. Most Asians had initially come to Kenya in about 1896, at the invitation of the British Empire, to provide labour for the building of the Kenya - Uganda Railway line from Mombasa to Kisumu.

Kenya was a pawn amid big powers. The East and Western Powers resolved to tear up Kenya like a carcass. It was thus torn by various predators; just like lions, hyenas, vultures, etc., each fought for and made haste to grab a big chunk and a massive piece.

The Missionaries, Sheikhs and other Religious Leaders, tore down the African Traditional Religion and culture. The White Settlers grabbed most of the land in the so called the 'White Highlands,' the fertile part of Kenya. The Asians took control of most of the commerce and trade in urban areas, market towns and places. Similarly, the White Imperial Administrators, seized more power and political control of Kenya, especially through the local African Chiefs.

Kenya was a British Colony – The British Kenya from 1920 – 1963. Ironically, I was born British. My grandparents and parents were British Subjects of the Kenya British Colony and Protectorate. In those days, as a subject of the British Empire, you were born British. Therefore, as my parents were British subjects, by default and birth, I was born British.

There was no need for documentary evidence unless you intended to travel overseas. As such, my parents never applied for or claimed their British Naturalisation Certificate or a British citizenship and passport for themselves or their family. Moreover, my parents and most Africans never bothered to register their births or acquire documentary evidence of their British citizenship.

Likewise, by the same default, I was stripped off my British nationality unceremoniously. Apparently, when Kenya became independent in 1963, and subsequently a republic in 1964, I lost my British nationality.

Seemingly, by independence time, to retain my British nationality, my parents were supposed to have opted to remain British citizens. They should have applied for

British passports and settlement in Kenya as British Citizens or immigrate to UK.

According to my parents, many Kenyan Africans in the rural villages even in cities like Nairobi, were never aware of this option or agreement between the British Empire and Kenya Government. This became apparent, when I tried to get my mother a Kenyan passport to visit me in UK.

The Kenya Government declined to issue my mother a passport due to her pre-independence date of birth. Conversely, Kenya Immigration Department reckoned that there were no subsequent records of my mother's birth in the Kenyan Registrar's Department or archives. I appealed against this decision. Unfortunately, she died before this was resolved and the chapter was closed.

As for me, I reclaimed my British nationality. I got it on 13 January 2000. Consequently, on the same day, I was naturalised British citizen. This was based on my over fourteen and a half (14.5) years residency in the United Kingdom (UK), rather than by default, based on my birth in the Kenya British Colony.

Prior to the Change of Constitution in Kenya in August 2010, the pre-2010 Kenyan Constitution forbade dual nationality or dual citizenship. Therefore, by the virtue of my acquiring British nationality and later acquiring a British passport, I lost my Kenyan nationality and citizenship.

I can recall, before independence, there was apparently a three-tier segregation system in Kenya. It was more apparent and distinct in urban areas, especially in the so-called '*White Highlands*', than in the Black African rural villages, far away from urban and White Settlers' area.

Sometimes, a four-tier system existed in some parts of Kenya, and especially in education.

As far as education was concerned, there were White Schools, Asian Schools and African Schools and Education, strictly in that order. It was more so, especially in terms of quality of education and resources. African Schools had extremely poor facilities and resources, therefore poor-quality education.

In addition, sometimes, some places, especially urban areas, had Arab or Muslims schools, categorised separately from their fellow Asians, based mainly on Islamic religious affiliation. Most areas in Kenya were also segregated, based on race or ethnicity, especially shops, buses and trains. This was also mainly, more distinct, in urban areas like Nairobi.

During my childhood, colonialism and the British rule in Kenya was at its peak. It was thus, the time when kaleidoscope of African culture was in collision with European, Western and Asian cultures. It was, a critical and significant period in Kenya's history, a time of great African education, to produce African clerks for the colonial administration. To the dismay of missionaries, most political activists, were products of the missionary schools, including Mzee Jomo Kenyatta himself, initially known as Johnstone Kamau, who later became the first president of independent Kenya.

I was born and grew up at a time of immense political awareness among Africans, a time for the rise of Kenya's liberators and freedom fighters. It was the era of the rise of Pan-Africanism, African Socialism, and African uprising against colonialism all over the African continent.

Looking back at this peak imperial colonial era, African resistance to colonialism and onslaught of African culture was inevitable. No wonder the fierce struggle for independence ensued, epitomised by the vicious Mau Mau resistance movement! Shaken and startled, the White Settlers, the British Empire and Colonial Government, viewed Mau Mau as a terrorist movement to be rooted out.

In retrospect, reflecting on my early life, growing up in Colonial Kenya, as a young African child, a few things stood out and some were very irritating. For example, we were not allowed to visit my father for more than one week in a whole calendar year.

However, on a few rare occasions, with the grace, grand and express permission of his employer, we would be allowed to stay with my father for about two weeks, but not exceeding three weeks. We were lucky if we managed to squat or hide and seek for one month. Such extended visits were generally exceedingly rare.

Nairobi was the hub of the British Empire in Kenya, and probably the whole of East African region. It was the headquarters of the Colonial British Empire in Kenya. It housed the home and office of the Governor, the Representative of His or Her Majesty the King or Queen of the United Kingdom (UK) and the Commonwealth of Nations. Consequently, Nairobi was the seat of power of The British Empire in Kenya and probably all-over East Africa.

Chapter Five: Fond Childhood Memories

Family Visit to my father in Nairobi City, Kenya. Frontline left to right: Shem, Ruth, my mother Atsinafa, Patrick in my father Charles Shabaya's arms, Agnes, Japheth and me standing elegantly at the back.

When my students attempted to side-track or endeavoured to distract me, they would often remark, 'most people have fond childhood memories.' They would laugh and say, 'we are making our fond childhood memories.' They would then ask me, 'Sir, what are your fond childhood memories?'

As for my early childhood fond memories, I can vividly remember, whenever we visited my father in Nairobi City, we travelled overnight on the 'nostalgic,' long train. As Africans, we travelled in third class coaches (wooden seats, no beds), not because the price was reasonable or affordable for my family, but mainly, just because we were Africans and black Kenyans.

The kids of my age called the long train, '*chuku chuku.*' Probably, this name was synonymous with its distinct character and the noise it made, travelling along the train tracks.

Indeed, like the snake's lateral undulation, it slithered and rattled, like a rattle snake. For this reason, the older generations referred to it as the 'iron snake', in Kiswahili '*Nyoka chuma,*' and in vernacular Luhya '*inzukha yi shibia.*'

From a child's perspective, it sounded and made '*chuku-chuku*' noise. The local kids, had a village kids' nursery rhyme for it: *Chinja kuku, tupa mbali, Chinja kuku, tupa mbali, Chinja kuku, tupa mbali,* literally, 'slaughter (kill) the chicken and throw it far away.'

In addition, it also spit fire, with extensive smoke. Its smoke could be seen miles and miles away, yonder in the sky; no wonder in Kiswahili, the train is called '*Gari la moshi:*' Literally Smokey vehicle or Smokey train.

The 'Smokey train' was unlike the current, fast luxury diesel engine train, Nairobi – Mombasa Standard Gauge Railway (SGR). Those were the days of the slow steam engine train, nicknamed the *'iron snake.'*

It puffed, negotiated, navigated, and traversed the plains and hills, into the hinterland, en route Nairobi. It rolled, undulating on the flat Lake Basin, through the Kano Plains, near Lake Victoria, named after Queen Victoria of the United Kingdom (1837-1901).

Up and down, the train went across the vast Rift Valley, up the escarpments, into the White Highlands. In between, it had an extensive stopover at Nakuru Station, in the Rift Valley, on the shores of Lake Nakuru, the haven of flamingo birds, an extra-ordinary tourist attraction, a must to see, especially for bird lovers. Thereafter, early in the morning, greeted by an awesome tropical sun rise, the *'chuku-chuku'* train, romped down, down into Nairobi, the Green City in the Sun (the popular nickname of Nairobi then).

The train was ever too slow; it always rocked me to sleep. As a child, I enjoyed looking at trees and objects outside, as the train went majestically, pass by, as if waving 'bye, bye.' Apparently, the objects outside appeared to move towards me and then majestically went by, past the train as if they specifically waved goodbye and wished me well, and a safe journey, to my respective destination.

I was always, mesmerised with this experience and wondered, 'how come trees, houses and other objects, move so fast, past the train or vehicles I was in?' Trains and auto-mobiles, vehicles, fascinated and hypnotised me. I longed to drive and steer such machines on their path, with or without passengers.

While in and on the train, seeing moving objects, especially the *'chuku chuku'* train, I wanted to stay awake, to witness, behold and lay eyes on the great contrasting scenery: The low land Lake Basin, the rising hills, the escarpments over the Rift Valley, the great, mighty and awesome Rift Valley itself, with its extensive beauty, and the highlands above it.

I wanted to glimpse the apparently moving trees, moving houses, other objects, etc. It was fascinating to spot the various scenic contrasts and places of great interest, en route to or from my father in Nairobi, the big city - the Green City in the Sun.

Apparently, the train puffed, winded, swayed, jolted, panted and rocked. Its sound was like lullaby to me, it rocked me to sleep. I could not manage to stay awake, open my eyes for a long time, even if I tried hard, whenever I tried harder to stay awake, it was all in vain, just futile attempts. All I wanted, seemed to be, doze off, and sleep....

Intermittently, I was occasionally rudely awakened by the blasting sound and horn of the train, hooting relentlessly and whistling fiercely, more like an angry lion roaring, requesting for its path to be cleared, so that it romps into, enter the next station.

At other times, it was a warning of its great majestic, eminent, pronounced approach to and at unguarded level crossings. It hooted like a roaring lion, in the plains of Masai Mara National Park. It whistled off motorists, warned anybody else in its path, by its loud, scary whistle, to keep off, as if they were fireflies, endeavouring to cross its path. If any children were playing nearby, it especially honked louder to scare the 'poor kids,' to keep off the path of the mighty one or else.....

Furthermore, the journey from Kisumu to Nairobi and vice versa, was mainly an overnight trip. We started off in the evening and arrived next day, incredibly early in the morning, most of the time at sunrise. Similarly, the journey was mainly in darkness, except for the dull light on the train.

That nostalgic train from Kisumu on Lake Victoria to Nairobi in the plains, in the highlands and the capital city, took over fourteen hours. Mathematically, the train covered about 215 miles (342 kilometres). Probably, the train travelled at an average speed of about 15 miles per hour (approximately 24 kilometres per hour).

Its persistence and unyielding negotiations of numerous corners, contours, meandering, climbing steep hills, roaring, rolling downwards and upwards bluntly, towards its destiny, with unstoppable determination were amazing. Retrospectively, this epitomised my own unstoppable determination, on the Incredible Journey of my life, towards my destiny.

I remember, the first class on that train was reserved for Whites only, with comfortable, cushioned seats and sleeper beds, attached to a dining car for dinner and breakfast. Second class was reserved for Asians, with better seats. The second-class passengers shared sleeper seats cum-beds and enjoyed facilities of a dining car.

The third class was always congested. In most cases, it was fully packed to the doors. Some passengers waiting patiently on the en route stations platforms, climbed through the windows to embark on the train, as the doors were sealed, locked by the sheer congestion of passengers.

Third class seats were just wooden benches, with nowhere for third class black passengers to lay their heads. There was no dinning car, except a kiosk. Most third-class passengers carried their own 'packed picnic' (food).

I loved the sound of the gong, the 'ding, dong' bell. The sound of the 'ding, dong' bell was the call to dinner and breakfast for upper class passengers and their respective coaches. Dinner was served in the so-called dining car. I only heard the 'ding, dong' sound and bell, whenever we were lucky enough to sit and board the third class coach, adjacent and near the upper class coaches, when goods and luggage coaches were not inserted in between.

Conversely, on most journeys, third class passengers were shielded off from having a glimpse of the upper-class opulence. Just in case third class passengers, may accidentally trespass into the upper classes' coaches, which would really have never, ever happened, however, a goods coach would be slotted in-between.

Thus, Upper Classes and Third-Class coaches, were distinctly separated from third classes coaches. Upper classes were thus sound and safe from their third class accompaniments and adversaries or would be apparent intruders. In fact, third class coaches were numerous and formed the bulk of the train, yet they were ever full, packed to the brim.

I yearned for the day I will be liberated and privileged to ride on the upper-class coaches. I always said to myself, 'what a joy it will be?' I also imagined and thought, 'What an elevation it will be?'

Unfortunately, I was a black African child, and as such, this was not going to be, or even happen soon and by then, it was not meant to be. Regrettably, black Africans including their children, were condemned to third class coaches, never to ride in the upper classes' coaches, for no other reason, except for the colour of their skin.

Each category, race or ethnic group used a different boarding gate. Third class passengers were constantly reminded; 'trespassing to the Whites only - the first class and Asians only - second class gates, region, platform and on the train itself, was prohibited!'

Any African or Black person caught, venturing into the upper class or accidentally striding in the upper classes area, would be arrested, prosecuted, and severely flogged. Finally, such trespassers would be jailed, then repatriated to their respective villages or home area. They were then banned from travelling to the city, outside their village and domicile.

Whenever we got to Nairobi, we always took a double decker bus to my father's ramshackle and residence in the Whites only suburbs of Nairobi. My father was accommodated in a secluded Servants Quarter (SQ) in the backyard, in a squashed shack and a tiny house.

Africans working for the whites as house helpers, gardeners, servants, etc., were called 'boys' or 'girls.' For example, the term 'house boy' or 'house girl' referred to all domestic workers, irrespective of their age. Whether they were over eighteen years old and even mature adults like my father, they were just 'boys' and if ladies, just 'girls.'

As such, they could live in shacks in their bosses' backyard and compound, but in a segregated, fenced off and hedged off area. Moreover, Blacks could not use the title Mr. or Mrs. For example, my father's documents, read Charles Shabaya s/o Malaya, s/o stood for 'son of,' while my mother was Atsinafa w/o Shabaya, w/o in full 'wife of.' All this changed at independence in 1963.

Like an active and excited child, I wanted to quickly get on the bus, grab the nearest seat, sit downstairs. However, I was always quickly shelved off by my mother, or if my mother was hesitant, struggling with our luggage and delayed to shelve me into my place, I was quickly shelved off, by the bus conductors and directed to the upstairs part of the bus, where I belonged.

The downstairs of buses, near the driver was reserved for Whites only, with comfortable and cushioned seats. Behind the Whites, at the back of the bus, near the entrance, was reserved for Asians only, also with better seats, though not as comfortable as the Whites only seats.

Upstairs deck on double decker buses, was the third-class deck. This was furnished with wooden, hard and uncomfortable benches. Just like the third class train furniture. Thus, it was reserved for Africans and Black Kenyans. Of course, in Kenya of those days, Asians were not regarded as blacks. Asians were in the class of their own - second class citizens, much more better off than Black Africans.

Whenever we were in Nairobi, we were often caught up, in what I recall as 'crossfire.' On several occasions, we were suspected and tormented by both the Colonial British Imperial Government and, and likewise by the Mau Mau Freedom Fighters.

Sometimes we got in real trouble with the Imperialists and Colonialists, for that matter. Apparently, they often suspected my parents to be supporting the Mau Mau, and vice versa. The Mau Mau also suspected anybody who worked for a *Mzungu*, plural *Wazungu*, (Kiswahili for Europeans and all the Whites), to be traitors.

As my father worked for the *Wazungu* (the Whites) as a house boy (colonial term for cook, chef, cleaner or house help, etc.), the Mau Mau used to come to our shack and house. They would of course harass us. They mainly came by night hours and occasionally daytime. Incidentally, they would come in our shack, be very friendly, and then they would request my father to replenish them with food and liquids, vital for their own survival and endurance of the struggle for independence.

While in Nairobi, we rarely finished a week without these constant encounters, interactions, harassments, and unwelcome interferences from either side. We were therefore caught up, 'the pawn,' in the middle of it all. As the saying goes, 'we could never win.'

As a child, I innocently, repeatedly and often asked my parents why the Whites and Mau Mau cannot sit under a tree or even at a table and talk to each other to resolve their differences. I often whispered a prayer, 'please God may this type of relationship end. Please God let it end soon before someone gets hurt!'

Truly I wanted the conflict to end, and end sooner than later! Little did I know so many people were already hurt and even so many were dead. Both the British Imperial Forces and the Mau Mau were vicious, and many lives were lost as a result. It is the civilians who really paid the higher price of extensive injuries and deaths. Referring to our dilemma, my father often said, 'when elephants fight, it's the grass that really suffers and hurts most'. My father had interesting idioms to home in, augment, and hammer the message home.

I remember one day, after I had said my prayer, my father looked at me with great bewilderment. He smiled as usual, but this time with a sarcastic smile, in a small still voice, whispered in my ear 'son, you don't know what you are praying about and praying for.' In the other ear, my mother complimented my dad and murmured: 'Son, wait until you grow up; then you will understand, then you will realise, we are up and against insurmountable force and great odds. Just be still! I pray that one day all this will come to pass.'

Since then, whenever I am in trouble or in any dilemma, I always pause.... Sometimes I can hear echoes of my late mother's small still voice and her clear words: 'son just be still and know.....' resonating with Psalm 46:10. Over the years, being illiterate, my mother had developed excellent oral tradition mnemonics. This helped her memorise, a lot of useful Biblical verses that nourished her faith.

However, unlike an Hafizi who memorises the whole Quran, she did not memorise the whole or entire Bible.

Being a woman of prayer, my mother also taught me how to pray at a tender age. In fact, she often celebrated my birth as an answered prayer. She often said that she had prayed for a child for a long time. She often told me, before I was born, my birth had been foreseen by one of the priests and prophets in her indigenous church, Prophet *Isaya Kituyi*.

Therefore, when I was born, a thanksgiving prayer was the first utterance on my mother's lips. Thus, at the beginning of my life, she whispered a benediction in my ear. Henceforth, she acknowledged God's graciousness and providence. She often reminded me that at about the age of four years old, I could say a little prayer. Later, I continued and horned in more prayer skills.

'It came to pass,' one day, sooner than later, just as my mother had prayed or even as my father had predicted, Kenya was 'free at last!' Ironically, the independence of Kenya was ushered in during my early years of age, in my adolescence. Reminiscing, I have always been so grateful the pre-independence unrest did not go on for so long or even forever.

Were my parents' prophets or future seers? I do not know, and I will never know. Did both parties, the Colonial Government and Mau Mau, hear my cry and my plea, my childish prayer, my mother's prayer as well? I am not certain!

However, retrospectively, I can just say, 'my cry, my voice, the voices of many young children, my childish prayer, and petitions, prayers of many people of Kenya then, praying, petitioning, crying, yearning for peace and freedom were heard.' By the end of 1963, Kenya was free at last!

Chapter Six: Beloved Illiterate Parents

The bullies in my basic primary school used to ridicule me about my parents. Their favourite so called joke, which was an insult to me was, 'you are just as thick as your illiterate parents.' For the bullies, my parents were just thick, illiterate and ignorant, hence, it hurt me so much.

As for me, they were 'my beloved parents.' Their illiteracy was apparently not just their ignorance or even their own fault, it was circumstantial. In view of this, as a child, while I regretted my parents' illiteracy, I wondered and often asked my parents, why on earth they were not educated as such.

My father was born in the 1930s. He was not born in an affluent city, but in the remote rural Ishanji Village, Idakho Location, Kakamega District, now Kakamega County, in Western Kenya. He was the third born of eight biological siblings and had a good number of step siblings.

My Grandfather was polygamous; he had more than three wives and several concubines. My father remembers vividly being told by his father (my grandfather) that with the coming of Europeans and Asians, the traditional African informal education will not suffice in the forthcoming challenging days and times, what he called, modern times.

In view of this, he insisted that education was a better option. 'White people's' education is vital,' he reiterated to my father. My grandfather, therefore beckoned my father: 'my son, you have to go to school.'

In view of this, my father was sent to the nearest Friends African Industrial Mission School, commonly known then by its acronym FAIM, later became Friends African

Mission (FAM). According to my father, Friends Mission had initially been set up at the neighbouring mission station at Lusui Village on the main Kakamega – Kisumu Road.

Thus, the initial school in our neighbourhood was set up by Quakers (Religious Society of Friends) from the United States of America (USA), ironically, not from UK. According to my grandfather, the school was meant to 'enlighten Africans' and 'civilise the villagers,' enable the African villagers to read the 'White-people's book: The 'Bible' and eventually be converted, not only to Christianity, but also to Western culture and civilisation.

Lusui was the home of Chief Shivachi, the paramount chief and ruler of Idakho clan and neighbouring clans and Locations. My grandfather reckoned that Lusui would have been the Quakers' Headquarter in Kenya. However, Chief Shivachi was suspicious of the Quakers' motives.

As such, Chief Shivachi did not want missionaries by his doorstep and for that matter, in his backyard. He eventually and cunningly condemned them to Kaimosi. This was a very remote place, on the border of Western Kenya and Rift Valley regions.

Kaimosi was in the Kakamega Equatorial Tropical Rain Forest. The Chief believed that the missionaries would not survive in the hostile Tropical Rain Forest, but perish and die there, one by one like fireflies.

Generations of my grandfather considered Kakamega Tropical Rain Forest uninhabitable. In fact, Kakamega Forest is among the very few surviving Tropical Rainforests in East Africa. It has an ever green, tranquil environment, with rare and unique bird species, a haven for bird lovers.

It also has a great diverse of animals, and beautiful tree species, with wonderful camping and tracking opportunity. I wonder why my people thought Missionaries would not survive in such a pleasant environment.

To Chief Shivachi and his subjects' dismay, Quakers did not vanquish in Kakamega Forest. Surprisingly, they did not just survive, but Quakers thrived at Kaimosi. In 1902, Quakers set up a Mission Station at Kaimosi.

Later a formal school, was established. In fact, apart from the Mission School set up in 1846 at Rabai, Kilifi County, near Mombasa, Kaimosi was among the oldest formal schools in Kenya, together with Prince of Wales, now Nairobi School. Quakers also set up a Vocational Training Centre, later, a Secondary or High School, a Teacher Training College, a Hospital and a Theological/Bible College.

Towards the end of World War Two (WW2), in 1944, the British Colonial Government in Kenya set up The Beecher Commission to design the African Education Curriculum. As a result, most African education was delegated to the Christian Missionary Schools, sponsored and managed by Missionaries from Europe, Canada and United States of America (USA), etc.

Apart from a few African District Education Board (DEB) schools that rebelled and were thus secular, all African schools were sponsored by Missionaries. Therefore, they had a Christian connotation and subsequent affiliation. These schools were supposed to convert, mould and produce superb African clerks for the Colonial Government.

The Rev Leonard James Beecher, an Anglican clergy sent by Church Missionary Society (CMS) from England, was appointed Chairman of the respective 1944 African Education Commission; hence, called The Beecher Commission. It was a milestone in the development of African education in Kenya.

CMS, that sponsored Beecher, was founded by the famous Clapham Sect, London UK. Original CMS founders in 1799 included Cambridge University Church of England clergyman Charles Simeon and William Wilberforce from Cambridgeshire, a vehement opponent of Slave Trade.

The same CMS Missionary Rev Beecher later became Canon and the Arch Deacon of Mombasa (1945). He was consecrated Bishop (1950) and became diocesan Bishop of Mombasa (1953). Subsequently, he became the first Anglican Archbishop of the Church of the Province of East Africa, including Kenya and Tanganyika, later Tanzania (1960-1970), to spearhead the autonomy of the Anglican Church from the CMS - Church of England.

Before independence, The Kenya Education system adopted a four-tier system: The White schools, Asian schools (mainly Indians), Islamic schools (mainly Arabs) and African schools (Black Africans), run by White Missionaries for Africans. However, as noted earlier, there were a few rebels who set up African District Education Board (DEB) schools that were for Black Africans and secular in nature.

Thus, African education was mainly supposed to enable Africans to read the Bible, liturgy, hymn books and consequently produce African Christian converts, equipped to work as clerks for the Colonial British Government. The local African administration was delegated to African Chiefs and Village Elders.

My father's education was curtailed, as African education was based on adherence and affiliation to a Christian Mission and denomination. In most cases African education was a missionary evangelistic tool, used for subsequent conversion of Africans to Christianity. In most Kenyan languages, no wonder, Christians were known as 'Readers' or 'Learners'. For example, in Western Kenya, in Kiluhya language Christians were called *Vasomi (Basomi)* – readers, learners.

Furthermore, according to my father, education was not totally free. Apart from adherence, Mission schools charged some form of fee as well, probably towards the running costs. You were excluded from school if you were not sponsored or could not afford to pay the set fee.

Some learners were lucky, especially children of chiefs and potential adherents. Such lucky learners were sponsored by the missionaries, but my father was not that lucky, for that matter, he was not among the lucky ones.

To avoid competition and duplication, in accordance with the 1910 Protestant World Missionary Conference, at Edinburgh, Scotland, Kenya was divided into 'spheres of influence,' or 'spheres of work.' Each Protestant Missionary Movement was allocated a certain area to evangelise, which was adhered to until independence in 1963 and subsequent Republic in 1964.

As a result, most Protestants predominantly belonged to one tribe or even one clan. For example, you could not find a Methodist Christian in Western Kenya. Methodists were allocated areas around the coast and Meru, on the slopes of Mt Kenya.

The positive ecumenical 'spheres of influence' apparently had negative tribal connotations, religious tribalism, or even segregation. This later developed into economic, manpower and leadership 'tribalism', as most early leaders were products of missionary movements and endeavours.

This became more obvious after independence and it is still 'a real thorn in the flesh' in Kenya, for many Kenyans and even the government itself. It is peculiarly exemplified more regarding the distribution of wealth nationwide and political leadership. It sometimes evokes great emotions and animosity within the Kenyan Nation.

It is embodied, resonates and is emotionally capitalised on by some politicians, more so during the National elections. During this period, the country experiences a spate of tribal clashes and violence. The Protestant churches themselves, particularly as regards to leadership, are not also exempted from squabbles. Sometimes, church squabbles are very bitter squabbles, resulting in legal wrangles and subsequent schisms, especially in Western Kenya, with remarkably high conglomerations of Protestant churches.

My father's parents (my grandparents) were not converts to Quaker Faith, predominant in Western Kenya, as a result of 'Spheres of Influence.' Likewise, he adhered to no other Christian Mission. Indeed, there was no hope of my grandfather converting to Quaker Faith.

My grandfather was a shrewd small-scale businessman, trading in hides skin, with Arabs from Kisumu on Lake Victoria and Kakamega town. He did not want to jeopardise his means of earning a living by converting to Christianity.

My grandfather's Arab Muslim clients had no business or dealings with Christians. Furthermore, for them, although Christians were *watu wa kitabu,* people of the book, especially the scriptures, however, non-muslims Africans and Christians were all regarded as *kafiri*, heathen and pagans.

I never dared to ask my grandfather, but always wondered why my grandfather never converted to Christianity or even Islam. He died a staunch adherent of African Traditional Religion, hence the traditional *mukumu* – sycamore tree was planted on his graveside.

Nevertheless, both my grandmothers were Christian converts. My father's mother was a member of an African Indigenous Church. She belonged to a rebellious African charismatic Church, opposed to the missionary type of Christianity and onslaught of African culture.

My grandmother's church was a schism, from Quaker Mission in 1927, known as African Church of the Holy Spirit (ACHS). It was nicknamed in Kiluhya language *Vahushi*: The Separate Ones, The Set Aside.

ACHS, was noted for its red cross, a cross symbol on members clothing, property, etc. My grandma's Church was permeated with African culture and resonated with the Old Testament part of the Bible. For example, their clergy were known as high priests, priest, prophets and seers, respectively.

My grandma's church loathed Quaker silent and meditation type of worship. Most African indigenous worship was more spontaneous and charismatic. With such exuberant worship, punctuated by dance and drums and occasional trance, Quakers and most western missionaries viewed African traditional worship and dance as erotic.

For that matter African dance and drums were condemned as evil, hence sinful, it should be discouraged and routed out completely. In fact, Christian conversion meant denouncing anything and everything African, even one's African name and taking up a new Western name. Thus, conversion, literally meant becoming a new creature, a new creation and a new person.

The indigenous churches deep-rooted Christianity into African 'soil'. African culture and Charisma were embedded in its worship. No wonder indigenous churches were vehemently opposed to Missionary westernisation and onslaught of African culture. As an onslaught of African traditional education and culture, Christianity was viewed with great suspicion.

Western formal Education pioneered by Missionaries was therefore also viewed with great suspicion by many adherents of indigenous church in my village. Overall, many Africans viewed Christianity and formal education as a colonial tool of oppression and westernisation, opposed to and against anything African. The famous Kikuyu saying, summed it up nicely: *'Gutiri Muthungu na Mubea,'* there is no difference between a white colonialist and a missionary or priest.

Despite the apparent conflict of interest, arrogantly and in defiance, my father joined formal school at Lusui Mission Station aged about thirteen years. He enjoyed Arithmetic and Literacy classes, especially writing in the dust, sand, or just on the ground. Learners were not issued with exercise books, until after significant time of schooling, at least more than six months of schooling.

According to my father, most of his classrooms were of dusty floors or makeshift open-air classrooms, some were taught under the canopy of a tree. Early Years of learning up to about three years of schooling were mainly in Vernacular, for that matter, Kiluhya language for schools in Western Kenya, my home region. During the rainy season, most teaching and learning was in the morning before the down pour of tropical rains or storms in the late afternoon.

In view of my father's interest in education and great passion for education and his height, as a tall lad, he was recommended to move to the Upper Primary Mission School, in the neighbouring village. This was in a different neighbourhood and clan where he thought he will excel more easily. It was at Bugina in Maragoli Location, now in Vihiga County.

Coming from Idakho Location and going to a school at Bugina in Maragoli Location, now in Vihiga County, was his best option and hope. However, he was soon identified and labelled as a 'an outsider,' on two fronts: A child of a non-member - a non-adherent learner, and an intruder from another clan. He was soon excluded, mainly based on non-conversion, adherence, to Quaker faith and lack of school fees, rather than an intruder from a non - Maragoli clan.

Just when my father was settling into his formal education, his father's (my grandfather's) business with Arabs collapsed. He therefore could not afford paying the required school fees for my father, a prerequisite for children of non-adherents. With great disappointment and humility, my father humbly bowed out and accepted the fate that befell him.

My grandfather's inability to pay school fees for my father marked the premature end of my father's beloved formal education, before homing in his literacy and numeracy skills, leave alone, other aspects of education. He had no choice, but to opt for subsequent diaspora, and exodus, out of his village, in search of a job and survival, not only for himself, but now for his family too.

Likewise, my mother was also born in the 1930's, a third child of eight children and several step siblings. My grandfather Agesa, my mum's father was also polygamous. My mother grew up when most African Education in Kenya was in the hands of Missionaries. As such, girls' education was not a priority, therefore it was not promoted much.

Like my father, my mother also experienced a lot of challenges in her endeavour to access education. However, unlike my father, there was a Roman Catholic Mill Hill Mission (MHM) School, right on her doorstep and in fact in front of her gate and homestead.

In view of this, my grandma, my mum's mother was a staunch Roman Catholic convert. However, just before my mother's school joining age, she was attracted by the Salvation Army and subsequently joined the Salvation Army Church, especially the Youth Group.

There Salvation Army (SA), noticed and encouraged, my mother with her passion, talent for singing and leadership ability, irrespective of her illiteracy, lack of education, gender or adherence. She was made an *Askari Kijana* (Junior Soldier - Young Salvation Army Soldier, youth member) and a Youth Leader.

Unfortunately, my mother's newfound joy became a great hindrance for her, to access education in the nearby Chamakanga Mill Hill Mission (MHM) School. As a Roman Catholic School, non-converts and those not interested in converting to Catholicism were not warmly welcome.

Furthermore, my mother usually recalled that anyone like her, who had converted from Catholicism to Protestantism, was not welcome in a Roman Catholic School or Mission Station. In addition, girls were not encouraged to attend mainstream education. Instead, they were encouraged to join convents, not to be married, but symbolically get married to the church by becoming nuns.

My mother longed to marry and have children of her own, as the plight of bareness was noted in her family. In fact, my mum's eldest sister Ezina Sambili was barren, a great anathema in Luhya culture.

As a Salvation Army convert, there were no Salvation Army schools in her vicinity. The nearest Salvation Army School then was SA Kolanya School, many miles away. It was in Busia County, Teso District, on the border of Kenya and Uganda, established in 1934.

To make the matter worse for my mum, Kolanya SA School was set up for Salvation Army Officers' children only, not for adherents. This was to minimise disruption of education, for Salvation Army officers' children's (SAOC), in view of the nature of their itinerant ministry that adversely affected their children's education.

In view of this, my mum never stepped in any school. She never saw the inside of a school, leave a lone a classroom, except during my school Parents Meetings. Unlike my father, my mother never tested the apparent sweetness of formal education. She did not attempt to develop, acquire any literacy or numeracy skills. She was literally, illiterate. At least my father knew some Arithmetic and could scribble his name and write a few words in Kiluhya (local Western Kenya Language).

My father's truly little or limited education, his short encounter with the Missionaries and my mother's illiteracy, meant a lot for me. It had significant ramifications for my own education and entire life.

Chapter Seven: Post Independent Kenya

On 12 December 1963, as a child, I witnessed the Union Jack being lowered. With a lot of Euphoria, the Kenyan National flag was raised at Uhuru Gardens, off Langata Road, near the famous Carnivore, next to Kenya Defence Forces barracks, Langata. As a protocol, the New Kenya National Anthem was played as the Kenyan flag was hoisted.

I also remember, the Kenya national flag being unveiled to the public, with beautiful colours: Black, Red, Green, with white stripes a cross the middle, a Masai shield and two spears, also superimposed in the centre. I also recall, we were later taught about the symbolism of the design and the colours of the Kenya National flag.

The black on the Kenya national flag represents the people of Kenya. Red represents blood, sacrificial blood, the blood shed for independence and probably blood as a symbol of life itself. The green represents Kenya's natural wealth, especially agriculture. Indeed, Kenya is an agricultural and horticultural country.

The white represents peace, probably, with a hidden representation of the whites and Kenya as a diverse nation, multicultural with diverse ethnic groups, including the White people. The Masai shield and spears also represents the fight for and subsequent defence of freedom and the entire nation.

Henceforth, in 1963, Kenya was at last emancipated from the shackles of colonial domination and slavery. Kenya was 'free at last' and the potential racial segregation and apartheid was defunct, extinct, over and out.

For me as a child, what stood out at independence was that from now on, and as I looked forward to growing up into an adult in Kenya, there was no more apparent tripartite system. There was also no more colonialism. Hence, there was no more war between the Mau Mau and the British Imperial Colonial Government. The British Imperial rule ceased and did not exist any-more. Additionally, there was no war between Black Kenyans and White or other Coloured Kenyans.

By 12 December 1964, Kenya was not only, no longer a British Colony, but a republic and Jomo Kenyatta as its first President. Prior to becoming a republic, at independence, in 1963, Kenya became a member of The Commonwealth of Nations, headed by the Queen. The Commonwealth of Nations was established in 1926 by Balfour Declaration, formalised in 1931 by the Statute of Westminster and finalised into Commonwealth of Nations in 1949 by London Declaration.

As a member of the Commonwealth, and former British colony and territory, Kenya increased its own self-government. Thus, within my adolescence, Kenya became not only an independent nation but a fully-fledged republic.

During my childhood, Kenya went through very many faces. With great euphoria, Kenya suddenly changed and became more like a rainbow nation: Whites, Asians and Blacks working, living, learning and being educated together, irrespective of their race or the colour of their skin.

From Independence Day in 1963, Kenya was determined to fight ignorance, poverty and poor health. This was a constant rhetoric from the politicians then, and especially the founding Father and the first President.

Apart from these three big agendas and a lot of rhetoric, I remember, our first President and founding Father Mzee

Jomo Kenyatta also constantly preached and encouraged forgiveness. He invited various races, tribes and groups in Kenya to forgive one another, almost like a homily on forgiveness.

Kenyatta beckoned the Freedom Fighters (Mau Mau), other Africans, Whites, Asians, to join hands, to live and work together like *Wandugu na Wadada,* brothers and sisters. He called for racial integration, tribal unity and harmony, and overall national unity. He also encouraged all people in Kenya as *wandugu* (brothers) and *wadada* (sisters), to join hands, to build Kenya, the ONE Kenyan Nation.

Recognising the diversity within Kenya, Mzee Jomo Kenyatta, upon independence in 1963 adopted the motto or slogan *'Harambee':* Let us all pull together; let us all push together; let us all work together. This became the National Motto.

Nowadays, you rarely hear much about *Harambee.* However, *Harambee* has been permanently inscribed and curved on the Kenyan Crest or coat of Arms, as a symbol of national unity. The crest or coat of arms stands out at

Government   Offices.

The Crest and Coat of Arms of The Republic of Kenya

Source: https://www.heraldry-wiki.com/heraldrywiki/index.php?title=Kenya
24 June 2019

Chapter Eight: Family Impact

I grew up in a ramshackle of a house. It was just one room house with no partition or privacy. It always leaked so badly during the rainy season. Sometimes, whenever it rained, we felt as if we were just outside, being rained on, yet we were indoors. I often wondered if we would have been better off sheltering outside under a banana plantation.

In fact, at night, the moon peeped through the big holes in the dispersed, sometimes rotten grass roof that it was difficult to sleep during full moon nights. In addition, the sun pierced and burst through the openings in the roof exceedingly early in the morning, beckoning us to 'rise and shine.'

Despite the dilapidated state of our ramshackle, we were happy; at least we had a roof over our heads. However, there were times I envied most of our neighbours who had nicely thatched roofs.

Since our roof was constantly leaking whenever it rained, thank God at least, there was one corner in our shack that was often in repairable state. This special corner withstood some rain when in repairable shape. We could cuddle into this corner, especially during the wet and rainy seasons, to be specific, between the months of April and July, October and November.

We also could cuddle into the same corner in the dry season, when it was too hot outside. As a child, my mother had wisely taught us to escape and shelter from the scotching tropical sunshine, especially in the dry season months of December, January and February. Hence, we tended to shelter from the sun whenever it got hot, especially in the afternoons. No wonder, none of our family members got skin cancer, melanoma, usually caused by too much sun exposure, in other words by ultraviolet (UV), the main source of UV light being the sun.

Growing and being in Western Kenya, on 0° Equator, there was plenty of sunshine throughout the year. We endeavoured to take care not to be sunburned. We sheltered under our beloved corner, as many of the shade trees in our compound, had been cut down into firewood or as building materials.

I am the eldest child, with five brothers and two sisters, and several step siblings. Like my grandfathers before him, my father was polygamous too. My mother had eight children biological children of her own. She took care of her siblings and several other children of her relatives from time to time. So, our housed hold was often big.

Against all odds, all of us survived into adulthood. This was amidst high child mortality rate. Surprisingly, this challenged the traditional perceptions and African beliefs of the times.

Most Africans believed that some children had to die, especially at birth. Therefore, most of our neighbours adhered to the counsel not to family plan. They purported to adhere to God's Biblical instructions to Adam, to simply: Be fruitful, multiply and fill the earth....' (Gen: 1:28). Therefore, produced as many children as they could, to ensure at least some survived.

For this reason, we were the envy of the village. Those families in my village that had lost many children at birth or early in life kept wondering and sometimes, confronting and asking my parents what they gave to the 'gods.' They often ignorantly asked my parents if and how they bribed the gods that they have not buried any of their children. Such ignorant questions really offended my parents. It pained and irritated my mother greatly, as she did not believe in the existence of the 'gods.'

As for clothing, we wore whatever rags or tattered clothes we got without any fuss of colour or gender. From childhood, I had no shoes for an exceptionally long time, up to and until extremely late into my life. I really started regularly wearing shoes when I finished my primary school and migrated to Nairobi. Even then, my shoes were shoes by name, only the top part was intact, but the sole was completely worn out and tattered.

When boys clothing was not available, I wore girls' clothing. Based on my attire and 'fashion', sometimes people mistook me for a girl and ridiculed me. This soften impinged on myself esteem and confidence.

During harvest season we had basic food, just something to eat. At least, I remember, there were times, figuratively, when we had 'food on the table,' but without a dining room and a dining table to dine on. As we were without a table, we had our food on the floor, the 'permanent, immovable table,' a picnic in the house, during all the mealtimes.

Moreover, there were times when my parents could not provide us with basic food. We literally went hungry and without food for several days, or weeks, especially during the dry season, usually known as *madukhu gi inzala*, literally hunger days, the hunger season, mainly during the dry season.

Being the first born, patience and hard-working ethos was instilled in me at a very tender and early age. I therefore learned to work extremely hard at whatever I did and did not need supervision or corporal punishment to scare and seemingly motivate me.

Besides, I resented and loathed corporal punishment type of sanctions with all my heart and might. For me, corporal punishment always had negative effects. No wonder I did not excel in my primary school education, as corporal punishment was rampant, indeed in plenty and the norm of the day.

In view of this, I vowed never to use corporal punishment if I ever became a teacher, hence, I have banned corporal punishment in my school: Atsinafa Education Centre. Moreover, nowadays it is illegal in Kenya, though in practice, it is still rampant and leashed out in many schools in Kenya.

As I spent more time with my mother than my father. I noticed that my mother was a woman of prayer. She was also charitable to others as much as she could; probably living out her faith or just reciprocating a lot of what she herself had received from the Ultimate Being - God and from 'others.'

Moreover, without help from 'others,' we could have never survived. I therefore learnt from my mother, that it is nice to receive, and likewise it is genuinely nice to reciprocate and give back. Furthermore, as humans, we are interdependent.

My mother always drummed into me that 'no human being is an island.' She often reminded me, 'human beings are perpetually in 'red,' indebted to others and are definitely interdependent.' She always said, 'we owe others a lot, we owe others a great deal that we cannot fully repay. Therefore, we are perpetually in red, especially to generations that preceded us and have gone before us; and even present generations.'

In my early life, I experienced abject poverty, especially the lack of a nice roof over my head, shelter, many a time, lack of subsistence nourishment, food, and decent attire, garments or clothes over my body. All the same, I received a lot of help from various people and organisations, including the church.

As a child, I was touched by the generosity of 'others.' I was also challenged by the philanthropy of people close by and far. Consequently, I noted the obligation to reciprocate at an early age.

The pinnacle and the greatest success of my life has been the extraordinary and exceptional opportunity and privilege to experience the luxury of a prestigious university, The University of Cambridge. A long my Incredible Journey I have also been privileged to interact with people from various backgrounds and almost all walks of life.

I have been privileged to interact, work and even walk with people who abound almost in everything, be it power, material wealth or possessions, and are happy and contended. I have also met, worked and walked with extremely poor people, yet so jolly, so happy, willing, enjoying and sharing whatever they have, the providence of life or what life bestows.

Regrettably, I have also met miserable people with abject poverty. I have encountered people, apparently rich materially, but miserable emotionally, spiritually, hence with a lot of bitterness, inner poverty and emptiness. Most such people are filled with discontentment and even despair. They have no faith, no hope for life, no love, and so forth, name it... Some, people are so disillusioned, depressed to the point of wanting to take their own lives, to the extent of attempting or even committing suicide.

On the other hand, I have also met people with a lot of internal and external negativity, not good for life or anything. I have encountered people who constantly complain and mourn, at almost everything in their lives, be it the weather or something else.

On my Incredible Journey, I have also met people who lack inner peace and joy. Likewise, I have met people who are really are too blind to see the good and bright side of life. Such people lack the ability to discern and put things in their appropriate and right perspective. A lot of people are too blind to see or notice how blessed they are. Some people are just not bothered to reflect, count their blessings, rejoice and be happy.

In view of this, I am grateful to my parents for instilling in me, not only the ethos of hard work, patience, but also exposure to the challenges, opportunities, realities of life, including various cultures, inner contentment, passion for education and the quest for truth. This is the ethos that gave me the impetus to pursue education at whatever cost.

Indeed, I have tasted and affirmed that good quality education and good knowledge, ushers in contentment and can open numerous doors and avenues. I have been helped by others, in return, I have also been able to help others and, in the process even helped myself as well.

While trying to help others, and particularly while endeavouring to transform my own life to another level, a better and higher level, the ethos imparted by my parents and education, the schooling I undertook, helps me immensely to jump huddles of life, whenever I encounter any.

Chapter Nine: Passion for Education

My sisters: left to right Agnes and Ruth in front of our mud hut in 1970.

While at the Mission School, my father enjoyed and developed passion for education, especially Literacy and Numeracy. In view of what he picked up within the short stint, my father must have been an enthusiastic and a good student. He always reminisced: 'I loved what I had tasted in the formal education at the Mission School; I wish I had gone further!'

Both my parents, especially my mum, always regretted to have missed out on schooling or formal education. My mum always said, 'I can't read, I can't write, and I can't count'. Sometimes, she would tearfully mutter, 'I am just like someone walking and living in total darkness. I missed the light education ushers in one's life, especially simple literacy and numeracy skills, vital for life.'

In view of this, my mother could not wait for me to get old enough to go to school. She wanted me to pursue education, acquire knowledge, find out more, explore the truth about Missionaries 'magic education;' the 'White-people's' education, as she often called it and endeavour to benefit from it.

Once I was about eight years old, my Mama took me to Bugina Friends African Mission (FAM) School, in Vihiga County, Western Kenya. While waiting for admission, my mama whispered to me, 'my son I have brought you here to school, because I don't want you to be as blind as I am.'

As I fiddled, my mother continued, 'I do not want you to walk in darkness.' She looked me in the eye and said, 'I don't want you to wallow in perpetual ignorance like me.' She then held my hand gently and said, 'I want you to get the 'White people's education.' I innocently retorted back, 'why mum?' She smilingly replied, 'I want you to see the light, travel the world and prepare yourself for these changing times, in which education is vital.'

My mum's lecture to me at that time was like a monologue lecture to me and I seemed disinterested but, the inside of me, was listening intensely. It resonated with my grandfather's talk to my father.

After a pause, my mum cleared her throat softly, with a calm voice, she continued, this time she decided to whisper: '*Mwana-ange*, my child, look at me, I haven't been to school, I am just good for nothing.' I remarked, 'not really mum, you are fine.' She replied immediately without any hesitation, 'my son, I am not better than a blind person.' 'Of course, not mum,' I remarked.

Mama again looked into my eye and painfully said, 'when your father sends me letters from Nairobi, I cannot read my letters; I have to get someone else to read for me.' She continued, 'I want you to get education. I want you to be able to read letters, I want you to be the one to read for me your father's letters.'

Mama paused for a while, as if contemplating for a strategic way forward. Afterwards, she smiled and said, 'I want you to read for me other writings too, like the Bible, hymn books from other churches.' She paused again, but this time with a sense of owe and wonder. The thought or mention of the Bible and singing always brightened my mother and brought out a big smile on her face.

The Bible and hymns, the two had a special place in my mother's heart. She continued, beaming with joy, 'I want you to also be able to read letters from my church, invitations and so forth, rather than begging neighbours to read for me,' my ignorance granting them permission to 'poke their noses' into my affairs, my private business because I have no choice.

My mother continued, 'when I get Money Order or telegrams from Nairobi, I cannot understand or decipher them, I cannot even decipher numbers, even money. I cannot understand figures.' After another pause, she sadly remarked, 'someone can swindle me, and I will never know or even understand. I have to get an educated person to help me out and read or decipher figures for me.' She paused again with great regret and said, 'my son, for how long will this go on? I am doomed. Please my child, do not be like me. Learn to read; learn to count! Love education for my sake and your own sake!'

My mother's not going to school gave her great determination to pursue her dreams through me. She encouraged me to wake up incredibly early in the mornings in term time, to go to school. She constantly reminded me that people who wake up late in the day are lazy and will die paupers. 'You therefore should never die a pauper,' my mother would say. My mother really believed in me whole heartedly and this imparted in me a great passion for education.

Being her first born child, though I was not a girl, she still taught me to help her with domestic chores. Being born in a poor family, when I was of age, I learned to help and work with my mother on other people's land day time, to get 'our daily bread' for the family and read late in the night.

My mother believed in 'burning the midnight oil'. As there was no electricity, no telephone communication or Wi-Fi in my village, my mother ensured I had enough kerosene to burn at night.

Whenever we ran out of kerosene, as we sometimes did, we borrowed kerosene from my neighbours to ensure I completed my school assignments and replenished our neighbours' kerosene when we were again able. However, there were times when we had no kerosene or paraffin, and likewise, our neighbours also had none. At such times, I used the fire flames to read and do my assignments.

The kerosene lamp was a makeshift tiny, tin oil lamp, sometimes known as oil burner. I always thought that it was a genius invention. It provided light in darkness. Conversely, it produced extremely poor light, but vital in the bleak darkness of our ramshackle, the mud hut that had no windows. Although it was dim, I was able to see and do my schoolwork. At least, in terms of reading, it was better than the moonlight.

Whenever there was a clear sky at night, especially with the full moon, lighting the skyline, the moonlight peeped through the holes in our poorly thatched roof. Our poorly thatched leaking roof let in and welcomed the moonlight at night. In our bleak dark mud hut shack of a house, when we had no kerosene, and therefore no light, the moonlight was simply good enough for me.

Regrettably, apart from its risk of being a fire hazard, poor quality light, our tiny, tin oil lamp, or oil burner produced smelly kerosene fumes. If it were in UK, in these days of health and safety concern, and great environmental awareness, it would have been banned, not only for health and safety reasons, but for its emissions and subsequent pollution.

Of course, the tiny, tin oil lamp or oil burner, polluted our poorly ventilated, dilapidated ramshackle house extensively. Our mud hut, ramshackle house being made of sticks or twigs, mud walls and grass thatched roof was also highly susceptible to open flames fire hazard. I often wondered how it never caught fire! Thanks to mama for instilling in me fire hazard awareness at an early age.

My mother seemed to have been aware of the potential of fire hazards from open flames. To manage such fire hazards, she always reminded me to be careful with open flames when in or near our house, to ensure our house did not catch fire.

Conversely, I now know that the kerosene lamp fumes, plus the extensive smoke were not good for my health. Apparently, the fumes and poor lighting were also detrimental for my eyes and my eyesight. There was no alternative or a better conventional light. Therefore, I had no option but to endure and prod on with my tiny, tin lamp, irrespective of the extensive safety and health consequences and ramifications. I endeavoured to survive and used what was available.

Maybe the poor light contributed to my vision impairment and subsequent wearing of glasses later in my life. Who knows? Conversely, that may not be the case or main reason why I had to succumb to wearing glasses later in my life. Currently, it is all but guess work and probabilities, what might have been or might not have been.

However, one thing I remember clearly and can vouchsafe, my tiny tin lamp enabled me to do my schoolwork and at least, lit our ramshackle. In addition, it was light in darkness, lighting the whole house and family, as much as possible. It illuminated our entire house and proverbially lit my family. Probably, it was the light that lit my entire world, life, future and passion for education.

Nevertheless, maybe, the poor lighting and inhaling kerosene fumes for a long time, had also extensive health ramifications for me, that may emerge later in my life. But for now, here I am, I have been fit and well, in fact, as the saying goes, 'I am as fit as a fiddle!' I seem to have survived unscathed. I must have developed robust survival resilience. May be the tough experience gradually gave me a proverbial body, 'John made of steel.'

On reflection, apart from inhaling the polluting fumes from the lamp, whenever we were cooking, our house was also filled up with smoke. In fact, the entire inside of the roof was covered with soot, smoke collected over a long period.

Over a long period of time, the soot turned into several black chunks of particles. The black chunks of soot particles filled the roof with hanging black fibres, tapering black pieces, that looked like black icicles, hanging and looking down upon me, almost about to drop over me. Indeed, sometimes they did drop, smothering me with black soot.

During cooking sessions and especially in the evenings, one would think our house was on fire. Not only was the inside saturated with smoke, but smoke sipped through the poorly thatched grass roof. From a distance, our house smoked and appeared as if it was on fire. Sometimes, especially on a cold wet evening, it smoked like a smoking volcano, pending to subsequently erupt into inferno flames.

We used open fire in our house, for cooking and warming ourselves. As our house had no chimney or smoke outlet, it had extremely poor ventilation. Therefore, whenever we were cooking on the open fire, or even warming ourselves, our ramshackle house was permeated with smoke.

No wonder, when mum was cooking, or we were warming ourselves on the open fire, we always cried 'tears of smoke,' rather than cry the proverbial 'tears of joy.' Retrospectively, they were probably 'tears of joy,' as smoke meant we will have some food to eat, when it was cold, smoke meant we will have fire to keep us warm.

We also tended to get apparent running noses, in the intensive saturated smoke, as if we had perpetual cold or flu. Amazingly, when we got out into the open, in the fresh air, as one may say, all was back to normal and the running noses ceased, the apparent cold or flu evaporated.

Moreover, cooking was on an open fire, in one of the corners in our one room shack. Due to lack of matches to light fire, as my mother could not constantly afford to purchase matches, we had a constant bonfire, like a 'scouts camp.' Incidentally, in view of the constant smouldering bonfire, sometimes, I felt as if 'we camped' perpetually in our own house, throughout the year.

The cooking pots were mainly *tsiynyungu* - earthen pots. Our cooker was just *mahiga* - a three stones fireplace, face to face, as if they were smiling at each other. We burned firewood or logs for cooking. Consequently, I have used the three cooking stones or fire place occasionally, to illustrate to my illiterate mum and rural village congregations, the complex and intricate Christian Trinitarian Theology: One God in three persons: Father, Son and Holy Spirit, yet One God. This formula is used at Cambridge University graduation ceremonies, but in Latin.

Despite the saturated smoke, we cuddled ourselves by the fire in the evenings, whenever it was raining heavily, especially on a very cold day or night. Additionally, at night, we cuddled by the same fire, not only to keep ourselves warm, but also to listen to mum and dad narrate traditional folk tales and sleep time stories, as we called them.

Since we had no beds or blankets, we just slept on the floor, stuffed in reusable sugar and maize sisal sacks that were to us sleeping bags. That catered for blankets or duvets. That is how we slept and covered ourselves at night. Therefore, I could not have bedtime's stories, but just evening stories.

More importantly, my parents were illiterate; therefore, they could never have read me bedtime stories. Incidentally, my granddad, my Nana, my father and mama were excellent story tellers. How I wish I had recorded some of their folklore, stories and oral tradition tales.

Surprisingly, my father's limited education and my mother's not going to school did not push me into the sociological false prophecy of vicious cycle of family illiteracy and ignorance. It even could not deter my mother from encouraging me to go to school. Even though she could not see great and immediate tangible gains from education within our village, she still insisted on me going to school and being educated.

In the absence of my father, she believed I could read for her, letters and other documents. Indeed, when I learned to read, the first extensive reading I ever did, was to read for my mother, letters and correspondence from my father, her church etc., especially mails from my father in Nairobi. That confirmed, I was now literate and whatever had been read to my mother before, was certainly a true record. In fact, some of the mails were romantic. Reciprocally, my mother also dictated to me and I scribbled her replies to dad. In most cases it was verbatim and great fun to write.

Deciphering dad's handwriting, reading and interpretation, gave me an insight into language and translation skills, later to become vital on my Incredible Journey. Scribbling mum's verbatim replies to dad, letters from her church, letters from far and wide, also became significant for my literacy skills, and passion for education.

I also undertook errands for my mother, like going, trekking to Mbale to post Mama's letters to dad, etc. The Mbale Post Office was the nearest, about six miles away at current Mbale town, Vihiga County. It was also the closest decent market or shopping centre. By going to the post office, at Mbale, I could 'kill two birds, with one stone.' That is, I could post mama's mail and shop and buy the necessary housed-hold groceries. En route, I would reflect on my passion for education and quest for truth.

Mum usually, sent me to the shop, including buying groceries. As a first-born boy, with no immediate sister who followed me, I collected and gathered firewood. I went to the river, to harvest water for the family. I also went to the power meal to grind maize for dinner, looked for and fetched *mboga* -greens, at the instructions of my mum. However, most of the time, I took other initiatives of my own.

Most transactions in the village were barter trade. However, there were also a lot of cash transactions. Therefore, my mother needed to decipher figures, count her money and ensure whenever she worked people's land, she received the respective wages. Whenever she transacted or shopped with cash, likewise, she gave and received the correct change back. This was an impetus for my mother to invest in my education so that I help her out.

My mother not only had faith in me, but trusted me whole heartedly, that I could do it! Later, when I was able to read, write and count, she even entrusted her life into my hands, especially her secrets. I became her Personal Assistant (PA), read mails for her from my dad and her church, etc. She dictated to me, replies to her letters and I also kept her accounts, as she had no inkling of figures and numbers.

My parents had a glimpse of the empowerment of education. My father endeavoured to support my education. Working away in the big city Nairobi, he got wages to provide meagre funds to support my mother in the village. Of course, my mother was a peasant subsistent farmer. Whenever she worked on other people's land, as unskilled labourer in the village, she was paid peanuts from her labour, especially for tilling other people's land.

Fortunately, most of my father's employers paid my school fees, as their charitable outreach and bonus to my father's exemplary service to them. I especially remember, the one who was called Patrick Jubb, Director of Kenya Broadcasting Corporation in Nairobi, later Voice of Kenya (VOK). Overall, my parents believed, 'with education I will have the prospects of a bright future; at least, I will have a choice and hope for the future, in the fast-changing world.'

My mother's observations and experiences had taught her that, not having education seals one's future to limited opportunities. She consequently believed, with education, I can access 'choice, alternatives and opportunities', resonating with experiences and beliefs of most mothers in developing countries.

The story of my passion for education therefore emanates from my parents' experiences: My father's foretaste of and passion for education, especially my father's fate of not completing his basic primary school education. It also emanates from my mother's non-schooling experience.

Consequently, the story of my parents' life, especially the challenges to access education and my own story of obstacles in endeavouring to pursue my education, is not only a tale of resistance, resilience, and so forth, but also a testimony of great determination. It is a dare to dream and a dare to try, fortunately with immense happy ending.

Thus, the enduring struggles and challenges that ensued, a long my 'Incredible Journey' in the pursuit of education, even when nothing positive seemed to happen or emerge immediately, in retrospect, have paid amazing dividends.

Not knowing how the future would unfold, my mother encouraged me to press on regardless and 'fight the good fight' of pursuing education, with hope and determination. My mother believed good education often drives someone to certain positive ends, to the unknown future.

She thus viewed education as almost a physical space, where the opportunity to choose an alternative state of being became accessible for her children. As a peasant, subsisting villager, who witnessed shrinking farmlands, 'education was like a garden where opportunities are likely to grow.' She thus actively encouraged me to pursue education amidst extensive challenges and struggles.

Even though my parents were not educated, they had insurmountable patience, commitment to education and hard work. They themselves worked awfully hard to make sure I had a roof over my head. My father worked whole heartedly, in Nairobi, with acclamations for exemplary service from all his employers.

From his meagre income, my father raised money to buy a small piece of land. At least we had a place we could call our own, our home, even though it was too small for our big family. He bought two (2) acres (approximately zero point eight hectares– 0.8 ha) of land in Lusomo, like the Biblical Mesopotamia, Lusomo is the land between two rivers.

By the time we settled in Lusomo, it was in the Tropical Rainforest jungle, that has now been deforested and merged with and lost into Ishanji Village. This taught me the significance of hard work, commitment and endeavours to be independent. It also instilled in me the vitality of being responsible, having the pride of providing for one's family and not forgetting commitment and continued passion for education.

Chapter Ten: Which School?

Punctuated by perceptible compliment, 'your English is so good', I am often asked, 'which school did you go to?' Since this question has been and is often asked, I have answered it several times.

My education and schooling spans over a long period, immense experience and across many continents. This chapter focuses on my schooling in Kenya, especially the background to my education, specifically my primary school experience and my basic education in Kenya. Other aspects of my education subsequently permeate this book and particularly the ensuing chapters.

I started my education at Bugina Friends African Mission School, my father's short-lived Quaker School in Maragoli Location, Vihiga County, in Western Kenya, aged about eight years. As stated earlier, my parents were not Quakers. Going to a Quaker school was thus bound to be rather challenging.

Until recently, my father, like his father, adhered to African Traditional Religion. Besides, by the time I started school, my mother had left the Salvation Army. She was now an adherent of an African indigenous church, the church of my grandmother, my father's mother.

As noted earlier, it was a breakaway church from Friends African Mission, Quakers, in 1927. It became a fully-fledged independent church in 1933, then known as African Church of the Holy Spirit (ACHS), nicknamed *Vaushi,* The Separate Ones, The Set Aside.

Within a few days of joining the mission school, I discovered adhering to Quakerism by regular Sunday school attendance on Sundays, was mandatory, yet it was during my non-mandatory contact time or non-school day.

Seeing that Sunday school attendance and keen participation in Quaker extracurricular activities was compulsory, I viewed it with a lot of suspicion. For me, by then, it was just a tool to convert me to Quakerism. I also saw it as a sign of adherence or potential conversion to the Quaker Faith. Therefore, my life at this Quaker school was bound to be short lived.

It was difficult to survive at Bugina FAM School for more than one school term, about three calendar months. My parents not being Quakers and by me not attending Sunday school, I was expelled after a few weeks of tasting the sweetness of formal education.

I was disappointed for being excluded for non-adherence of my parents and my potential conversion to Quakers' faith. I had just tasted the sweetness of education and developed a passion for education.

Still determined, my mother decided to try home county school and took me to the neighbouring Ivonda School, in Idakho Location, Kakamega County. I was welcomed with both hands and registered at the school, but on one condition, I had to attend the respective Missionary Sunday School, every Sunday during term time, when the school is in session.

The Ivonda School was sponsored by the Pentecostal Assemblies of Canada (PAOC), later known as Pentecostal Assemblies of East Africa (PAEA), now Pentecostal Assemblies of God (PAG). Pentecostal Missionary schools were more sympathetic to children of members of indigenous charismatic churches and even the so called 'pagans', non-Christians.

I was incredibly lucky to go to a school not extremely far away from my home village. It was about two miles only from my village then. In view of my experience, I could not allow Sunday school attendance to deter me completely, from my passion for education.

My determination to pursue education was now unstoppable. Rather than being singled out easily as a non-adherent, and later expelled, I decided to concur to attending Sunday school, in order to secure my place at the mission school.

This was my best option and hope. I did not want the same fate that befell me at the preceding Quaker Mission School to occur again. Exclusion within a few days for non-adherence or potential conversion would have been devastating to my mother.

Determined not to let my mother down, I decided to try hard to attend extracurricular activities, including Sunday school attendance and any other ensuing expectations or requirements that guaranteed and facilitated my pursuit of education, except conversion to Pentecostalism. From my tender age, I had a quest for truth, with an inclination to a faith that would appeal to my intellect as well as my emotions, mind as well as my spirit. Figuratively, my head and my heart were significant for my adherence, convictions and subsequent conversion.

Facilities and structure wise, Ivonda School was in an unbelievably bad and poor state, worse than Bugina where I had been expelled. It was made of dusty floors, leaking grass thatched roofs, very poorly constructed classrooms with dilapidated mud walls.

Construction of schools was and is still, of course the responsibility of parents and guardians. Therefore, particularly good school structures or buildings in the villages of poor parents or guardians, were and are next to impossible and not easy to have or find nearby. Ivonda was therefore no exception.

My mother standing elegantly, celebrating the impressive strides and progress our family has made.

As there was lack of space at Ivonda School, we alternated and shared classes. Lower Primary (Early Years) came early in the morning (08:00 - 11:00), while Middle Primary started later in the day (11:00 – 14:00), after Lower Primary had gone home. Upper Primary had a long day, (08:00 – 16:00), with three breaks in between, so long as it did not threaten to rain in the afternoon.

If it threatened to rain, we were dismissed forthwith earlier than usual or normal school day. On such a day, the whole school had a half day of learning. Of course, Kenya being on the Equator Latitude 0°, predicting when it was going to rain is very possible. The formation of the clouds into rain, if observed closely, gives ample time, to prepare and take the necessary appropriate action, in most cases, in good time. Very often, it rains late in the afternoon or at night, up to early morning hours.

We usually came one hour early to clean up classrooms and arrange the learning space, under the supervision of Class Monitors and Prefects, before the teachers arrived. We also stayed on after lessons, for about an hour, clearing classes and tidying up the compound under the supervision of Prefects and Teacher on Duty before the evening parade and break off to go home. Class Monitors and Prefects were chosen by Teachers and the Senior Prefects by the Headmaster.

There were no female Head teachers in my primary school days. In fact, female teachers were very few; two out of ten teachers in my school were female. Moreover, they only taught Lower Classes or Early Years Learners.

For unknown reasons, most of the female teachers left school or signed off and went home by lunch break i.e. they just taught for a half day but were paid full day wages. They only stayed longer, whenever it was rumoured that the Government Inspectors or the Education Officers may be calling, visiting the school for inspection.

I was just dropped in the deep end of primary school education, without any initiation through Nursery or Pre-primary Education. I therefore never savoured introduction to education, through Nursery and Reception or Pre-School classes. My school was no exception; most 'African schools,' schools for blacks in Kenya and Blacks education had no Nursery Schools, Kindergartens or Reception classes.

On admission, we were all heaped in one group of a class, based on our date of arrival, the date one joined the school, rather than on our date of birth, our respective age our ability, or even height. During registration, nobody bothered to ask me my age or record my date of birth. Of course, I had no birth certificate or any form of identification document. Birth Certificates and Birth Registration in Kenya became obligatory in 1968, well over after Kenya's independence and well over, after my Primary School education.

Most of the Lower Classes were taught by elderly ladies, teachers who were about to retire. We usually called our lady teachers 'Madam' and male teachers 'Sir.' Failure to address our teachers appropriately and with due respect was an invitation of storms of canes, flogging and some ridiculous punishment, depending on the gender, age and stature of the teacher.

We never knew our teachers' names or call them by their names. One thing I can remember and still lingers in my mind is that, my teachers were well fed, huge and scary. They rarely smiled, always had a cane in their hand or beside them waiting, or longing for kids to err, so that they can rain on them numerous thunderstorms and thunderous canes and flogging.

Whenever we erred, made a mistake or could not understand what had been taught or said, we seemed to give our teachers great joy. Indeed, it gave them the greatest opportunity and the joy of raining numberless canes on us. They flogged us, belittled us, and dehumanised us. We also gave them the opportunity of name calling us, pouncing on us like a leopard pounces on an antelope. All this was in the name of instilling knowledge and discipline in us and on us, as if we were just empty vessels, like empty containers, like a *debe,* a tin to be filled.

Our teachers appeared overjoyed and filled with great satisfaction for instilling and inflicting a lot of pain on us. I wish they would have accessed our innermost beings! For inside us, we were boiling, fuming with rage and resentment, the resentment of and for the inflicted pain and punishment. Moreover, we were hopeless and powerless. We felt reduced in size and to size, we often shrunk at the encounter with the teachers, and even sometimes we felt the belittlement reduced us to nothing, it reduced us just to feeling smaller than we were.

Indeed, in primary school, I was very helpless. My parents and guardians belonged to the same 'old school' or 'battalion.' As most parents belonged to the apparent same 'old school,' the same 'old school' of thought, they could not care less. As far as schooling was concerned, I was handed over to the teachers. My parents never ever came to my rescue or defence. Even if they did, that would have created more problems for me, than intended.

I was always expected to salute my teachers like soldiers saluting their senior officers, in school and out of school, whenever and wherever I encountered one of my teachers. Failure to salute my teachers, meant I will be punished on the spot, i.e. being flogged, irrespective of where you were. If I managed to run off, then I was in greater trouble. My punishment was doubled and applied whenever I got back to school, or wherever I encountered the teacher again.

On Mondays and Fridays, I had assembly in the morning. Thereafter, there was also an assembly in the evenings, at the end of the school day. I stood on the parade in a big semi-circle, according to my classes. Teachers and prefects gave various notices and then always came the rain of canes by the Head teacher on villainies, including those who had not saluted teachers out of school encounters or those who had not attended church Sunday school as well.

Afterwards, I stood with my class at attention, like in the military, while the flag, the Union Jack, the British flag, was hoisted in the morning and lowered in the evening. Guided by the scouts and girl guides, we sang 'God Save the Queen,' the British National anthem, after hoisting or lowering the flag. However, after independence, in January 1964, this colonial ritual was replaced by the national custom. We now sang Kenya National Anthem and hoisted the Kenyan multicoloured flag on Mondays and Fridays.

Our classes were mixed gender, but boys outnumbered girls. I was the youngest in my class, underweight and the skinniest boy in the entire school, up to and until in my final year. My peers and teachers alike, took advantage of this. I was therefore by all means, the most bullied boy and learner in the entire school.

With the epiphany of Francis, at least and at last a much weaker boy than me, joined Ivonda School from Lusui School. Having had the full brand of bullying a lone for a long time, at least and at long last I had someone, with whom I had a common foe: the bullies. I had someone who shared my plight. However, this was in my last year at Ivonda School.

This bullying from peers and teachers alike made my life at school rather difficult, at times unpleasant. Sometimes I felt like being in hell, without the gnashing of teeth. I believe this had significant implications and ramifications for my education and to me as a person. It must have affected my concentration, self-esteem, consequently impacting my schooling, educational performance and achievement too.

Chapter Eleven: The Greatest Blunder

Just before I joined upper primary, in 1964, the Kenya Government took over all mission schools, changed them into Public Schools. However, the government allowed churches to maintain sponsorship of their former missionary schools and subsequent new church schools. In the same year, Ivonda Upper Primary School was closed due to lack of minimum numbers of learners, set by the new requirements, introduced by the Otiende Education Commission in 1964.

In the same year 1964, my mother had to look for an alternative school for me. She sent me to her homeland school, Chamakanga Mill Hill Mission School (Roman Catholic), in Maragoli, currently in Vihiga County. This was the school she could not go to herself, perhaps she took me there as a sign of defiance.

Based on my grandma's membership and adherence to Roman Catholicism, I was accepted at Chamakanga Mill Hill Mission School (MHM) without many further questions. However, the School was three hours walk, one way from my village. I ridiculously spent six hours every day to and from school, time I would have used for my studies and even relaxation, as necessary.

Despite the long distance and arduous journey, to Chamakanga School, it was at Chamakanga that I met my best friend. Later he probably became my only real friend, particularly when I had hit the rock bottom. When I was in great need, he was there, as a friend indeed. He later stood by and with me through 'thick and thin.'

My Chamakanga friend, became my stronghold, much later in life, amidst the challenges that ensued, after my primary school and later my secondary school. He protected me in many ways. Unfortunately, or fortunately,

I was just at Chamakanga for one year, but our friendship started, prospered and never really ended, until death do us part. However, our paths did not cross sooner. Nevertheless, our paths did cross later, after my departure from Chamakanga School and successive migration to Nairobi.

In 1966, Ivonda Upper Primary School soon got on its feet; suddenly and certainly, it had the required number of children and reopened. Conversely, Chamakanga was extremely far. I wasted about six hours en route daily, with adverse effects on my performance and achievement. I opted to return to Ivonda.

Once again, I was glad to be back at Ivonda School. Now It was much nearer to my home, as we had moved to Lusomo, later to become part of Ishanji Village. It was much nearer, less than fifteen (15) minutes' walk to school.

At last, I could come home for lunch, rather than 'fast.' There were no meals provided in my school then. Sadly, I gave up carrying packed lunch. Whenever I carried my lunch, it was so often nicked, stolen, that I gave up carrying or taking lunch to school. I therefore opted to fast instead.

In all the schools I had been to, nobody really bothered to know, if I had some form of learning disability, if I were a kid with Special Education Needs (SEN), or if my eyesight had issues or was a problem. I was never tested for any learning disability or eyesight issues, in any of the schools I attended.

I just struggled with my eyesight and overall reading and learning issues unnoticed by anybody or any school I attended. Instead, I was severely punished. I was scolded and even flogged if I did not understand what I was reading or what was being taught. Regurgitation learning was the order of the day, particularly information and numbers, historical dates, the whole of learning and overall education. Of course, in those days, in Kenya where I grew up, there was nothing like SEN.

Moreover, teachers focused on the group, rather than individual learners. There was no differentiation or Individual Educational Plan (I E P). The learners in each class were so many that I cannot even remember the number count. I never noted how many we were in each class, probably eighty or even one hundred kids per teacher, leave alone the entire whole school.

All said and done, around me there were numerous negative vibes. I constantly heard deafening voices of failure, both from my teachers, aunts, uncles and peers alike. I constantly heard demoralising voices such as, 'you are a failure! You are always daydreaming. Don't dream young man, dreams don't always come true.'

My teachers knew my family background so well. They had read me and my family like a fascinating story book. You would have thought my entire life and whole story had the potential of being turned into a set text for literature lessons, or even converted into a feature a movie show, motion pictures or feature films. Most of my teachers reiterated negative voices, that commensurate with such words: 'just like your father; you will never make it!'

Such ridicules used to really pierce my heart, feelings and hurt me so much that I decided not to succumb to their false prophecy. I promised myself that one day; the future will unfold to show and prove them wrong. Indeed,

I constantly hoped that I would be able to prove my adversaries wrong when I grow up.

I promised and solemnly vowed that I would show my 'false prophets' of doom and critiques, 'I can, and I will change my life for good.' The more I was put down, the more I became determined. I made up my mind that I will walk in my father's footprints but carry them beyond and yonder.......'

Once I have made up my mind, there is no turning back.

With the imminent independence of Kenya, I was caught up between the old and the new, the Colonial and the Independent Kenya. I did not sit for the Common Entrance Exam (CEE) to move from Lower Primary to Upper Primary. As I approached the Upper Primary, the National Curriculum changed, without ample warning or preparation.

Bravo, my stay in Primary School was cut short and significantly reduced. Instead of spending another two years at Ivonda Primary School, I just had to stay for one more year in the Upper Primary School. These changes were imposed by educational changes in the independent Kenya. That was my warm welcome, back to my school, after the return from the exodus, from Chamakanga School.

After my primary school, I dreamed of joining Duke of York School, now Lenana High School or Prince of Wales, now Nairobi School. This was because, both schools were former Whites only schools, with the best resources, facilities and teachers. This was one of my big dreams. After independence, both schools had just changed to National high cost schools.

I also dreamed and had wishful thinking of joining Alliance Boys High School, that is if I could not get into Lenana School or Nairobi School. Alliance was renowned, as the pioneer and best Protestant African School in Colonial-days Kenya.

Alliance Boys School was therefore among the best schools nationally. It was founded by three missionary churches: Church Missionary Society (CMS) - Church of England (nowadays Anglican Church of Kenya (ACK), Methodist Missionary Society (MMS) – Methodist Church and Church of Scotland (CSM) – Presbyterian Church.

Therefore, the name Alliance, was an Alliance of these three Missions that founded the school and reflects the three churches getting together, founding the school as joint venture at Kikuyu and later working together to run it. I dared to choose it, as one of my national schools against the wish of my teachers.

Most leaders and great people, including medical doctors, lawyers, etc., in Kenya were and are alumni of Alliance Boys and Alliance Girls High Schools. It was highly selective, incredibly competitive and incredibly stringent in its selection, picking the best brains in the country, the highest performers and kids with the best grades, based on regional quotas.

After my choice, I realised, getting a place at Alliance was next to impossible. This was probably one of my unrealistic dreams, but once I have made a choice, I rarely regret it. Furthermore, in this incident, once the choice had been sent off, there was no turning back, I was stuck with it. I had to explore alternatives later. No regrets, I had made up my mind.

My final year at Ivonda Primary School went so fast and just evaporated like water vapour. The curriculum had just been suddenly changed from eight years Primary education, four years secondary, two years Advanced/A level education, and three years tertiary education (8 4 2 3) to seven years primary education, four years Secondary, two years Advanced/A level education and three years tertiary (7 4 2 3). Thus, in total, primary education was reduced by one year, from eight years to seven years.

I cannot recall, and even then, I never understood for whatever reasons, in my final year, teachers instigated numerous strikes. I just wanted to pursue my education and finish my primary school education, move to Secondary School, Sixth Form and university, in due course.

Unfortunately for me, teachers went on strike, just a few weeks before our final exams. Most of the interior village schools with poor roads and poor infrastructure, including Ivonda Primary School were closed. We had to carry our desks to Makhokho on the main Kakamega - Kisumu Road, over about five miles away to complete our education there.

I sat for my final Primary Education Exams in the month of November 1966. Believe it or not, I cannot remember the exact dates. The only thing I can remember is, at least it lasted for about three days, amidst chaos and confrontation between teachers and the government.

Our final Primary Education Exams were invigilated, guarded and supervised by the Kenya Police, armed with big guns to safeguard us against our very own striking teachers' interference. The peace loving Roman Catholic Nuns from Mill Mission at Mukumu, Kakamega were recruited as the invigilators and helped with the management of our exams, especially paperwork.

Hence, for me, taking my primary school final exams, was a nerve racking and scary experience. It reminded me of my childhood visits to Nairobi. It un-archived the agony of being caught up in Nairobi, in the middle of the conflict between the British and Mau Mau, whenever I visited my father in Nairobi.

Despite the scary environment of my exams, after three gruesome days of great tension within me, I managed to complete my exams within the stipulated timetable of three days. However, I never ever remembered any single question, or the multiple choice answers I chose for each question. That was the time that multiple choice questions were introduced in the final Primary School Exams in Kenya.

Indeed, I did my last school exams with great trepidation, fear, and trembling. Instead of focusing on my exams, I kept asking myself what if the striking teachers storm our exam centre. Someone could be hurt; someone could die in the confrontation that may ensue, reminiscent of my thoughts in the apparent colonial forces' and the Mau Mau crossfire, I used to encounter in Nairobi as a young child. The conflict and confrontation between the Mau Mau and the Imperial Colonial Government was vicious from both sides.

Retrospectively, I must have been a very responsible pupil. Knowingly, I had completed my primary education; I could have cared less about Ivonda School furniture. For sure I knew I would never have to go back to Ivonda Primary School again as a pupil. However, with the help of my friends, I still carefully carried and took back my heavy desk, scaling over five miles downhill from Makhokho across the terrifying Yala River Bridge and yonder to Ivonda.

After returning my heavy desk back to my school approximately five miles away, I had to patiently wait for the results that would take about two months to be released. Anyway, I cannot remember how long it took and even when the results were released. But overall, it felt as if it had been an exceedingly long, long time.

Probably it was an awfully long time, but to the best of my knowledge, I have no recollection of how long. Perhaps my mind deliberately forgot to register and archive how long it was, and even much better, I do not remember at all what transpired in that limbo time.

When the results came out, they were displayed on the rough uneven muddy wall of the Headmaster's Office, almost reminiscent of Cambridge University results, being pinned on The Senate House boards in the open, especially in the Summer time, when there are so many tourists around Cambridge City, for everyone to behold.

Unlike nowadays, thus our KPE results were public; everyone who dared to see was welcome to look at them. Those who had passed celebrated. Those who had failed moaned for almost eternity.

I really did not feel like going for the results, but my mum and grandma insisted. Therefore, I had to go. Of course, my education mattered a lot to my Mum. With great tribulation and anxiety, I went and looked at the display wall more than three times.

After a while, shaking and trembling, I noticed the Headmaster was looking at me smiling sarcastically. I remarked: 'Sir, what does this mean? My name is not on the wall, it is not on the exam results list, Sir?'

'The list spells your failure!', the Headmaster murmured. This time with great laughter, he continued, 'This spells out the end of your journey in life. It means you do not have greater openings or a bright future. Of course, you have failed to get your KEY, the opener of your future: KPE exams. Your dreams are over! Do not dream again! You have no hope, your future is doomed!'

I would have fainted, I even I do not know how I did not crumble or collapse. Failing KPE rubber stamped one, permanently with the stigma of failure. Failing KPE wrote off the learner and condemned the learner to eternal failure in life. It was the end of the learner's Journey – period! The learner was supposed never to resurrect or rise again.

I paused, thought for a moment and asked myself, now that I have been declared a KPE failure, from now on and forever, does it mean I cannot, and I will never ever move on? I felt as if my passion and dreams were now completely shattered.

Chapter Twelve: The Day of Reckoning

On that fateful day, on the day of my KPE results, the very day I received the sad news of my subsequent failure, for a moment, if you asked me, I could not remember or recollect, even for a minute, my footsteps to and from my school. I could not recall, how I got back home from that encounter with my Headmaster at my Primary School.

I thought for a while, then I could not think any more. My mind went blank. Even though the sun was shining, all I could see, was darkness, a bleak future, that was all and what I could see in-front of me. It was total darkness for me.

'Maybe my memory, my inner computer had just shut down,' I thought for a while. Maybe I was daydreaming! I could not even remember the ticking of the clock, '*tik tok, tik tok*', or even the counting of the clock. I could not remember the days of the week, not even the months of the year. On that cataclysmic day, my whole world sunk into oblivion. I felt as if everything, including life itself, just died beneath my feet, in front of my horizon, around me and underneath my entire existence. My hope had almost been turned into real despair.

However, as if that were not enough, to add injury to insult and to make the matter worse, when I crawled home, I found my mother and grandmother waiting for me. They were eagerly waiting for me to deliver the 'good news,' the 'good news' of my exam results. They were zealously and keenly waiting and ready to celebrate my apparent success.

My mother had prepared the traditional Luhya delicious cockerel stew, with ugali, a cooked dough of maize meal, in addition chapati. Thus, the dish of honour and success, my favourite dish was already prepared, just waiting for me to dig in and celebrate.

I silently whispered to myself, 'How can I celebrate, when I have just failed my Primary School Exams?' 'How can I celebrate when my dreams have been shattered? 'Despite my failure, the stew was seething, simmering with a genuinely nice smell, and flavour of local spices. There was the exotic mixed tropical fruit salad for dessert. In addition, my grandmother had brought me a gift, hidden under her pouch.

I did not know how to break the atrocious and awful news I was carrying. Indeed, how could I proclaim the abominable, despicable tidings of failure, I was bearing upon my shoulders. I could not come to terms with myself: I was the bearer of the dreadful news, the unspeakable, terrible news of my failure.

When I got home, I just slumped onto the floor, dropped down, almost dropped dead like a heavy sack of maize, or a heavy sack of beans, offloaded from, and relieved off and from the carrier's back. My mama retorted 'Why did you not go to check your results? You would not be in that bad and desperate mood! What happened to you? Who died?'

'Maybe I had died' I thought for a moment. Then I gently put my hand on the left-hand side of my chest, I touched my heart, it was still pumping, but rather differently. It was pumping, almost the way my grandpa's pumped and he was gone within no time. I said to myself, I wish mama could know the inside of me was dead. My mother fired simultaneous questions that I could not answer promptly, leave alone answer one by one adequately or even reasonably at that time.

'No one is dead Mama!' I replied. 'Nothing happened on the way to school mama,' I muttered. 'Of course, I have been to school mama, I could not have missed to go and check my results,' I softly replied, almost in the tone of a dirge, a lament tone and voice.

'The Headmaster told me; my Incredible Journey had ended.' I retorted. Before mum chipped in, I said, 'Mama, my name was not on the wall.' I re-joined impatiently, as if to implore her not to ask me any further questions.

In a creaking voice, I said, 'I failed my KPE mama, I failed my exams! I have lost my "key to life" and the will to live.' Thus, in a creaking voice, I had declared and proclaimed the fateful and dreadful news of my KPE failure. I had no other choice.

For a moment, there was dead silence in our ramshackle. It felt as if the bugler, had just sounded the final sound, the 'last post.' There was a moment of enormous vacuum of silence, as if in honour of the dead, we had bowed, buried our heads in momentous silence. Maybe it was in the honour of 'the demise,' the end of my primary schooling or the seed of education, had just been laid in the soil, just planted, later to germinate and grow ...

'No, it's not the end of your Incredible Journey, but the beginning of another section on your journey of life', my mama broke the silence. 'Maybe it is just an uphill to climb,' said mama empathetically and emphatically, in a cricking but soft voice.

'The road that leads to success has hills, slopes, valleys, several corners, straight stretches and even mountains to climb', mama pronounced...' Grandma reiterated in another soft voice, a real calm soft voice, 'of course it can't be the end of your Incredible Journey in life.'

Mama then said; 'Let us have the nice lunch we had prepared for you.' We ate the meal in somehow a sombre mood as if it were the Last Supper, or the Passover Meal. 'Was I the Passover Lamb to be sacrificed?' I asked myself. 'No!' I said to myself quietly. After the meal, my mum and my grandma escorted me, about four miles, approximately six kilometres, to Chavakali, in Vihiga County.

I was not allowed to use our usual Bus Stop, lest I bump into or meet my Headmaster. I might be spotted, anyone else may spot me and detract me from my destiny. The usual road to the nearest village common stage and bus stop was en route and passed in front of my Headmaster's gate.

'We are going to Chavakali in Vihiga County,' my mother explained. 'My son, I would rather you go into a self-imposed exile', she murmured. 'Go to your father in Nairobi, you'll be in '"nobody's land", away from our community, and ostracise yourself.

'Nobody there will talk about you and your apparent failure, or you and the supposedly end of your life's journey,' she comforted me. She continued, 'When you get there in Nairobi, you will start anew, you will start afresh. You will embark on your Incredible Journey again. It will be a new beginning to start life, far away from the so-called home ...'

With the help of grandma and my mother, aged 14 years old, I left my village secretly by the night bus; this time, not by the nostalgic chuku chuku train. Thank God my father was far away in Nairobi. At least I knew my father's address. I knew, I had a place to escape to, run away from home of the sad KPE failure news. I could not wait to escape there, to go into diaspora and take refuge there.... at my father's place and residence.

Despite my failure, my grandma still gave me the gift that she had brought me for my success, hidden in her pouch. It was a small bag of Kenya shillings notes and coins. She had saved this money for me from her selling bananas. She instructed me to humbly accept the present, not to count it and never divulge to anyone now or later how much it was. She continued, 'Whatever is inside, it is my gift to you, use it one by one, to help start your new life's journey, indeed, life itself is a journey.'

My grandma assured me that on her own word and said, 'By the time this gift runs out, for sure, you will be up and back on your own feet, able to survive.' This was the perceptible gift of success turned inside out into my bus fare, pocket money, and anything else necessary for my survival. The bus fare was not to Alliance Boys High School, it was not to Lenana Boys or Nairobi School. It was to Nairobi 'City in the Sun', to my supposed 'self-imposed exile.'

In my mind, I was embarking on a trip almost to nowhere. I was probably heading to *sheol*, the abyss. However, on a second thought, I was at least heading somewhere.... or to some place I didn't even know very well. I was going to open a new and another chapter in my life, along the road to my destiny.

With nil academic qualifications and no school certificates in my pocket or grandma's given pouch, even a School Leaving Certificate, not knowing what lay ahead of me or for me, I left my village. I left my comfortable zone to Nairobi the big 'City in the Sun', a jungle for me. I was very, very scared. I had never felt like this before. I was a very miserable and vulnerable Young man, thrown in the deep end of life and amid the urban jungle.

I recalled the unwillingness of my Headmaster to support my application for a high school. This had affected my morale, to the extent of the loss of the will power and even the 'courage to be.' It may have impacted my memory and subsequent studies. In those days, I thrived on encouragement and praise, rather than challenges and ridicules.

My failure and the constant ridicules that were already so many this time and in numerous past times, had almost suffocated me. Luckily, by this time I had lost count and was no longer bothered any more. In view of this, after the shock of my life: KPE failure, I started acknowledging ridicule as a form of motivation for me, a challenge to be overcome.

Similarly, I had started exploring and reading about people who had turned failure into success. I had started taking to heart my mother's stories of people, who had turned futility into opportunities and possibilities. At this juncture I recalled the encouraging story of David Livingstone's background and life, who later became, a great Scottish Missionary and explorer.

At times I thought, maybe I was synonymous with *Yohana Musilu* - Foolish John, my namesake in Kiluhya. In the 'Foolish John's' story, he followed his mother's instructions and always did his best and what was expected. I loved this character most in my Early Years Vernacular lessons. I empathised with Foolish John very much.

'Foolish John's' best was not always necessarily successful. There was apparently always another challenge ahead that he had not anticipated or prepared for. So, he made so many blunders overall, but also learned so much from each blunder.

This story had imparted in and on me the love, great passion for reading and improving my literacy skills. I always endeavoured to read more pages to try to find out what 'Foolish John' will do next. Additionally, it had also taught me that life is full of surprises.

Occasionally, with no offence, my peers jokingly, and sometimes the bullies too, called me *Yohana Musilu* - Foolish John, to ridicule and put me down. Surprisingly, I could identify myself with 'Foolish John's' blunders. I could also empathise with his resilience and relentless attempts to do his best in the next unexpected situation, demand, new encounters and challenges.

Amidst the challenges 'Foolish John' encountered on his errands for his mother or parents, he was willing to take another errand, another challenge again, and again, regardless of the blunders he made up early on. He never grumbled. He just endeavoured to improve and learn from each of his apparent 'foolishness' or carelessness.

Sometimes 'Foolish John' made reckless mistakes. However, even if his good intentions backfired, he went forward without hesitation. This was succinctly displayed, demonstrated and characterised by each of his next move and action. He went forth on the next errand, without any excuse, complaining or even grumbling.

As I mentioned earlier, my Primary School fees were actually paid for by my father's employers. Most of them sponsored me directly. One of them Patrick Jubb, continued to pay my fees, long after returning to UK, until I finished my Primary School.

My Headmaster updated my sponsor regularly and particularly every term, after my every three months assessment and exams. This included my effort, performance and progress. Once I was able to write, I communicated with my sponsor regularly, especially during the Christmas Season and the New Year. He was my first pen pal. Later, I enjoyed communicating with pen pals from all over the world, whose addresses and contacts, I got from Reader's Digest magazines, discarded by my father's bosses.

Just before my fateful exams, I suddenly lost contact with Patrick Jubb, my father's former boss and my sponsor, who was paying my school fees and other expenses. Apparently, he was going through an acrimonious divorce, hence his quietness. Once he remarried and was on his feet, he re-established lines of communication again. However, by this time, it was rather too late. My school years were almost gone, over and out.

The new education system introduced by Otiende Commission in 1964, seemed to have had no alternatives or equivalent of KPE. To be able to move on in future, register for the next level exams, I would have to produce KPE certificate. Without it, I was really stuck for life.

I cannot remember anyone else from my village, leave alone my entire location, whose name literally never appeared on 'the wall.' Equally, those who had failed in my school or village never moved on, never ventured or made it outside our village. They never ventured or made it beyond or on the far side of the globe.

Chapter Thirteen: What Next?

As I boarded the night bus (coach), after the fateful KPE failure, the inevitable question on my mind was 'What Next?' Indeed, the next chapter in my life was about to begin. I myself, 'How was I going to live in a strange land, far away from home?' I also wondered, 'How am I going to survive in my forthcoming strange environment?'

While on the bus, my mind continued to be bombarded with many more thoughts and questions: 'How will I ever realise my dreams and my destiny? With my plight, my apparent failure, what can I do next?'

In view of this, I made up my mind to live one day at a time. Of course, when I left my village, I headed towards Nairobi, as advised by mother and my grandmother, apparently, my destination, to The City in the Sun. I wondered, 'Is the City in the Sun going to shine on me, with a bright sunny future?' Seemingly, it also rains a lot in Nairobi. Besides, I thus wondered, 'Will it also rain on me showers of blessings or pour on me storms of destruction?'

En route, while pondering about the many questions in my mind regarding my destiny, I randomly and unconsciously opened the Bible my Mum had given me. I landed on the book of Exodus in the Old Testament.

Exodus is a Greek word that literally means going out. It is the movement of the people of Israel from Egypt. It is the story of liberation and freedom, from slavery to the Promised Land, Canaan; the 'land flowing with milk and honey.'

Was I likewise, being liberated to 'my promised land, my Canaan?', I asked myself, if so, how was life going to be in my apparent promised land?' Astonished, I marvelled,

'Will I have a bright and even *any* future?' I continued to ponder and ask myself 'Do I have any hope of a better life in this land I am migrating to, away from my home, my comfortable zone?'

Moreover, whenever I felt dejected, my mother had always encouraged me with stories of heroes with humble background. I was mesmerised by how the apparent failures, rose from nowhere, to unbelievable achievements and destiny. She also often narrated to me and reminded me of heroic biblical characters that fuelled her faith. I often reflected on these stories too. Amazingly, I had taken them on board subconsciously. I took them with me everywhere I went, especially the stories of Abraham, Isaac, Joseph, Moses and David, to mention a few that often sprang to my mind.

I often remember the story of Abraham, who left his homeland in Ur of the Chaldeans for an unknown destination. The story of Joseph, dragged from his homeland, his comfortable zone, and sold into slavery by his own kinsmen, his own brothers - and thrived.

I loved the story of David, a humble shepherd boy, from a humble poor background to a mighty King. Moses, the boy born into poverty, born into slavery, born with speech impairment, but became the confident liberator. Surprisingly, de facto, I was reading the story of Moses: The Exodus, and its liberation theme.... Was this a coincidence?

I reflected on this story, while waiting for the bus to Nairobi. While on the bus, before sunset and before darkness blanketed the bus, I enjoyed reading the story of Joseph, the subsequent slavery and the dawn of liberation via Moses.

When I woke up early in the morning at sunrise and the crack of dawn, the theme on my mind was liberation. While waiting for the bus, even on the bus to my father, the theme was liberation.

So even though ostracised from my village by my unmistakable patent failure, the theme on my mind was - liberation. I thought to myself, 'This time it is actually the more needed liberation, my liberation.' Deep inside me, I felt as if I had already been liberated, set 'free at last.'

In Nairobi, I boarded the bus to my father's ramshackle dwelling: this time I could sit anywhere and everywhere on any vacant seat on the bus, irrespective of my colour. Unlike UK, in Kenya, you do not excuse yourself to sit next to someone on the public transport like buses, coaches, trains and even *matatu,* the public minibus vehicles.

I could sit anywhere on the bus because segregation in Kenya was over and defunct. Kenya was now an independent country, a home of all races. In fact, I sat next to an Asian young man. Both of us were alighting at Broadway bus stop off Nairobi-Thika Road. He was going to his father at Tusker Breweries and I was going to my father's shack, in the middle of nowhere. My father's shack was in a vast, immense, monumental coffee plantation. It was on the edge of Nairobi and Kiambu Counties.

My father's boss was a researcher at Ruiru Coffee Research Station. He had decided to rent a house in the middle of a coffee plantation in Kiambu and commute to Ruiru, rather than live in the Nairobi City suburbs. His home was extremely far from the main road, far-flung off, far away, inaccessible, what I called 'in the middle of nowhere.' It was in a coffee plantation that belonged to a white settler and farmer: George Ramsay.

My father's abode was therefore far off the road. It was past Honourable Paul Ngei's home, a renowned Freedom Fighter veteran, imprisoned with His Excellency Mzee Jomo Kenyatta Kenya's first President. By then, Hon. Ngei was a senior Government Minister. For that matter, he was a no-nonsense man, and was feared by many. His home was fortified and heavily guarded by Kenya Police. You could dare not peep in or linger around.

There was no public transport from the main Nairobi-Thika Road to my father's employer and residence in the Kiambu County bordering Nairobi. My father lived in the Servant Quarter (SQ), in the backyard of his boss, in a corrugated iron sheets ramshackle that was ridiculously hot on a hot day, and very cold in the night and on a cold rainy day.

My father's house was a single room, with cooking and shower facilities outside. It was in a quiet place, but as noted earlier an exceptionally long walk from the main road. For the subordinate staff and their families, who had no means of transport of their own, this was an arduous trek, especially when trekking with groceries and luggage.

Of course, in those days, the days of my youth, even so, more recently, Uber and *boda boda* (motorcycle) was non-existent. Therefore, no public transport to the main road. Taxis only operated in the main city precincts of Nairobi. Without company and something to focus on, one would find it difficult to endure the long walk, arduous, trek to and from my father's abode.

This time, I was on my own; I had no company except my ever-arching question, 'What next?' The stories my parents narrated to me in my early childhood lingered in my mind. I began to reflect in my mind. I reflected on my childhood memories. This was supposed to keep me going and focused on my arduous journey.

I decide to "walk down the memory lane", my old rugged road. For a while, it kept my mind off the questions in my head. It broke the monotony of thinking and worrying about the scorching tropical sun and the road that still lay ahead. This would have just drained my energy and the will to go on.

I also had time for wishful thinking and reality check. By the time I got to my father, it was clear in my mind that I still had a passion for education. I still dreamed and wanted to go on with my education to secondary school, high school and even to University.

I wanted to have letters after and behind my name: *John Shabaya Malaya (BA).* I had failed my KPE. 'How was that going to happen or even be possible?' That was the recurring question and, always lingering on my mind, and lingered on my mind for an awfully long time.

My father was a bit surprised to see me. Of course, he was not expecting me, and he never ever thought I could make it alone to Nairobi and to his home. On this occasion and juncture in my life, I truly dreaded to encounter my father. However, he welcomed me warmly and just enquired of me: 'What is the urgency of your abrupt journey and visit?'

I replied, 'Baba no urgency or emergency.' I stammered, 'Baba, I have come to be taken to school.' He tried to solicit more information from me, and asked, 'Do you have your result slip?' Trembling with fear, I responded, 'I do not have any, Baba.' 'In that case we can look for the nearest newly established private school, the Asian private schools don't require any certificates, or pieces of paper, so long as we can afford to pay', he remarked. Your uncle Nuhu is attending one in the city.

My father was usually a strong and determined person. He was a no-nonsense man, with no emotions, the military type. However, unlike my other uncle, his younger brother, my father never joined the army. As a child, I feared my father. His face and look were enough. It said it all!

Whenever my father came home on vacation or leave, I had mixed feelings. While I was excited to see him and receive many nice presents from Nairobi, I was also scared stiff, for the apparent 'discipline' that would ensue.

My father's presence would usher in an extremely strict regime, but just for a while. On several occasions, he would rain canes on me in the name of discipline. My parents had this biblical belief and admonition, 'spare the rod, and spoil the child,' therefore, they spared none, lest they spoil the child.

Mama would therefore archive in her wonderful memory almost all my misdemeanours for even over a year. Believe it or not, my mother had an incredibly good and splendid memory. She would then report my misdemeanours or misdeeds, one by one, in graphic details, to my dad spanning all the time he was away.

My father would then pull out his 'rod' and cane, and subsequently give me words of wisdom, as if he had forgotten to rain and inflict the long-awaited pain. He would reprimand me. Then, suddenly, spring up on me, 'surprise and owe strategy,' bang! there he was. He would stretch his rod and rain on me numberless canes, never to forget, until he returned in another year or so.

However, to my surprise, this time, my Dad was calm and empathetic. He neither quarrelled, pulled out his rod, or cane, nor even scolded me at all. Amazingly, he never even commented on my failure, and my apparent let-down of the family. As *Mwana wa mbeli,* the first-born, the future of my family, my mother and my siblings, hinged on my success.

To my astonishment, this time, I discovered the real caring and fatherly side of my father. Indeed, I felt like the Prodigal Son. This time he was not judgemental towards my failure, my apparent doomed future, with all its implications for my family, his family.

Instead, my father warmed for me water on the *jiko,* the charcoal burner, for me to wash myself. He gave me his clean clothes to wear, even though they were oversize for me. He then took my dirty clothes and washed them together with the laundry of his boss.

Unlike my father, the father I had in my mind, the one that lingered in my childhood memories and mind, he gave me a nice cup of tea. He also gave bread, with butter and beans on toast as well, the apparent 'crumbs under the table,' leftovers from his boss's breakfast.

My father was so economical and noted for never wasting food, like throwing leftovers. He would, for economic reasons, encourage us to clear leftovers. We therefore learned to first use leftovers, before embarking on preparing a new dish or meal.

Being a superb cook, my father would even reuse leftovers, turning them into another delicious, starter, main dish, or just a dessert. However, on this occasion, he later laid on a big traditional meal for me. It was a combination and mixture of *ugali* maize/corn meal, with *sukuma wiki,* kale and chicken. In retrospect, it was indeed a celebratory meal, a 'homecoming,' away from home, yet at home.

In those days, people from upcountry, particularly, Western Kenya, where I was born, never saw Nairobi or other cities and towns as *ingo*, home. Most people from Western Kenya never retired outside their home village or were interred outside their roots area.

For most Luhya's and Luo's, *ingo, nyalgunga* – home, was in the village of their roots. Home was therefore in Western Kenya. Nairobi was a place to work, and residence in *inzu,* a house. Therefore, my father's residence was just *inzu*, a house, not a home, a temporary place to stay at and live in, waiting to return home, yet I felt as if I had arrived home.

On this occasion, I felt as if my father treated me like a prince. We reminisced over the meal. He assured me that he was willing and going to help me pick up the broken pieces and rebuild my life and my future.

He comforted, encouraged me and remarked, 'You will pursue your passion and destiny my son.' With more assurance, he continued, 'This is not the end of the road, but just the beginning of an uphill climb.' He cleared his throat and continued, 'It is a sharp bend to be negotiated on the road to your destiny.' He advised me not to worry about my failure or linger on the bad patch of my past, but focus on the emerging possibilities and opportunities, awaiting to unfold in the future.

By nature, my father was overly optimistic. On the following day, my father asked for a day off. We went off on our expedition. We trekked for over ten miles on school hunting in Nairobi and the neighbourhood. Unfortunately, none of the city schools were willing to accept me.

Apart from his optimism, my father was also a man of great determination. He never gave up easily. He requested me to give him more time to find me a school on his other day off. The following Monday, he got a day off.

This time round, we headed to the neighbouring Ruiru town. The Red Lion Hotel had been converted into Ruiru High School. The new school was owned by some Kenyan Asians in conjunction with the son of our President Jomo Kenyatta. He was called Peter Muigai.

Ruiru High School had boarding facilities. I was offered a place to board. The only qualified teachers on the staff were the Headteacher and his deputy. The rest were unqualified young men and women; majority being Kenyan Asians, who had just finished secondary school education. They were waiting for their results, and subsequent university intake.

Thus, most of the teachers were looking forward to joining the university or further education. However, unlike my preceding primary school teachers, they were patient, with no canes in their hands. There was no harassing and scarring of learners. So long as I could understand their accent, all was well. As the school had limited resources, teaching was more teacher centred, rather than learner centred.

At last, and at least, I had found teachers who believed in me. They often encouraged me with such statements like: 'determination has got no barrier', 'the sky is the limit', 'work hard and reach for the stars', etcetera.

This made a great difference to me. Indeed, I realised that a good teacher or mentor, can make a big difference in a learner's life. I made up my mind to become one of them, teaching became my passion, my next ambition and career.

However, my time at Ruiru High School was short lived. My father's former employer Patrick Jubb paid my fees for about six months, for about two academic terms, approximately one semester, then we lost contact again.

My father could not afford to pay my fees. When Patrick Jubb stopped paying my fees, that was the end of the road for me. Due to financial constraints, I soon dropped out of school. Once more, I was on the road again.

By this time, my mother had joined my father, to explore possibilities of making some contribution to the increasing family expenses. My father was finding it difficult to manage single handed. As my father lived closer to Kiambu County, my mother was able to secure a temporary coffee picking job in Kiambu County, close to my father's one room, corrugated iron sheets ramshackle.

Coffee pickers pay was based on how much pounds or kilos of coffee one harvested daily. Most coffee pickers were temporary, unskilled casual labourers, on incredibly low wages or pay. It was cash at hand job, without any employees' rights, benefits, such as annual leave, holiday, and so forth.

I moved in with my parents, in their one room shack. I joined my mother in the coffee picking, as a casual labourer. At least now I had some income and I could contribute to the family pot. I also raised funds and paid for correspondence courses and continued with my passion for education.

The nice twist to my failure story, is that I established, forged and formed awfully close relationship with my father, whilst I was nearer him and with him in Nairobi. I now had a male role model, a father figure close by. This meant a lot to me. It had a significant impact on me. It transformed my whole outlook to life and motivated me to focus on my studies and make the best of my situation. As I bonded more with my father, I realised how important a father figure is in any child's life.

Aged 15, I studied privately and whenever possible. I used public libraries, mainly over the weekend. Nairobi had a good number of public libraries, like the British Council Library, McMillan Library, Kenya National Library and Nairobi City Council Library.

Most of my weekdays study time was at night, after a day's hard labour. As for most weekends, after a long week's labour, I studied daytime. While working, picking coffee in Kiambu County and studying privately, day after day, time after time, the question on my mind was now, 'where next?'

Chapter Fourteen: On My Own: Where Next?

After Christmas celebrations of December 1967, aunt Ezina Sambili, my mother's eldest sister decided to help with my plight. Auntie had no children of her own. She worked as an ayah girl, with meagre income, but she was very generous to her nephews and nieces.

Even though my aunt was a grown up, an adult mature lady, she was always referred to by her bosses and their friends as the 'ayah girl', reminiscent of colonial terminology for female domestic servant or female house help servant, a European families' care giver, mainly caring for the kids and even the elderly parents if any.

Like my Mum, auntie was illiterate. She could not literally read or scribble anything. She used thumb print to sign for her wages and all other vital documents and transactions. Nevertheless, unlike my mum, auntie Ezina was conversant with, and fluent in English. She had picked up English over many years that she worked for Europeans and with European kids.

My auntie was amazing. Moreover, although she was illiterate, she had learned English, without stepping in a formal language school or classroom. Her English was oral, spoken language. She mainly acquired her English, from the various European kids she took care of, interacted with and encountered in her line of duty and work as an ayah.

As auntie had to communicate in English with European kids and their parents, one way or the other, English being the lingua franca for her job, she had no choice, but to learn it orally and by all means. This in return, secured her jobs and future career as an Ayah.

Auntie was inspiring, passionate, loving and patient with kids. In fact, I was always amazed and wondered, how she managed kids of a different ethnicity and culture. Even though auntie Ezina did not have any kids of her own, she was always exceptionally good with kids. Her relationship with us her nephews and nieces, said it all.

Moreover, even though she was illiterate, she was also a good teacher. She taught most of the European kids under her care basic life skills and Kiswahili language. As such, she was a great inspiration to me. I learned a great deal from her. I loved my auntie Ezina.

Aunt Ezina lived in the Servant Quarters (SQ), in the back yard of her employers' compound. By this time, she worked and resided in Lavington, particularly Bernard Estate Area. It was a pity my aunt was not allowed or supposed to live with anyone else in her residence. Moreover, her SQ or abode was a tiny house, a one small single room, in the backyard of her boss, almost like my father's ramshackle.

Like my father's shack, Auntie's room was also, only partitioned by *kitenge* fabric. Therefore, there was no room for me or anyone else at my auntie's. Auntie Ezina was a very loving aunt. Among all her nephews and nieces, she especially loved my little sister Agnes to bits.

Auntie even tried to adopt my little sister, but all was in vain. As my aunt was employed as a 'Miss', with no children of her own, her bosses did not allow her to foster any children, even her needy relatives like her nephews and nieces. Hence, she tried to help her many nephews and nieces, by contributing towards clothing and any other essentials.

By Christmas 1967, it had become exceedingly difficult for me to live with my father in his squashed one room. In

January 1968, I moved out of my father's ramshackle to my auntie's. Little did I know, my Auntie's abidance had a lot of restrictions. Therefore, it was a 'hide and seek' game, to ensure her bosses did not find out.

The 'hide seek' game became a difficult game to safely play. Most of the residences in Lavington and up market suburbs of Nairobi, had *mbwa kali* – fierce dog signs all over the gates. This was not only meant to keep off intruders, but in reality, several residences had huge, well fed, fierce dogs.

Part of my hide and seek game was to make sure I do not encounter my aunt's bosses' humongous fierce dog. However, one day, I turned up as usual, but this time the *mbwa kali*, the fierce dog, was still outside and bounced on me unaware.

With its 'surprise and owe,' it suddenly tore into my leg. My aunt rushed to my rescue, at least to stop my being devoured with other dogs that were about to join in the feast. I still have the mark, the permanent scar on my left leg.

I could not complain to anyone. I just hoped that it did not have rabies. Of-course, it was my fault hiding and living with my aunt. I was an unwanted and unwelcome guest. Furthermore, I had blown out my cover, my hiding place. My hiding place was now gone, in fact, gone for good. In view of this and many other challenges in my game of 'hide and seek,' I could not live with my aunt anymore.

My Aunt was determined to help me. She rented a room for me in Gatina. Later, my uncle Ernest Keya, joined me, while he was studying Accounts in Nairobi City. Gatina was a slum area, not as large as the populated and the famous Line Saba Kibera slum.

Contrastingly, Gatina was just a Shanty Town. On one side, it was overshadowed by the magnificent Lavington Green, a posh area in Nairobi and Bernard Estate. On the other side, it was fringed by Kawangware, another slum area in Nairobi, and Riruta, renowned for its National High School, a high performing nationwide Roman Catholic Girls School: Precious Blood Girls High School.

My grandfather Vudohi Malaya when on a visit to my father in Nairobi, just before his demise (picture bequeathed by my grandmother Shamola Sambili.(

In those days, Lavington Green was mainly a White dominated suburb, with a few emerging African elite, mainly, University Professors, Cabinet Ministers, Senior Kenya Government officials, Representatives and Ambassadors of recent Independent African Nations.

In contrast, Gatina and the surrounding area were upcoming slum areas, with cheap shacks of houses, made of mud walls and rusty roofs of corroded, and corrugated iron sheets. The rooms were small, partitioned by card boards or filthy mud walls.

Each room in the neighbourhood was rented separately, to a different tenant and sometimes multiple tenants. Thus, my neighbouring house or room was just separated by a cardboard. In the other neighbourhood, most houses were just separated by muddy walls.

In view of this, Gatina was a real shanty town, mainly for the poor. It was indeed a poor housing area, primarily housing subordinate workers, working for the White population and a few elite Africans of Lavington Green and the surrounding suburbs.

While in Gatina, I volunteered to fetch water for residents in the neighbourhood. I especially targeted, male neighbouring tenants. Most of the male tenants, were ashamed to carry water in jerrycans. Most could not carry water on their heads from the distant tap. Some found it difficult to stand in long queues with women. Most women enjoyed the long queues, to have excuses for idle talk.

Water-supply was centralised on one, low pressure, tap. It was, almost just a dripping tap for each slum area. It took so long to fill up a few litres of jerrycans. Patiently I waited for my turn, drew the water unashamedly. I was not bothered by the said ladies' idle talk. I just minded my 'own business.' I drew the water and supplied the water to my clients.

In return, I received some small gratuity or a tip, which I used to pay for my correspondence courses. Meanwhile, I continued to figure out how to return to full time education. By April 1968, I had figured out and mapped a way forward.

I talked to my Aunt Ezina. She agreed to support me to go back to school. My Mum's coffee picking job in Kiambu County, consolidated with my auntie's support, I was able to pay my fees. Therefore, I was able to go back to full time formal education.

In May 1968, I applied for a place at President Kennedy Memorial High School (PKHS). Initially, I was attracted to President Kennedy Memorial High School because it was mentioned in the Kenya Parliament, The House of Representatives circa May 1966.

I had a lot of interest. The debate focused on the introduction of Kenya Junior Secondary School Examination (KJSE). The exam was supposed to help students who did not do well in their KPE. PKHS was used as one of the private schools allowed to progress to Form IV, to take Cambridge School Certificate, 'O' levels.

In May 1968, I was admitted at President Kennedy High School, Mfangano Street, Nairobi. It was on top floors, on the top of shops, in the middle of town, on a remarkably busy street. Again, it was a private, commercial day school. Like my former school, it was also owned by Kenyan Asians.

On the opposite side, was Haile Selassie Avenue, named after Emperor Haile Selassie of Ethiopia. There was also a big noisy agricultural produce market. Nairobi Railway Station, the headquarter of the defunct East African Railways, now Kenya Railways, was on the same road.

The Kenya Bus Station was just a stone throw away from my new school. It was also next to a Sikh Gurdwara, temple. Break time was spent in the car park below overlooking the school and the Bus Station. It had no fields, no playgrounds or Physical Education area. As such, the school was in a very noisy distracting area, and not a particularly good or conducive environment for learning.

To maximize profits, it had two streams. With its limited space, one stream came in the morning and the other stream in the afternoon. I was allocated an afternoon slot. I found it exceedingly difficult to concentrate in the afternoon tropical heat of Kenya, but it gave me ample time to walk to the school and arrive promptly, without any haste. Most of my peers were from mixed backgrounds. They were 'don't care' type of young people, who were not bothered and cared less about education.

Moreover, most of the teachers were young untrained teachers, still figuring out their future. Majority of them also cared less about quality education, or even quality teaching or learning. However, there were three inspiring teachers. One taught me both English Language and Literature, the other taught me Humanities, especially History. The third teacher passionately taught me Religious Education and Kiswahili.

Most of the students did not like Christian Religious Education and Kiswahili. They were considered dead subjects by my peers. However, as the teacher of these two subjects was passionate about her subjects and teaching, her subjects always came a live to me.

Like my aunt, the three good teachers, inspired my passion for languages. Unlike my illiterate aunt, they also instilled in me the passion for Humanities, especially Religious Studies and the quest for truth. I feel sad I cannot remember my teachers' names, as we always addressed them: Sir or Madam, a sign of respect.

The English Language teacher co-ordinated the Debating Society, the only available extra-curricular activity, in a school without much space or field. Inspired by his teaching, I joined the Debating Society. I really enjoyed it and in return, improved my command of English language, including communication skills, self-esteem and confidence, that would become vital later, in my ensuing career.

Fired and inspired by my three best teachers, as I had no bus fare, come sunshine, come rain, I trekked to school miles and miles away. I trekked day in, day out, day after day, term after term, time after time, not to miss any class or lesson. President Kennedy high school acknowledged and commended my effort, hard work, punctuality and debating interest.

Although I had no opportunity to proceed to National Examinations, at least, this time, I left school with a School Leaving Certificate. This for a long time, was the only certificate and recognition I had from my young schooling age and experience.

As soon as I joined formal school again, my mother returned to the village in Western Kenya. My aunt's employers had returned to their home in Europe. My aunt was made redundant. She could not get another job quickly and was now unemployed.

The fee we had raised, just paid for two terms, about one semester. My aunt being unemployed and my mother back in the village, I could not raise funds to continue with my full-time education. Come January 1969, in view of my financial constraints, I had no option but to drop out and try to get a job to survive. Incidentally, in such a short span, I dropped out of school again, hence, I was on the road again.

To make the matter worse, my uncle with whom I was living with, who was by now employed and helping with paying rent, eloped with his girlfriend. Subsequently, he moved out, and moved in with his girlfriend to her house in the adjacent Kawangware slum. This left me with the whole bill for the room, excluding upkeep and living expenses. Suddenly I was on my own; now, truly on my own.

Our family had increased to seven kids. My father was now really straining to manage; therefore, he could not help me. My aunt and uncle who were chipping in with my rent and upkeep were now nowhere to help.

Now I literally had nobody to support me. I had no money to pay rent for my ramshackle in the Gatina slum. I was about to become homeless. Having dropped out of school once again for having no money for fees, my future was once bleaker. I was doomed!

There are no State Benefits, Social Services or Public Funds to recourse to in Kenya. The society is hinged on African Socialism. Family, friends and communities endeavour to support each other, like my aunt Ezina and Uncle Keya had done.

Suddenly being on my own was becoming very tough - hard. However, I was a healthy, strong young man. So, I tried to get a job in Nairobi City. I whispered to myself, 'when the going gets tough, the tough get going.'

The following day, I woke up incredibly early in the morning. I trekked to Nairobi Central Business District (CBD) area, a journey that later became an everyday event. I figured that, if I stood by the familiar Uchumi Supermarket entrance, between Taifa Road, Harambee Avenue and Aga Khan Walk, not extremely far from my former school, I could earn some money. I could volunteer to help shoppers, more like the Nairobi City Parking Boys do, and earn some money to support myself.

That is exactly what I did. I volunteered to assist shoppers, especially the elderly, by carrying their heavy shopping bags to their cars, bus stop or railway station. Most reciprocated with some gratuity from their remaining shopping change. These were real handouts, but vital for me. These were hard times for me.

After a few days at the job, I noticed some shoppers found it difficult to get a parking space in the nearby car park. It paid more to help with car parking than 'poll bearer' job of helping shoppers with carrying their luggage and shopping.

I had developed a good rapport with some shoppers and knew who would stay for a shorter period or longer period. I began to juggle between carrying bags to cars and helping customers to find parking space. In other words, I opted to also become a real *chokora,* a parking boy,' the most loathed street job. On a more positive note and being streetwise, in the entrepreneurship language I had diversified my business.

Unlike a lot of young people, who tended to fear the judgement from their friends and families when they do not do well and end up in menial jobs, or on the street, I was proud of what I was doing. Of course, it helped me make ends meet. Naturally, and simply, I was now virtually on my own, surviving on my own and had no other option.

Competition with proper 'parking boys,' who were more streetwise than me in Nairobi, became stiffer and my gratuity dwindled. As there was a demand for selling and delivering charcoal, door to door in the neighbourhood, I opted to go for that. I rented a bicycle from a friend and embarked on selling and delivering charcoal door to door in the neighbourhood. While I was concerned about my job's contribution to deforestation, I had no choice, no other option. Moreover, it was hard work.

By the end of the day, or my work-shift, I looked more like a mineworker, mining gold in the defunct Roast Mines, near my home, in Kakamega County, Western Kenya. I was soiled daily, with black charcoal residues and soot.

This job was also short-lived. It was a temporary casual job, bound to end anytime, sooner than later. The friend whose bicycle I hired while he was at work, lost his job. For this reason, he left the area. Similarly, by his abrupt departure, I lost my means of transport to supply goods to my clients. That was it! It was the subsequent demise of my entrepreneurship, business acumen and hope. I had to wind up. I wound up, gracefully 'throwing in the towel' and bowing out.

Chapter Fifteen: The Rock Bottom

Having hit the rock bottom, my mother's admonition 'be still....,' came to the forefront of my mind. A lot of domestic and sub-ordinate house servants in Lavington, Kileleshwa, Kabete, up to Westlands, in Nairobi, lived in the Gatina slum. I therefore lived among a lot of these staff.

One day, as I was on my usual errands of drawing and supplying water, I bumped into my long-time school mate and best friend. To use my father's figurative language, 'our paths had not crossed' since our primary school days. Here and now, they at last crossed. We had not seen each another, for over three years. Here we were face to face with one another.

It was a nice surprise and a great joy to encounter each other again. Unlike our encounter before, in a school environment, at Chamakanga Primary School. This time we met again in a strange land, far away from my home, sweet home and comfortable zone. It felt like a haven without the school bullies, including some bully teachers.

We reminisced over our past experiences, so long that I almost forgot my errands. Apparently, my friend had been informed by my uncle that I was residing within the Gatina slum. It was a rainy day. I dreaded being in Gatina slum on rainy days.

Gatina was usually very filthy on rainy days. In fact, I always carried two pairs of shoes to the main tarmacked road. When venturing beyond Gatina, it was advisable to be street wise. Lavington Green, our main bus stop area, linking us to the city centre and yonder, had tarmacked all weather neat roads. From Gatina, one looked like a stranger, an alien from Mars, with filthy, muddy shoes.

My friend told me about his new life. He had been converted. He was now worshipping at Lavington United Church on the Lavington Green, adjacent to Lavington Green shopping centre. I enquired more about my friend's newfound faith and church.

My friend expounded more about the new church he had joined. He informed me that it was an Ecumenical Church: Anglican, Methodist and Presbyterian Churches, united to form a united church. The church was mainly, built by The Methodist Missionary Society (MMS).

Based on 'spheres of influence,' The Methodist Church had no footing or missionary work in Nairobi, yet Nairobi was the capital city. Through Lavington, The Methodist Church initially endeavoured to set foot in Nairobi. The church was exuberant, beaming with various outreach activities like Study Groups, Urafiki Club, Scouts and Girl Guides, Youth Club, Badminton Club, Cine Club, Drama and Acting, Table Tennis, etc.

He also talked about his job. Of course, unlike me, he had a job. He was a subordinate staff member. working as a Shamba Boy, a colonial term for a gardener. He worked in the new upcoming estate between Lavington, the Old Strathmore College, off St Austin Road, St Mary's School and Kileleshwa, also bordering Kenya High School.

The New area was just set up mainly for expatriates. Most of these expatriates were providing specialist knowledge, skills, service, etc. They were apparently helping the newly independent Kenya, to get on its own feet. Some Kenyan critiques, viewed expatriates, with a lot of suspicion. They were perceived as neo-colonialists and expatriates aid or apparent help as neo-colonialism.

As it was getting late in the evening, and with the abrupt tropical sunset, and impending rain, we agreed to meet again the following evening, to pick up our story again. We exchanged addresses. I discovered, in fact we lived close and near to each other, just a few metres apart.

The following evening, we met at my friend's house and continued where we had stopped. This time, my friend told me more about the Weekly Discussion and Bible Study Group on Tuesdays 20:00–22:00 (8 – 10 PM). My friend invited me, to go along with him to the group. It was usually held at the Manse. The Rev John Myer was then the Minister of Lavington United Church at that time, he himself was a Methodist Minister.

I enjoyed the discussion and the freedom by which, we explored and talked about life issues, faith, hope, love, theological questions, ultimate questions, existence of God and overall, the quest for truth. The atmosphere in the room and among the group members, was reminiscent of my debating experience at President Kennedy High School. This was unlike my mother's church, which by now I had abandoned.

In addition, this group was more focused on real life issues. The Rev John Myer, presided. He gently, skilfully and pastorally, guided the group through the various topics and questions. He ensured discussions were focused, acknowledging various diverse views, opinions and personal convictions.

He guaranteed that the group did not digress from the set topic of the respective evening. He also made sure that there was no offending of one another. He encouraged respect across the board, irrespective of ethnicity, age, class or gender. I felt the group adhered to the Biblical teaching: 'There is neither Jew, nor Geek, there is neither slave, nor free, there is neither male nor female, for you are all ONE...... (Galatians 3:28).

On the following Sunday, my friend invited me to the Sunday Services: English Service at 10:30, Kiswahili Service at 14:30 (2.30 PM) and later English Evening Service 18:30 (6.30 PM). All the three services were very impressive and appealing to me. I was spoiled for choice.

Even though all the services were mixed race services, Kiswahili Service was more appealing to Non-English speakers' resident, in Lavington, those from the surrounding neighbourhood, and as far as Dagoretti Corner. Both Morning and Evening English services were mainly for those more conversant with English.

For convenience, the Lavington Green area subordinate staff, also attended the Kiswahili Service. Most of them worked early Sunday shifts as house servants or cooks. As such, they were only available in the afternoons.

Urafiki Club also met weekdays in the afternoon 14:00 – 16:00. It focused mainly on helping illiterate people in the neighbourhood, to again and improve their literacy, numeracy and life skills. Attendance and membership included subordinate staff in Lavington area and the neighbourhood.

Majority of the beneficiaries of Urafiki Club were subordinate staff in Lavington Green and the neighbourhood. A lot of people from the neighbouring slums like Gatina, Kangemi and Kawangware also benefited from Urafiki Club, and extensively improved their numeracy, literacy and life skills.

After a few days of attending the worship, helping at Urafiki Club, Discussion and Bible Study Group, I was invited to an Open-Air Meeting in Nairobi CBD area. It was an Ecumenical Service, in the Central Park, between Kenyatta Venue, Nyerere Road and Uhuru Highway, near YWCA, St Andrews Church and Nairobi University.

The park was filled to the brim. In fact, the dais or podium was pitched on the grounds of the current Serena Hotel, Nairobi. This was well before Serena Hotel was built on part of the Central Park. The preacher was the late Bishop Festo Kivengere from Uganda.

During the preaching, towards the end of the service, I had a strange experience. I had a 'strange feeling.' I felt great inner peace. The inner part of me was at an exceptional peace. I had inexplicable, immense tranquillity within me. Thereafter, there was a significant paradigm shift in my life. It was 'an about turn.' Henceforth, I started perceiving life and the world I live in differently. My pursuit for knowledge and quest for truth was further enhanced. This was coupled with my new life's motto: 'All for God.'

Afterwards, I was nurtured by Lavington United Church, joint Anglican, Methodist and Presbyterian Churches. That was the beginning of my extraordinary interest in the quest for truth and subsequent zeal for my pursuit of Theology.

So, as I had hit the rock bottom, I remembered my friend. I regretted why I did not share with him my plight when we met. We always used to encourage each other, with maxims like, a 'problem shared', is 'a problem solved.'

On our next encounter, I decided to share my plight with my friend. Without any hesitation, he invited me to move in with him. His abode was just a shack of one room in Gatina slums. Like 'birds of the same feather, flocking together,' we had a lot in common. Although my friend was over six years older than me, we were both young. We were both far away from home, from the green, green grass of our sweet home of Idakho. However, I was penniless, jobless, and hunting for a job.

Therefore, that was an offer and a great opportunity that I would not hesitate to grab with both hands. Of course, I was on the verge of being thrown out of my shack. My rent was long overdue, and the Landlord was threatening to act. As I had 'hit the rock bottom,' I appreciated my friend's generosity, and seized the 'opportune moment.'

I moved in with my friend. As I was impecunious, penniless, my friend gave me free accommodation. In return, I offered to do all housed-hold chores for him and his companions.

In due course, my friend was promoted to another job. He asked me if I was willing to do his job before someone else grabs it. If so, I can take over his dirty job, as he was now surrendering it.

He had been employed by Mr. Frank Lund, a British expatriate, who worked for the prestigious East Africa Railways, later Kenya Railways, probably as an Accountant. His compound was among the new houses in the newly set up estate, mainly for the new breed of post-independence expatriates.

Mr. Lund was the Treasurer and Organist at Lavington United Church. In fact, I later discovered, he wielded a lot of power. Mr. Lund controlled almost everything at Lavington United Church, including kids club, and so forth. He was also particularly good at Do it Yourself (DIY) for the church.

I jumped at the opportunity. I took up the job and thanked my friend from the bottom of my heart. The following day, he took me to my new prospective employer. He introduced me to Mr. and Mrs. Lund. I was briefed about the job and given the relevant tools for the job. Without any hesitation or a signed contract, I took up the job and embarked on my duties.

With a spade, a fork, a wheelbarrow, other bits and bobs, in my hand, off I went, as duty called. During the day, my responsibilities were mainly landscaping single handed. For a young lad like me, aged 17, this was a bit too much to handle, but I did not mind. I was overjoyed just to have a job.

My job included levering and moving earth. It also involved digging up big and heavy rocks, uprooting humongous and gigantic trunks and stumps of trees. There was a lot of red soil I had to carry, move around and spread all over the ground.

The grounds were about one acre - 0.5 ha. I moved the soil and worked like an earth mover machine. I worked like a tractor commonly known as caterpillar machine. Friends who passed by and beheld my work, nicknamed me Mr. Bulldozer. Others called me Caterpillar or JB, the earth mover.

I planted and watered various species of plants. I planted the green grass of home, beautiful tropical plants, flowers, thorny key-apples, bougainvillea, cypress trees, shrubs, roses of various colours, etc. Within few months, I transformed the barren land, open vast space, into a 'perfect garden.' It had exotic plants and a beautiful, mowed and tidied up garden.

Once the hedge grew, it was opaque, insulating the occupiers from the outside world, also keeping off the 'peeping toms' and unwelcome intruders. The garden made the new home tranquil, peaceful and a haven of peace. I was indeed immensely proud of my work.

My other duties included washing and cleaning, including, morning car hand-wash and regular polishing of the bosses and madam's cars and thoroughly cleaning in and out. Car wash and polishing was a regular daily duty and routine, every Monday to Friday. This was irrespective of whether the car was dirty or not. It also did not matter whether it rained or was dry. Come rain, come sunshine, I just had to do it.

Another daily routine was also polishing their shoes every morning. From 06:00-16:00 hours, I was up on my heals, running a round Mr Lund's compound, like a yo-yo or mad person. I ran all over, up and down, roaring like a lion, or for that matter, like a bulldozer moving earth. By the end of the day, I was so exhausted from head to toe, and completely written off.

Compared to the job I did, I was paid 'peanuts.' The payment was cash at hand monthly, unlike my former jobs of cash at hand daily. I had to learn budgeting, to manage my meagre finances to last me through the month, share and support my mother and my siblings as well. For whatever I earned, I shared with my mother in the village, to supplement my father's meagre income for the family budget.

Like most homes, the shamba boy job at Mr. Lund's home and a few of other newly constructed upcoming homes, had only one SQ, mainly for house boys or ayah girls. Between the ayah girl and the house boy, whoever worked longer hours, especially late into the night and early in the morning, was allocated the SQ on the premises. As such, most shamba boys – gardeners, did not reside at their workplace. Likewise, I continued to stay with my friend.

As Mr Lund's and the neighbouring compounds were each over one acre: 0.5 ha., the shamba boy or gardener's job was therefore tough. To get going on this tough job, I had to get tough as well. Of course, it was a promotion for me. I had been promoted from my earlier jobs in Kiambu and Nairobi: coffee picking, potter, parking boy, charcoal delivery and water distribution.

Furthermore, I had been reduced to nothing, having been unemployed for sometimes, to the extent of being literally impecunious and helpless. I just wanted a job, any job, anything that would help me put food on the table, and literally just survive.

I was therefore, thrilled to get a job. For that reason, I put in all my might. I walked countless miles every day to my place of work. I also walked a lot of dead mileage, distance at my workplace. I literally walked up and down at my place of work. Building on my school days experience of walking to Chamakanga Primary School, I developed the necessary stamina, required to make ends meet and survive.

I also built up a lot of muscles, my friends nicknamed me 'Muscle Power,' vital for lifting and moving stuff, a lot of stuff. Others just nick-named me 'Mr. Muscle.' I had to move a lot of stuff at my workplace. Therefore, I needed more muscle and muscle power became inevitably significant. Additionally, I was as fit as a fiddle, another vital outcome, and a necessity for the tough job.

This experience later, became vital and indispensable for long distance walk and my heavy-duty jobs. Later, my tough shamba boy experience, became vital for my future career, including military training, subsequent military service and field exercises as an Officer-Chaplain.

In view of my commitment and exemplary service at Mr Lund's, I was later promoted to *Toto jikoni*, literally, 'kitchen child,' hence, a colonial terminology for Kitchen Assistant or helper. *toto* is a distorted version of Kiswahili – *mtoto,* a child.

Etymologically, *toto* was from Indians pronunciation and used more during the colonial period, referring to the subordinate staff as '*toto*', either assuming 'm' was silent or they were just lazy and arrogant. If so, they could not be bothered to pronounce *mtoto* correctly.

Maybe it was sheer and mere arrogance that Black Kenyans and Africans for that matter, did not matter. Thus, they were perceived to be mere kids to be tossed around. I leave that for linguistics indulgences and historians to decipher and ascertain.

Whatever the meaning, connotations or etymology of *toto jikoni*, I can only remember, it paid better than any of my preceding jobs. In comparison, any jobs I had undertaken before, could not match, nor beat *toto jikoni*. Comparably, overall, its duties were lighter.

For example, I had the luxury of working in-doors most of the time. Moreover, I had a lot of cups of tea in the morning, at break itself, lunch time, in the evening, and not forgetting after supper or meals. Kenya being numbered among the top tea growing countries, as *toto jikoni*, I lived out the Kenya saying and belief, 'any time is teatime'.

As a *toto jikoni*, I also had the privilege to dine on the delicious 'crumbs,' the leftovers, the so called 'crumbs under the table'. And surely, I was guaranteed of some delicious leftovers, from breakfast, lunch to dinner. Most *toto jikoni* and house helps, chefs, ayahs, fed from 'crumbs under the table' - 'the leftovers.' Hence, most sub-ordinate staff in the Middle-Class homes were usually chubby and plump.' So, I joined them, and became rather chubby. However, I was healthier, compared to the prior 'skinny Billy long legs' that I was in the preceding and foregone times.

Moreover, as *toto jikoni*, I was also terrorised and bullied by the house boy and ayah girl. Likewise, sometimes, I was also bullied by the bosses themselves. Most of the time, I was bullied into doing most of the work, while the house boy, kitchen helper and ayah girl just enjoyed themselves and took the praise that was really mine and rightfully so. I never dared cross the paths of my 'bully' colleagues or report them to the boss, lest I get into a lot of more trouble to the extent of losing my job, my one and only job.

Good work, good rapport and relationships, meant chances of recommendation for a better job, better opportunities. *Toto jikoni* was usually an apprentice job. It was a chance and an opportunity to learn and demonstrate one's ability. It was an opportunity to rise and shine, then move on, move on to greener pastures.

At the recommendation of the house boy and other house helpers, *toto* jikoni, could catapult you into a greater future, especially like-me, if KPE did not. In most cases, the *toto jikoni* understudied the house boy and took over later. If not, *toto jikoni* being like a steppingstone or ladder, slingshot one to a bright, greater and more promising future

Chapter Sixteen: Greater Promotion

The Caretaker at Lavington United Church finally retired in 1969. By then, my friend had become a regular attender and worshipper at Lavington United Church. Furthermore, my friend had been confirmed as a full member of Lavington United Church. On the retirement of the Lavington United Church Caretaker, my friend was employed as the Caretaker of the prestigious Lavington United Church. My friend was thus elevated to what we called 'Greater Promotion.'

In view of the services I was rendering my friend, he vowed not to leave me behind. He beseeched me to move together with him to his ' Greater Promotion' residence. Thus, I was offered the opportunity to partake in the opulence of the accommodation that came with my Friend's job.

The accommodation then, according to us and our standards of that time, was fabulous and fantastic. It was a stone-built house, situated behind the Lavington United Church hall, on the scenic Lavington Green.

The house was one bedroomed with a foyer, dining room-cum lounge and a cooking place. It had running water, therefore, had a shower and flushing toilet. Moreover, it had electricity and was furnished with basic furniture. As a matter of fact, we were so excited to have such a magnificent and luxurious residence.

The house being behind the church, and on the beautiful Lavington Green, it had a special mien. It was just next and adjacent to the then stunning Lavington Green Shopping Centre. Unlike the dusty and muddy filthy roads of Gatina slum, Lavington Green area roads, were tarmacked. Alongside, the main roads, there were exquisite, nicely paved tarmacked footpaths.

Prior to independence in 1963, Lavington Green area was a 'Whites only area.' It was dotted with Black African subordinate workers, who served and worked for the whites. In contrast, Gatina slums was a Black African area.

The Lavington Green shopping centre was therefore formally a 'Whites only' shopping area, setup in the gorgeous beautiful, bonny gardens. People from the neighbouring slums often had various names for it: The Garden of Eden, Hanging Gardens of Babylon or even heaven come down to earth area. It was stunningly beautiful.

As a former colonial 'Whites only' area, Lavington Green was a very developed area, unlike Gatina and surrounding Black African slums. It was pretty, adorable, beautifully landscaped, with exotic plants and flowers.

Lavington Green was reminiscent of racial colonial segregation of 'whites only' luxurious environment, vis a vis Black Africans undeveloped surrounding area. However, by this time it was a mixed and interracial area, even though majority of the residents and homeowners were in effect Whites, many being expatriates.

In Gatina slum, come rain come sunshine, I had learned to be set. I was ever ready. In contrast, with our new residence, there was no need for two pairs of shoes during the rainy season: One for the muddy, filthy roads and the other for the decent town roads and so forth. In fact, unlike Lavington Green, imagine Gatina slum, was a place, where, 'streets had no names.'

Suddenly, we were resident in Lavington Green, where the roads were tarmacked, streets had names the famous being Lavington Road, gateway into Lavington Green. Thus, roads were all weather roads. Come rain, come sunshine, the place was well drained as well.

Residing in Gatina was unbelievably a useful preparation for my life to come, including residing in UK. Life in Gatina was in many ways unpredictable, like the UK renowned unpredictable weather. Of course, often, life itself is unpredictable, no matter where you are. One never knows what the future holds. Literally, 'life, is like a box of chocolate, you never know, what you gonna get' (words of Forest Forest Gump, 1994 comedy-drama film *Forest Gump).*

In fact, being in our new residence, it felt as we were reliving a children's fairy tale, a folklore story. The environment and atmosphere of my newfound blessings and residence could have been described as mythical, yet it was real.

For me, coming from the Gatina slum, my newfound residence was more than mythical. It was. but truthfully grand, fabulous, awesome, and a stupendous accommodation. I had no better adjectives, to describe it.

Lavington United Church was remarkably busy during the day, weekdays and weekends alike. It was almost occupied day and night (twenty-four seven - 24/7). It was booming with activities like, three Sunday Services, including two Sunday Schools on Sundays.

During the week there were ongoing activities, such as, Urafiki Club, Youth Club, Community Meetings, Kindergarten, Scouts, Girl Guides, Children's Saturday Cinema Club: especially watching kids cinema films or movies, weddings, funerals, etc. Overall, it was in fact, a lively church and community with extensive social outreach, an exemplar city church.

In view of this, my friend worked more in the night. Sometimes he worked extremely late in the night. Some church activities extended into and went on, until the late hour, dead in the night, while some other activities ended past midnight. As my main duties at Mr. Lund's residence were daytime, I frequently helped my friend out with caretaker chores and duties through the night.

Consequently, I learned a lot from the voluntary service and subsequent charity work. Apart from helping my friend with his duties, I also volunteered for various activities at the church.

I helped at the church with translation services: English into Kiswahili and vice versa. I taught Sunday Schools at both English and Kiswahili Services. I helped with Boy Scouts and Cubs. Believe it or not, I also taught Urafiki Club adult literacy and numeracy, including general knowledge.

As this was a 'handful' of activities, I developed good organisational skills and time management. Likewise, I earned another nick name: 'Busy Bunny' or Mr BB.

By this time, the perception that KPE was crucial in determining one's future, had dwindled and almost evaporated from my mind. It had evaporated like warm water evaporates, rises above up in the sky, cools down over the hills and later produces or gives back relief rain.

My 'relief rain,' was just beginning to precipitate, soon to shower and rain down on me. It was beginning to pour down into 'greater storms of greater knowledge and even greater service. The more I was blessed, the more I gave, the more I reciprocated. Some people would call it 'greater promotion.'

The stress about my failure was diminishing, it was becoming non-existent in my mind and in my entire life. I was beginning to exist and manage my life without KPE certificate and even secondary school certificates.

The key role schools play in making sure pupils are well supported and equipped for later life, was emerging. It was coming from my real-life experiences and encounters. It was being played by myself and by my real-life experiences, rather than from the luxury of a school and the classroom.

The school and Classroom were now non-existent for me. Being positive, determined and motivated became the more likely option, to get me through it all, the life encounters and challenges. For me, the world and life experiences, became decorous, a real comme il faut, an etiquette for positive learning environment.

In addition, I was beginning to acquire a lot from 'Home Learning:' The school of life and the university of life. Anxiety was no longer an issue for me. The key question on my mind was how to respond to patent anxiety and challenges ahead.

Most young people tend to fear the judgement of and from their friends (peer pressure) and families, when they do not do well in exams or life. Unlike most young people, for whom friends and families add further stress and pressure, I picked up the best from my friends and family. This fuelled my ambition and desire to move on and get on with my Incredible Journey and 'business as usual,' regardless of peer pressure.

Chapter Seventeen: The Higher Call

In life one must have something one strongly believes in and vehemently believes. My friend had discovered early on in his life, what he strongly believed in and vehemently believed. He thus followed his heart.

In pursuant of what brings him more joy and inner satisfaction, while working at Lavington United Church in 1969, my friend developed a great feeling for higher calling. He offered for outreach service within the Church of the Province of Kenya (CPK), now Anglican Church of Kenya (ACK), a member church of Lavington United Church, as an evangelist.

My friend was accepted for training, at Church Army Training College in East Africa, Jogoo Road, Nairobi, Kenya. Church Army is an outreach arm and evangelistic organisation of the Church of England and Anglican Church worldwide. It trains evangelists, known as Church Army Captains and Church Army Sisters, to work within parishes and various outreaches of the Anglican Church. My friend started his training in January 1970.

On his departure, I was the next in line of the call of duty. I was appointed and elevated to 'take over' his duties of the Caretaker of Lavington United Church. Taking over and being employed as a Caretaker was a great responsibility and considerable achievement in my life.

Contrasting with my KPE failure in 1966, and subsequent struggles, I had encountered thereafter, en route my Incredible Journey, I now felt that I was on the right track. I was on my way up, not down. I was on my way upwards, not downwards. I was on my way forward not backwards. In fact, I felt as if I had reached the end of my journey. I felt as if I had found what I was looking for. I was at the peak, the pinnacle of my life. I was on top of the world, now just looking down. The only exclamation I could make, was 'nothing else to look for!' I had reached the 'mountain top' of my life's journey.

After the Nairobi Central Park 'strange feeling' I experienced, mentioned earlier, I had quietly resolved in my heart, from there on, my Incredible Journey was going to be: 'Forward ever, backward never.' Here and now, I was moving forward. I let God 'take over.' My prayer was, 'God, take control, lead and I follow.'

The duties of the Caretaker were not new to me. I was already familiar with the job. I had been helping my friend most of the time. In fact, I was probably unknowingly, doing most of the job as I was a 'sort of' an apprentice. What was new to me now and upon my friend's departure, was handling the Saturday duties.

Saturday obligations included, managing the Kids Club cinema activities, including showing films, using the old photographic reel tapes film projectors, which often snapped. This was the 1960s, at the time when digital projectors were either not yet there, or just non-existent in Kenya.

On Saturdays, I also managed the selling and distribution of snacks to the Kids Club. I received and accounted for drinks and sodas from Coca-Cola Bottling Company. In retrospect, this was something that would come to haunt me later.

It was through the Saturday duties that I met the football legend, the late Joe Kadenge, the famous Kenyan and East African football (soccer), finest footballer and thus a real legend. We became particularly good friends. By that time, Mr. Kadenge was working for Coca-Cola Bottling Company. Kadenge was my childhood hero.

I was mesmerised to meet Kadenge in person, not even on TV. Indeed, he was real, not just a made-up entertainment name on the radio. I just used to hear his name and fame over the radio. In radio adverts, would often hear, *Kadenge na mpira, Kadenge na mpira, goo.... oolu*! Literally, Kadenge with the ball, Kadenge with the ball, go...al!

Whenever I played football with my friends, I imitated and pretended to be the greatest footballer, Joe Kadenge. He was indeed my hero. I had no access to TV. Therefore, I had never ever beheld my hero. Although in those days' TVs were only black and white, I had none.

Joe Kadenge oversaw distribution for the Coca-Cola Company. He distributed Coca-Cola brand sodas like Coca cola itself, Fanta orange, Fanta lemon, Sprite, etc. For the Kids Club and Theatre Club, I was the recipient and manager of this department at Lavington United Church. Through our friendship, I discovered and learned a lot about football in Kenya. For example, he was not paid much, but just had passion for football.

In Kenya, Football was a hobby. Kadenge therefore, was not a professional footballer as such. He only played during his free time and particularly when he was granted permission from his employer, especially during National marches and games.

Kadenge also played for AFC Leopards Club. He was indebted and grateful to AFC Leopards Club, initially a tribal Luhya football club, our fanatically home club. This is the club that launched him into fame.

Having a friend like Joe Kadenge, with first knowledge of football in Kenya, I made up my mind not to ever think of becoming a footballer in Kenya but enjoy my football as a hobby. We became particularly good friends with Joe

Kadenge until I left Kenya in 1985 and lost contacts. Our 'paths never crossed' again, until his death, 7 July 2019. May his soul Rest in Peace (RIP)

Saturdays also involved preparing for weddings and occasional community events. Any Saturday activity or extra activity like weddings and funerals, meant more work for me. However, there was also some compensation in the form of extra gratuity, tips or extra pay for each activity. Hence, my pocket was reasonably flowing on Saturdays.

While working as a Caretaker, almost my entire income was going towards supporting my mother and siblings. I took in my sister Agnes Shabaya, now Mrs Masengo. When my Aunt Ezina got a job, she later took my sister Agnes and fostered her temporarily. That gave me some relief, to take her follower, my brother Shem Shabaya on board.

Due to my exemplary service to the Lavington Church Kindergarten, my brother Shem was offered a whole year scholarship. This gave Shem a wonderful foundation and a head start in education and schooling. When Shem went back to our village to start school at Ivonda, my former school, he exceeded expectations from day one until his last day there.

In those days, most of the kids in our village never went to nursery school. Like me, they were just dropped in the deep end of the primary school. So through me, my brother Shem was privileged to have been in a nursery school and for that matter, a multi-racial nursery school in Nairobi, 'the Green City in the Sun.' Probably this was a great preparation for his long time future career in the United Arab Emirates (UAE) and globe-trotting experience.

Unlike me, my brother Shem excelled in his basic Kenya Primary Exams (KPE). He scored all the points, the maximum marks and scores 36, out of 36 points. He was an A* student. In view of this, he was awarded Jomo Kenyatta Foundation Scholarship and Joined Kabete Technical Secondary School, Nairobi.

Again, unlike me, Shem knew what he wanted in life early on. He was interested in an Engineering career, hence joined a technical school, instead of National Schools like Alliance Boys.

One day, in view of the passion I had for education, displayed in my voluntary commitment in my teaching illiterate Urafiki Club adults, at Lavington United Church, Rev John Myer enquired about my life, my background and my past experiences. Surprised with my story, he encouraged me to resume my correspondence studies. He volunteered to pay for my correspondence course, the distance/home learning. I enrolled at The University of Nairobi Extra-Mural Studies Department, Kikuyu Campus.

Thus, while continuing to volunteer, helping with the various activities at the church, I resumed my correspondence studies. Initially I focused on basic English Language and Literature.

I encountered Black and African writers like George Lamming: 'In the Castle of My Skin.' Chinua Achebe: 'Things Fall Apart' and 'No longer at Ease.' Ngugi Wa Thiong'o by then known as James Ngugi: 'The River Between' and 'A Grain of Wheat.' Alan Paton: 'Cry the Beloved Country' to mention but a few of classic Black and African Literature in English then.

Chinua Achebe's 'Things Fall Apart' was my favourite. I could empathise with Okonkwo's character and dilemma.

A lot of Okonkwo's expectations, experiences and culture, resonated with my own culture and experiences. It encouraged me to courageously press on regardless.

Later, in preparation for Kenya Junior Secondary Examination (KJSE), I increased my choice of subjects. I took those subjects I could manage to study on my own at home, without the help of a teacher, going to school or attending classroom lessons.

KJSE was introduced in Kenya in 1966. It intended to help kids who had not done well at KPE and may wish to take up a job without going up to Form IV to take Cambridge 'O' Level Examinations. This exam was taken at the end of Form II. It was mid secondary school exams, compulsory for private schools (urban), like the ones I attended, and Harambee Secondary Schools, (rural self-help schools), now defunct. KJSE was later scrapped.

I found it difficult to study Mathematics and Science on my own. I therefore decided to study traditional arts subjects like Geography, History, including Ancient History and Ancient Civilisations (Classics), General Science, Kiswahili, and Religious Knowledge (RK). Lack of a Mathematics certificate would come to haunt me many, many years later, when I opted to become a secondary school teacher in UK.

By this time, I had just fallen in love with reading. Apart from the set correspondence courses, I read anything and everything I could lay my hands and eyes on. This enhanced my literacy skills and overall general knowledge. I homed in, particularly, more English and Kiswahili languages.

Unfortunately, before I completed my KJSE course, it was faced out. So, I never ended up taking KJSE exams, that

I had extensively prepared for, but I retained the knowledge I had gained. As for me, studies are not just an examination preparation exercise, but a quest for knowledge and subsequent truth.

To home in, my learning and general skills, I shared most of what I studied, in my voluntary work, including teaching Urafiki Club Adult learners. I also utilised my knowledge and skills in my encounter with young people through the Youth Club, Sunday School, Scouts, Cubs and occasionally, Girl Guides and Brownies.

Many people started referring to me as *Mwalimu* - teacher, others called me the Untrained Teacher (UT), others referred to me as a Community Worker (CW). I also participated in the Sunday Services, especially Kiswahili Service.

I helped the Social Worker with the outreach to my former Gatina slum and the neighbouring Kawangware slum. Therefore, to others I was known as the *msaidizi*, the helper, the Social Worker. To the others I was *Mwalimu* – the Catechist, also known as teacher in Kiswahili. I was almost 'a jack of all trades, and a master of none.'

Through the outreach and translation services, especially sermons, etc., I developed an interest in homiletics. I decided to take a Local Preachers course – Lay Preachers course. Soon I became a fully-fledged Methodist Local Preacher, nowadays Lay Preacher.

In the same year, The Rev John Myer, came to me after one of the Sunday Services I had taken. He looked into my eye with a big smile and said, 'I have sat in a lot of your services, observed you working with adults and young people alike, and I have a question for you.' He paused then continued, in fact it is actually a proposal for you.'

The Rev John Myer was a jovial padre and with pleasant personality. He always wore this big smile. He paused and as usual, smiled again. Thereafter, he continued, 'have you ever thought of being a church minister like me?

Again, he paused, then continuing, he said, 'perhaps you would like to follow in your friend's footsteps and join Church Army in the next intake in 1972?' He again smiled and paused, 'or would you like to join even the higher call, the ordained ministry as a Methodist minister?'

I was dumbfounded. Amidst my daze, stunned confusion, as if to inflict more pain, he continued, 'the choice is yours.' Trembling and astonished, to block him from asking me further questions of that nature, I answered quickly, 'no, no, no Sir.' He stared at me as if to prod more. 'I have never thought of that, nor have I had such an idea in my mind,' I retorted quickly.

With a squeaking voice, I beckoned The Rev John Myer, 'please Sir, give me more time to think about your questions.' I felt as if I was being interrogated in a Police Station or a Supreme Court. I needed a lawyer, I needed an Attorney, lest I implicate myself and get into deep trouble, deep waters that I may not get out of easily and for that matter, a live. But no one else was around. It was just the two of us.

I continued to tremble with fear and a sense of owe and wonder for a few more minutes. The words of my headmaster when I failed my KPE in 1966 rang into my mind: 'The list spells your failure!'.... 'this spells out the end of your journey in life.'

I reflected further. 'It means you do not have greater openings or a bright future. Of course, you have failed to get your KEY, the opener of your future: KPE exams. Your dreams are over! Do not dream again! You have no hope, your future is doomed!'

Several questions, also simultaneously ran through my mind: Why, why me? Can I really make it? Should I take up another challenge of this magnitude? Can I handle it?

After a long pause I requested The Rev John Myer to give me some more time, more time to think about the 'bomb shell' he had dropped on me. In my mind, I had reached my 'promised land' as a Caretaker. Of course, I was really enjoying my job. I did not feel like moving again.

After our encounter, when The Rev Myer left the scene, I thought to myself, 'was I dreaming?' If I was not dreaming, and the encounter was real, 'Should I make another move? Is this the opportune time, the right time to get on the road again?' I thought for a while, still speaking to myself, I asked myself again, 'Should I go now, or should I stay now?'

I quietly asked myself all these questions and many more that I cannot even remember now.... I felt that I really needed more time to 'be still........,' before I could make any decision of such magnitude.

After a week, I met with The Rev John Myer again, this time in his study and office. I told him, 'I have thought, reflected and prayed on the question, 'beckoning me to a higher call,' and found it daunting.' I paused, for a while and then continued, 'however, I am willing to give it ago. I will take the plunge. I will take the 'bullet.' I will take the challenge.'

When I looked at Rev Myer' face, there was this broad smile. His shoulders had expanded. He stood, with open arms. Likewise, I stood up. He gave me a big hug and punched me hard in the stomach (tummy).

Whatever that symbolised, the hard punch in my tummy, I do not know. I never dared to ask the symbolism. I can only recall the big broad smile on Rev Myer's face. I had never seen such a big broad smile on his face before.

He then asked me, 'which option will you go for? I answered, 'I can definitely enjoy either or even both. I am spoiled for choice.' I threw the question back to him.

After a brief pause to get back my breath, I asked him, 'If you were me, or imagine being in my shoes, position and knowing me, which one would you go for?' He replied, 'of course the ordained ministry.' He continued, 'I am an ordained Methodist Minister and therefore more conversant with and familiar with the Methodist Church ministerial and candidature process.'

As I appeared startled, he stood again and held my hand. He assured me that he was convinced that I can make it. I can make it not only as an ordained minister, but a charming particularly good clergy. He reckoned that my volunteering, Lay Preaching undertaking, demonstrated I have what it takes.

My background, the experiences I have had and displayed, including The Story of My Life, were vital for the ordained ministry. Finally, he was in no doubt, I will make a good minister. I replied, 'sincerely, I am humbled, and I couldn't concur more.'

I thought and paused for a while, then I joyfully erupted, 'I will go for the ordained ministry.' Rev Myer stood as to beckon me for something higher and reiterated, 'then go for it, go for the ordained ministry!' He gave me another 'brotherly' big hug, this time without a punch in the stomach. I had made the decision. No turning back, no turning back, the deed was done. The process began, just like that.

Chapter Eighteen: What Did I Study?

In my taxi and in my cab, people often remark, 'you look educated' and often ask me, 'what did you study?' 'Theology of course,' it was my major, and various other subsidiary subjects along the way, including Education,' I normally reply. Many of my clients get surprised and look at me with a sense of owe and wonder.

Majority of my clients have never heard of the word theology, leave alone the subject. So, I must explain. 'Theology is an academic subject pursuit. However, it is also a personal and pastoral reflective pursuit,' I normally explain. Attempts to explain, opens ensuing interesting questions and discussions. My taxi/cab suddenly turns into a classroom and even lecture hall, for that matter and place in time.

As I pause to embark on a further explanation, some clients likewise, pause for a while, then budge in and ask, ', what is theology?' This gives me the opportunity to delve briefly into the subject matter of theology. If there are a few more minutes left on the fare, the taxi/cab journey, I explain and outline the synopsis and etymology of the word theology, which is a combination of two Greek words.

Simplified, the combination of two Greek words: $\theta\varepsilon o\varsigma$ - (theos – God) and $\lambda o\gamma o\varsigma$ – (logos – word or study), make up the English word theology. Therefore, theology is the study and exploration of the nature of God and religious beliefs, systematically developed. It is a 'God-talk', a God encounter, systematised over the ages.

With such an explanation, some just, switch off into dead silence. Others just sink into stupendous thoughtful quiet muteness of reflection. More often, others pose the second question: 'Where did you study theology?' Just like the 'British ice breaker,' the 'British weather', with such a question normally ensues further questions, remarks, subsequent advanced and interesting discourses and pedagogy.

In my initial encounter, with the editor of this series, in a taxi in Cambridge, towards the end of the fare or journey, the subject of theology, also emerged. This time, I initiated the discussion. As they say, 'curiosity killed the cat,' I was rather curious and wondered, why my passenger had travelled all the way on X5 Bus, Oxford - Cambridge, to a BB - Bed and Breakfast.

I rarely dare ask my clients personal questions. It is the expected etiquette of cabbing or taxi job. With such questions some clients may be intimidated and feel or perceive me to be 'poking my nose into their affairs or business.' So, I am often reluctant to ask personal questions, lest I 'step on my clients' toes.'

This time I was ready for the repercussion of my question. I picked up the guts, I picked up the courage and asked, 'what have you come to do in Cambridge? Expecting a rebuff, however, I was surprised not to be snubbed.

Instead the fare replied, I have come to interview The Most Rev Dr Rowan Williams, former Archbishop of the Church of England and the Leader of the Worldwide Anglican Community. He is currently, the Master of Magdalen College, Cambridge University.' She continued, 'do you by any chance know him?'

'I am going to... to interview him tomorrow, to contribute to the series I am editing: 'Hearing Others' Voices,' she concluded.' I was excited about her series and the forthcoming interviewee. Being in my position, who wouldn't have been excited?

I remarked, 'I sat under the feet of Dr Rowan Williams. He was my Lecturer. He taught me Ecclesiastical History, especially the Early Christian Thought.' She remarked, 'so you are a theologian.'

I paused for a while, wondering what to say next. No one had ever referred to me like that before. Undoubtedly, life is full of surprises. She continued, 'you should write a book.' I thought to myself, 'Surprise, surprise!'

Surprised further, by her statement, I asked her, 'write about what?' She replied, 'your life, your story.' She carried on, 'many people, especially young people would like to read your story.' She further remarked, 'I am a writer and a lecturer at The Open University.' We exchanged email addresses. She handed me one of her own book 'Black Inked Pearl.' She personally autographed it without a date:

'So good to meet you

and to learn some of your story.

Ruth X X'

Believe it or not I cannot ever remember the day we met [it was mid-November 2018, Ed.], when 'our paths crossed,' and 'our paths parted.' I never knew we could ever meet again. I have exchanged many contacts, emails addresses, with celebrities without any follow ups, from any one of them.

Ruth made me feel nervous, but also at the same time made me ponder for a while about being a theologian.... If theologians are people who lecture at universities or theological colleges and seminaries, famous scholars and prolific writers, who have published a lot, then I am not one of them.

I further pondered, but if theologians are people who wrestle with God, almost like Jacob did, then I could be one of them. If theologians have a quest for truth; enjoy studying, including Religious Studies, then I could be a theologian. If theologians probably study and lecture in the 'University of Life,' like I do in my taxi, in most cases unrecognised, or even unnoticed, then I am one of them: I AM A THEOLOGIAN.

It was in 1972, when for the first time, I encountered theology or in-depth encounter with 'God Talk' at St Paul's United Theological College, Limuru, Kenya, now St Paul's University. This was after I had been selected for ordained ministry within the auspices of The Methodist Church in Kenya in 1971. I was then offered an opportunity to study Theology commencing in January 1972.

My caretaker job, Urafiki Club teacher (UT), Voluntary and Community work, ended abruptly, the same year in November 1971. I was on the move again, and since then, I have been on the move.... I have continued to be on various relocations and moves, literally and symbolically, all over and about, en route 'My Incredible Journey.'

There was a fire at the church, just before I left my post. The Church Hall was extensively burnt down, especially the area housing Kids Cine Club activities and the Theatre Club. A lot of property was damaged. There was substantial and extensive loss of property, with a lot of church items unaccounted for, especially items stored or kept in the Church Hall and adjacent rooms.

The sanctuary and the entire church building were left unscathed.

However, Mr Lund the Treasurer, Lavington United Church felt that as a Caretaker, I had to vicariously compensate for the damages of the Church Hall and the extensive loss of property therein. Moreover, I had resigned, and my resignation had been accepted, prior to the firebreak.

Lavington United Church Treasure, Mr Lund, my former employer as a *'shamba* boy,' gardener and subsequent *'Toto jikoni,'* kitchen help, insisted I must suffer the consequences for the extensive damage and loss. He requested the church to appeal to the Methodist Presiding Bishop, through The Rev John Myer, to rescind my candidature and subsequent training. For him, as a vicarious compensation, I should be summarily dismissed, without any benefits, including revoking my candidature.

Thus, Lavington United Church, the church that had initially sponsored, supported and recommended my candidature, had now just turned against me, with a lot of animosity, bad feelings and bad blood of revenge. In contrast, instead of just summarily dismissal, this time, it was now an application for and petition for cancellation of my ensuing theological training.

Thanks to the resolute and firm stand of The Rev Lawi Imathiu (Presiding Bishop). Supported by The Rev Johana Mbogori and The Methodist Church Standing Committee they adhered to the Methodist Standing Orders.

The Rev Lawi Imathiu and the Standing Committee were inclined that the decision of The Methodist Conference, in August 1971, prior to the fire break was final. Such decision, they reckoned, can only be altered, revoked, varied, repealed and rescinded by another Annual Conference, the final authority of Methodism, due again in August 1972.

Meanwhile, they insisted I embark on my theological course, pending the decision of the Annual Conference in the following year. So, in January1972, I commenced my course without knowing and not being sure of what the future held for me. Everything was in limbo.

I was left hanging in the balance, pending the August 1972 Methodist Annual Conference, to deliberate and decree on my plight: Should I go now, or should I stay on?

In August 1972, The Methodist Annual Conference met, deliberated, confirmed and re-endorsed my candidature. It decreed that I should stay on course and steer my course towards the end of my training and subsequent ordination.

Later, Dr John A Newton replaced The Rev Tom Beetham. He advised me, to carry on as if nothing had happened. He was by then, the Methodist Tutor at St Paul's United Theological College. He thus, encouraged me to stay on the course, and on course on my Incredible Journey. That was another huddle jumped along the way.

Thereafter, I prodded and ploughed on with my course, wounded, but not maimed, wounded but not mutilated nor destroyed. I just remained positive as ever. Contrastingly, the incident just bestowed on me more determination to once again, 'carry on regardless.'

At St Paul's then, the total training cost of my training, was borne by the Methodist Church in Kenya. I was endowed with some upkeep money, the so called 'pocket money'. This was very handy for me.

With the given allowance, I continued to supplement my father's meagre income. I supported my mother and my siblings in the village back home in Western Kenya. Thus, I shared out my allowances. Furthermore, I used my allowances and gratuity to build my mum, a much more needed improved newer thatched house. I also continued to help her with basic domestic needs.

In fact, at St Paul's I was a Methodist Probation Minister, a Minister in the making. Time spent at St Paul's United Theological College, counted towards my probation period, seniority, and ordination date. Hence, I was paid about half or more of the respective allowance of a Methodist Minister's stipend. Thus, I had acquired a new title at the front of my name, though not at the back of my name yet.

In the Methodist Church, my new title was The Rev John Shabaya Malaya. Due to the contrasting negative connotation in Kiswahili for my last name then, *Malaya* – prostitute, harlot, I had to change my name. In 1983, by Deed Poll in the Kenya Gazette, my name changed to John Lisamula Shabaya.

I was accepted into Full Connexion and affirmed by the August Methodist Conference of 1974 and subsequent ordination in January 1976 at Kaaga in Meru, in the hills, high-grounds and slopes of Mt Kenya, the Home-country and real Home-land of Methodism in Kenya.

Chapter Nineteen: At Limuru

Without the mythical KPE, which was supposed to catapult me into a bright and greater future, I was endowed with other great opportunities and eye openers. These were substantial, appreciable opportunities, greater than all school certificates: KPE, East African Certificate of Education (EACE) and Kenya Certificate of Education (KCE). If anything, St Paul's United Theological College catapulted me into unbelievable and unfathomable world. It was a 'bird's eye view' into a different world, 'the world of opportunities'.

Being in a United Theological College, set up in 1955 by the three main Protestant Missionary Churches in Kenya: Anglican, Methodist and Presbyterian churches, I was at home. It was just and more like my former Lavington United Church. Additionally, by this time, in the 1970's, the Reformed Church of East Africa (RCEA) had joined in and became a constituent member of the college, extending St Paul's United Theological College wings and umbrella.

Incidentally, the higher percentage of the student population and members of staff, was mainly from the member churches. However, other denominations, including indigenous churches, especially member churches of The National Christian Council of Kenya (NCCK), also sent their students here, particularly for advanced theological pursuit.

The college also partnered with other colleges, especially exchange programmes, academic and pastoral pursuits. This included resident students from East Africa, Central Africa and countries beyond, as far as Europe.

Most partnership was with Mukono Theological College, now Uganda University at Mukono and St Mark's

Theological College, Dar es salaam, now St Mark's Centre, part of St John's University in Tanzania. Academically, the college partnered with and was a credited by Makerere University, Uganda and Nairobi University, Kenya.

Besides, St Paul's United Theological College, interacted with Scots Theological College, Machakos County, an African Inland Church (AIC) College. St Paul's United Theological College also had reciprocal arrangements and undertakings with other various institutions of higher learning in Kenya and yonder.

Culturally and academically, I had great exposure at Limuru. It gave me a wonderful environment and opportunity to pursue my passion for education. Being in the former White Highlands, set in a pleasant high-altitude area, overlooking the lowlands of Nairobi, it had an ambiance of its own.

Limuru had particularly good and conducive environment, not only for wonderful pastoral and personal opportunity for growth, but also academic pursuits and endeavours. It was also pleasant for refreshing morning runs and jogging, an opportunity I made the best off.

The college had expansive grounds, with exotic gardens, neatly maintained by full time gardeners, since 1903 as CMS Divinity School and even more so since 1955, when as such, St Paul's United Theological College, was established. To me, it was almost a replica of the Lavington Green area in Nairobi.

Apart from the conducive academic environment, it was a celestial setting, for group, personal reflections and quite times. It also had a ranch and a farm. Initially the farm was set up to train and prepare the clergy for rural ministry.

Most of and the bulk of Kenya's population is made of the wider rural communities. Of course, Kenya was and is mainly an Agricultural country. As Kenya, is a country with extensive rural communities, any ministerial preparation or training for the ministry could not have ignored this fact. However, more recently some oil has been discovered in Turkana County, in the Lake Turkana area. This might influence the future training and preparation of the Kenyan clergy.

Indeed, St Paul's United Theological College was a great ecumenical attempt in East Africa. It was an οίκουμενη. The Ancient Greek word *oikoumene*, literally means, a habitable and civilised world, both in terms of secular and religious civilisation. As such, St Paul's United Theological College was a place with its own distinct mien. It made one feel as if, and almost the whole entire world converged there, at Limuru.

St Paul's United Theological College was like a family, a brotherly and sisterly Christian family. It was open to and participated in the world. Grounded in the world, grounded in the Christian faith, yet not limited to the world.

For me, St Paul's United Theological College, was a foretaste of the universal church, the united Christian existence. It was focused on outreach, mission to the world, mission for the world and the entire human race.

St Paul's United Theological College was probably a preparation. It was preparation, with great expectations and prospects. It ushered in the anticipated East African ecumenism endeavour and Church unity. Sadly, that was never to be. Church Unity was never, ever realised. After independence and freedom from shackles of colonial rule, actual church unity and ecumenism as such, in East

Africa, was shelved into archives, for researchers, if interested.

At Limuru, as a potential minister and 'a man of the cloth,' I learned, realised and affirmed that in life, 'you never know, what you gonna get' and whom 'you gonna meet.' I was therefore frequently reminded, in my work, I will meet people in need, and even grieving families.

The word of advice was, 'in all circumstances be with them, empathise and grieve with them.' I was also reminded, I will meet people celebrating wonderful endowments and achievements of their lives, abundance, and so forth, 'rejoice and celebrate with them.' I was constantly reminded to encourage those 'with,' to share with those 'without.'

I was also cautioned that, some people will be hostile, while others will acknowledge my service. Some will accord me wonderful warm welcome and extend hospitality and even respect. I should be prepared to accept with gratitude, such extended hospitality and kindness. Most of all, I should always-be alert, on the lookout. I should always be aware.

I was occasionally warned, 'the job you are taking, will give you a feeling of inner self-satisfaction, while at other times, it will be a real uphill with numerous challenges.' The august and most considerable, distinguished word of advice was, 'be always prepared, be ever ready...' With such words of advice, again and again, time after time, I kept asking myself, 'what type of a job am I really getting into?'

At Limuru I touched almost on any and every subject in the world. Of-course my time at Limuru, was a preparation, real preparation. I was being prepared for my encounter with the *oikumene*, the world, the real world, the whole world. The world with various real people, with various needs, diverse backgrounds, different professions, contrasting academic qualifications and distinct heritage.

After a few weeks of arrival at Limuru and some introductory teaching, students undertook exams, to help the college assess their potential and ability. The college was flexible, with an inclusive diverse curriculum.

The courses available at that point in time, were Certificate in Theology and Diploma in Theology, respectively. The college Certificate in Theology was undertaken by all students and awarded by the college, after the three years training.

There was also an opportunity to pursue some basic academic Certificate in Theology, offered as a distance learning course by University of Nairobi, an equivalent of 'A' Level qualification or standard. The Diploma in Theology was more advanced than both the St Paul's United Theological College Certificate and University of Nairobi Certificate.

The Diploma was awarded by Makerere University, Uganda. I passed entrance exams for both, the Certificate and Diploma in Theology. I was enrolled for the advanced Makerere University's Diploma in Theology.

Apart from Theological studies and Pastoral studies, I was able to pursue other subjects as part of the college curriculum. I also pursued extra-curricular activities, utilising the available time and resources within the campus.

In view of this, on top of my Diploma studies focused on Theology and Religious Studies, I also studied subjects like English Language and Literature, Swahili, Ancient and Modern History, including World History.

I also studied subjects like Commerce and Economics, Politics, Sociology, Psychology, Theatre and Drama, Communication and Media Studies, Bookkeeping, Accounting, Leadership and Management. Thus, at Limuru, my cup was full and overflowing.

There was also an encounter with the 'World Programme.' This included work experience in a variety of jobs and settings. For example, I was exposed to Police duties for two weeks.

I observed front line and station desk duties at Central Police Station and Kamukunji Police Station in Nairobi, respectively. I also overshadowed patrol police officers on their respective duties including day, night duties, and surveillance in Nairobi.

I attended Court of Law's sessions, House of Parliament deliberations and the enactment of statutes and laws. I also spent time in Prison Service, Night Clubs and Casinos, including 'Red Light' Districts of Nairobi. In those days, these were mainly Majengo and Koinange Street, respectively.

I encountered and worked with young people on the urban streets, *chokora* – parking boys and their sisters, including Young Offenders Rehabilitation Centres. I visited and worked with schools, especially secondary schools and tertiary colleges, including University of Nairobi in term-time and vocational Work Camps.

I exposed young people to real rural disadvantaged communities. I took such groups to Work Experience in remote areas of Kenya. This included secondary schools, such as Alliance, Lenana School, formerly Duke of York,

Nairobi School, formerly Prince of Wales, State House Girls, formerly Delamere Girls High School, Kenya High, formerly European Girls School, Butere Girls, etc.

In August 1973, I took one group of secondary school kids to Ngao, Tana River County. The group included young people, from a variety of backgrounds and religious affiliations, for example, Muslims, Christians and so forth.

The trip from Nairobi to Ngao, to the farthest coastal region of Kenya, was a two days journey. For four weeks, the young people were exposed and involved in Community Development. The Work Camp, at Ngao Village, on Tana River, largest and longest river in Kenya, involved building a Village Community Hall.

I raised the funding for such trips, through my industrial experience and links. It was worth the effort. For most of the young people from urban areas, upcountry and especially those from the middle-class homes, it was an eye opener.

I also experienced and tasted the work of Social Workers and Probation Service. I shadowed several Social Workers and Probation Officers. I was also attached to Kenyatta National and Mathare Mental Hospitals, Nairobi. This gave me hospital experience and working with the sick and even the dying.

I had a stint of upcoming care work, and opportunities to relive my experience, in *Mji wa Huruma*, the Mercy Home and Nairobi slums. My slum exposure and experience were at Mathare and Kibera slums. My colleagues from upcountry were in absolute shock, more shocked with the encounter with various Nairobi slum dwellers. This exposure and training had a significant impact on me.

Then there was the Industrial experience. This lasted at least for over two weeks. I worked night shifts at places like Coca-Cola Bottling Company and East African Breweries, now Kenya Breweries. I observed and worked shifts on the conveyor belt.

I did jobs I had never undertaken before. I encountered first-hand experience of the impact of such jobs on personal lives and subsequent human relationships, people's beliefs, etc.

On Sundays, I was attached to various churches and Christian institutions, in both rural and urban settings and environments. I also made friends from the various ethnic groups represented at Limuru. By the time I graduated from Limuru, I had almost 'seen and heard it all.'

At St Paul's United Theological College, I earned another nick named. I was known as 'Mr. Accident.' This was because I was an 'accident.' I was the only and probably the first Methodist from Western Kenya.

As I mentioned earlier, due to 'spheres of influence' Methodism was predominantly at the coast, along the Indian Ocean. It was therefore mainly in Mombasa, Kilifi, Kwale, Tana River Counties and later in Lamu, especially Mpeketoni area.

In Tana River Methodist churches were dispersed along the River Tana itself. Most adherents were mainly from members of former Lutheran Mission stations and therefore, formerly Lutheran converts. These were handed over to the British Methodist Mission Society (MMS), now Methodist Church in Kenya, after the end of World War Two (WW2) and subsequent surrender of Germany after WW2, the Homeland of the Lutheran Church.

Up-country Methodism was mainly in Meru on the slopes of Mt Kenya. As Christianity did not deep root itself at the coast, the highest population of Methodist members were and are from Meru. Of course, I had encountered Methodism accidentally or more so, providentially in Nairobi. Thank God, the Methodist Church had come to and established itself in Nairobi by the time I migrated to Nairobi and subsequently, became a candidate for the Methodist Church ministry.

My leadership skills started emerging at St Paul's. Towards the end of my course, I was elected a student leader as the Secretary of the Student Body. This involved student welfare, grievances, representation and negotiations for and on behalf of the students with the staff, the College Council and external relationships, including other partner colleges in East Africa and Europe. I met secular dignitaries, including Kenya Government Ministers and respectable church leaders, including the Roman Catholic Archbishop Ndingi Mwana Nzeki, etc.

In view of my responsibilities, in Summer 1974, I was selected to represent St Paul's United Theological College, on the East African Theological Students' Exchange Programme, with European Theological students, mainly from West Germany. By this time, Germany was still divided into two countries – East: Communist and West Germany: Capitalist.

1974 was my first time to fly out of Kenya. At last my childhood dream came true. The inspiration from and by my uncle, who had travelled extensively during World War 2, became a reality for me. What a feeling of great happiness! I had no words or adjectives to describe how I felt, or to articulate the great joy inside me, now that I too, I was travelling overseas.

By then, Jomo Kenyatta International Airport had not yet been built. I flew from Embakasi Airport, now a military Garrison. I took KLM Dutch Royal Airline via Entebbe, Uganda, Cairo, Egypt and Schiphol Amsterdam Airport, in Holland, The Netherlands.

I spent a few weeks in Amsterdam, including observing its transport system and urbanisation. The programme included night visits in the city. I visited the Amsterdam 'Red District' and exposure to the commercialised Sex Industry. I also encountered and observed almost the liberal use of *bangi* – hemp, marijuana, cannabis sativa, being smoked on the streets with no police arrests and its consequences.

Afterwards, I flew to Hamburg, West Germany. The Berlin Wall was still standing, dividing Germany into two parts: East and West Germany, respectively. In view of our tight schedule, I never managed to see The Berlin Wall. I spent more time at Missions Akademie, University of Hamburg. There, I delved into in-depth theological encounter with outstanding German scholars and theologians.

Most of these scholars' work and publications had been translated in English and were set texts, a must to read for my Diploma in Theology course. Later, I went to various Germany cities and villages, excluding East Germany. I experienced the extensive work of Lutheranism.

I came across first-hand history, especially how the Lutheran Church started and how it currently operates in Germany. I heard stories about the protest of Martin

Luther the reformer and his subsequent excommunication from the Roman Catholic Church in the 1520s.

It was encouraging to hear about Martin Luther's courage, in his homeland. I beheld the work of his hands, his protest, hence the name 'Protestants,' for non-Roman Catholics and the results thereof. Additionally, I was surprised, to learn that Germans paid church tax to either Lutheran Church or Roman Catholic Church, the established churches in Germany.

After a few weeks, I travelled by train from Hamburg to München - Munich. I had a reasonable exposure to German culture and Christianity in Obermenzing area, Munich, Bavaria. I witnessed the Bavarian Beer Festival in Munich.

Then I travelled by train through Austria, to Zurich and finally Geneva in Switzerland. This for me, was a real memorable journey. I traversed the mountains, hills and valleys of Germany, Austria and Switzerland, that resonated with my nostalgic childhood memories of the *'chuku chuku'* train experience. However, unlike the *chuku chuku* train, this train was modern and moved fast.

In Geneva, I encountered United Nations offices and personnel. I also visited the World Council of Churches Headquarters and met the General Secretary Dr Philip A Potter, a Methodist minister from Dominican Republic, West Indies. I also 'sat under the feet' of great International renowned scholars.

In the suburbs of Geneva, Switzerland, I met face to face the outstanding African Scholar Prof John S Mbiti, a Kenyan, a graduate of Cambridge University, and Director of Bossey Ecumenical Institute, Geneva, Switzerland, our host institution. Professor Mbiti inspired me to work hard, towards furthering my studies at Cambridge University, by then an almost impossible dream.

The same year 1974, I travelled to Uganda to scheduled Meetings and Conferences to represent my college at Makerere University and Mukono Theological College. The Meetings and Conferences were cut short by the terror and sheer madness of Field Marshall, General, Dr Alhaji Idi Amin Dada Oumee, the self-made and self-declared President of Uganda.

Uganda-Kenya relationship had deteriorated and was turning sour. In view of this, I was informed that the borders were about to close. I therefore left Uganda in haste. In fact, by the time I got on the border, at Malaba, the relationship had deteriorated further. The Ugandan soldiers were not allowing anybody to pass the border check point into Kenya with any possessions. Thus, they took all I had on me including money.

Chapter Twenty: In the High Grounds

On 30 November 1974, it was a beautiful and gorgeous day. It was not so hot, but just cool and pleasant. The sun was shining. It was shining brightly, lighting the paths, at the same time, warmly gazing into the eyes of the beholders. Present were the dignitaries, the invited and uninvited guests alike, the on-lookers......

It was unlike, the wonted November, with its normal short heavy rains and tropical storms, as the season dictated. The day was noticeably clear in the high grounds, the former White Highlands, overlooking the plains of Nairobi. The other side, overlooking the Great Rift Valley, the cradle of humankind was also bright, waiting for the evening fantastic sunset.

The invited guests were impeccably dressed and closely knit together, bound by the occasion, with bright eyes eagerly waiting to witness this great occasion and event of the day. The uninvited, but warmly welcomed guests stood yonder, gazing in owe and wonder.

They gazed at the beautiful day and the colourful occasion. The wonderful breeze fanned and graced the occasion, in the graceful pulchritudinous - beautiful scenery, with serene and ambience atmosphere.

It was St Paul's United Theological College, Annual Graduation Day. It was an alluring, beautiful, ecstatic, rhapsodic and joyous day! The graduation ceremony was outdoors. It was in the expanse and beautiful exotic grounds and gardens of the college, well-tended gardens, since the establishment of the college in1930, initially as CMS Divinity School, later in 1955 as an ecumenical venture.

In attendance, was my mother. She was flanked by her sister, my barren aunt Ezina, my father and my step uncle Petro Mugangai, and the Pastor of my mother's indigenous church: African Holy Spirit Church (AHSC). There was also an entourage from my mother's AHSC indigenous church. They had come to witness the occasion. Like the 'doubting Thomas, they wanted to 'touch the marks.' Thus 'seeing and touching the marks was indeed believing.'

My mother was still reminiscing the 'Day of Reckoning,' the fateful day of my KPE failure and the ensued disappointment. That disastrous day crisscrossed her mind. She kept muttering to herself and whispering to my father, 'is it true, is it real? And My father whispering, 'yes, yes! Our son is graduating today.' He continued, 'it has been a long walk and An Incredible Journey.'

There were many dignitaries, including the Chairman of the College Council, The Rev Lawi Imathiu, to award the certificates and respective credentials. It was indeed befitting and rewarding for the graduation of that day and that year to be graced by the Chairman.

The Rev Lawi Imathiu's determined contention, was commendable. His adherence to The Methodist Standing Orders had enabled me to partake in this graduation. Here I was graduating.

I graduated from the college, with St Paul's United Theological College Certificate, highlighting my four favourite subjects: Survey of World History, English, Swahili and Introduction to the Bible. It also recognised that I had sat and passed Special Entrance Examination for Makerere University, Diploma in Theology.

Lastly, I had sat the External Examination for Makerere University Diploma in Theology. The College Certificate was signed by The Rev John Riddlesdell (Principal) and The Rev Lawi Imathiu (Chairman College Council). The deed was done, dusted and truly done with. It was finished.

In January 1975, I took up my station in Kaaga Circuit, Kambereu Section, on the other side, in the highlands below Mt Kenya, in Meru. I had been to Meru before. As part of my college attachment, like the disciples of Jesus, we had annually been sent out one by one, on missions to various places and churches.

Earlier on, I had been sent out to Meru for six weeks, in the Meru Highlands, on the slopes of Mt Kenya at Kirwa and Kibirichia, high altitude areas. I had also been sent to the coast, low attitude area. This included Mombasa and Kwale Counties, with a visit to Rabai, on the high grounds, in Kilifi County.

I had to pay tribute to the founding Mission station by Johann Ludwig Krapf and Johannes Rebman. With my passion for education and interest in Charles New, I had to visit the remnants of Rabai, especially the site of the oldest school in Kenya, set up in 1846. I was rather disappointment by its run-down state.

I also visited Frere Town, another significant historical place. This was a place where St Paul's United Theological College was first established as CMS Divinity school, before transferring to Limuru. It was also significant for the end of slave trade, especially for mission and end of slavery.

Unlike my earlier attachment during the rainy season, this time I arrived in the highlands of Meru in the dry season. Those were the days before the extensive 'global warming,' when the weather in Kenya was predictable.

We used to have four distinct seasons: two dry seasons and two rainy and wet seasons: short and long rains, respectively. They alternated between, dry and rainy, accordingly. The day and night were generally divided equally into twelve hours each, throughout the year: twelve hours night and twelve hours day.

Kenya being on the Equator, Latitude 0° degrees, there is no Winter, Spring, Summer, or Autumn (The Fall). In Kenya, snow is only beautifully peached on the peak, far high, on the top of Mt Kenya, throughout the year. Even though Mt Kenya is right on the Equator itself - Latitude 0°, the ever-present snow on its peak, affirms, 'the higher you go, the cooler it becomes,' no matter where you are.

Comparatively, Mt Kenya is high, seventeen thousand feet (17,000 ft), over five thousand metres (5,000 m), above sea level. Therefore, snow on it is too high and too sacred, to be trampled upon by the ordinary people, typical human beings, who rarely dare climb Mt Kenya.

The ordinary people who dare not climb Mt Kenya, are probably, wise. This may not be just because they have acrophobia, scarred of its height. They may not just be afraid to be hit by high altitude sickness, or cultural sacredness of the mountain. They are but just wise overall.

So, most people in Kenya and around Mt Kenya, have not been on top of the mountain. They have wisely not gone on the peak, to look down, and behold the surrounding beauty. I also have not dared to do the same.

However, at least I have flown above and over it, severally, en route Europe and vice versa. I have beheld its magnificent beauty, but from a distance, a safe distance.

Some people in Kenya have not encountered and beheld the real beauty of Mt Kenya. There are many people in Kenya who have not glimpsed, the snow on its peak. Moreover, many Kenyans have never come face to face with snow at a close range. In Kenya, the beautiful rhapsodic snow, is therefore up there. It is far removed from reality and far from humans' regular encounter. Snow is just on the top of the mountain, high up there, high, at the peak of the mountain. I beheld and stepped on my first snow in Cambridge, UK in 1985.

In 1975, the only tarmacked road in Meru, was the major road, between Nairobi and Meru via Nanyuki. The anti-clockwise road through Embu, though shorter, was a winding, meandering road, along the slopes of Mt Kenya.

The Embu-Meru Road by then was just a dusty road. It was easily passable in dry season, though very dusty. It was impassable during the wet season. In fact, it was a very, very slippery road and an imaginable, scary road during the wet, rainy season.

Therefore, I used the more convenient longer route. I travelled around Mt Kenya clockwise, following contours, via Naro Moru, Nanyuki, down and below the mountain, into Meru high grounds.

Working and staying in Meru, I learned a lot. I learned to observe and plan my day and work accordingly. In dry season, I worked far and wide. Likewise, in wet season, I worked closer to home. I commuted to closer places. I only went to places, I could walk to if necessary, in case the roads were impassable by automobiles. Thus, time and season dictated my schedule.

To my surprise, when I arrived in Meru, the most common form of transport and vehicles in Meru, including matatu –

public transport, were four wheel long base land-rovers. That spoke louder about the nature of the roads. Most roads were 'off-road tracks. Electricity, piped water supply and telecommunication was primarily limited to Meru town.

I was warmly welcomed in Meru. As such, I immediately settled down to work. I really felt at home fast and embarked on learning Kimeru, the local language. One family (Harriet Nkirote) took me in and adopted me, not necessarily legally. Of course, I was already over eighteen (18) and had an Identity card (ID).

I moved to Meru with my young brother and immediate follower, the late Japheth Shabaya in his final year of secondary school. I took him to Kaaga Harambee Secondary School. It had boarding facilities. I paid his fees and upkeep. He stayed with me during the holidays and vacations.

I was immensely proud of him because he completed his secondary school successfully. I later helped him to join The Kenya Police Force, and later, teaching career. Thereafter, he finally, determinately became The Senior Chief, Idakho Location. Therefore, as far as government administration goes in Kenya, he was my boss, until his death.

While in Meru, my jurisdiction and my area of responsibility, was Kambereu Section, neighbouring Tigania, with rich volcanic type of soil. Most of the area, was very fertile, so fertile with unbroken ground. Almost anything could grow over there.

However, on the other side was Tharaka, more-like semi-arid area. It was dry most of the time but produced wonderful honey. Therefore, my area of operations and service, had amazing contrasting scenery and economy.

I was the first residential minister in the section. Within the first quarter, I had encouraged and motivated the members to complete building the minister's manse. Water pump was installed on the Kambereu River, just next to the Manse.

In dry season, water was pumped from that nearest river, into the elevated water tank. During the wet rainy season, I had a massive water tank. I harvested the rainwater from the roof of the house.

I, therefore, had running water and a flushing toilet in the house throughout the year. The house was spacious, incorporating a study and a kitchen. There was a chimney, servicing the kitchen and the lounge.

In the evenings, during the cold evenings, especially in the wet, cold seasons, I used to sit in the lounge, next to the fireplace, under the chimney. This often reminded me of my childhood three stone faced open logs fire, by which we cuddled around, for warmth, whenever it was cold. Unlike my childhood house, that was filled and saturated with a lot of smoke, the Kambereu Manse had the luxury of a chimney and a smoke outlet.

Cooking at Kambereu Manse and heating water was by logs of firewood. Unfortunately, rural electrification and improved infrastructure, had not yet reached Kambereu and most parts of rural Kenya, Meru included. So, I had no access to electricity, telecommunication and all-weather roads, or good tarmacked roads.

In the evening and at night, I used a kerosene optimus lantern. Unlike my childhood 'tiny tin smoky lamp,' with blurred fuzzy grey light. The kerosene optimus lantern was bright and less smoky. It was a more civilised light. It lit the room, the whole room and even beyond, almost as bright as an electric bulb.

There were no mobile phones or computers in those days. So, for instant communication beyond and far, I had to travel all the way to Meru town. Hence, it was an ordeal to make a phone call.

The other quickest means of communication was by telegram. Nevertheless, I had to go to the post office, miles away in Meru town, to send, likewise, to receive and retrieve a telegram, if I had been sent one.

Most telegrams were used for emergency communication. Whenever I saw a telegram, I usually panicked. Most telegrams announced demise of a close relative. However not all telegrams bore bad news.

Incidentally, some telegrams were also used for faster transfer of money, Money Order Telegraphic Transfer (MOTT). Unlike Mpesa, mobile money transfer in East Africa, Money Order Telegraphic Transfer was not instant as such. It took at least a day or two to arrive.

Those were the days, when Mpesa and instant money transfer and delivery was non-existent. The Mpesa, online and Mobile banking era, had not dawned in Kenya and in the world.

While in Meru, on 14 March 1975, I graduated in absentia at Makerere University, Uganda. I was awarded Diploma in Theology by Makerere University, Kampala, without attending any ceremony or any celebration. A few days later, I went to collect my credentials at St Paul's United Theological College, Limuru.

The subjects I pursued included: Old Testament, New Testament, African Theology, Research Paper, African Church History, Biblical Theology, Contemporary

Theology, African Traditional Religion and Pastoralia. I skipped Islamic Studies, Philosophy of Religion, New Testament Greek, Hebrew and Latin. Missing out on Greek, Hebrew or Latin was apparently not a wise decision; it came to haunt me later, but overall, it became a blessing in disguise.

I learnt Kimeru whole heartedly. I read a lot, including any Kimeru writings, stories and folk tales like '*Ngono Cia Nyomo,*' 'The Animal Stories,' etc. Hoping to stay longer in Meru, I endeavoured to master the local language, dialect and accent. Within six months, I was conversant with Kimeru language, especially - Ki-Imenti dialect of Kimeru.

When in Meru, I quickly learned that, unlike the 'Wameru' of Tanzania, the 'Ameru' of Kenya are not causally related to those in Tanzania, especially the language. The Kenya Ameru are nine sub-tribes, with distinct language characteristics and dialects: Chuka, Igembe, Igoji, Imenti, Mitine, Muthambi, Mwimbi, Tharaka and Tigania, respectively.

Within the churches in my jurisdiction, I gently and slowly introduced lively singing, including playing of guitar, etc., in the services and fellowship meetings and so forth. I had taught myself to play a guitar and local drums. I was encouraged to do so, and more so, at St Paul's United Theological College as a hobby and as an extra-curricular activity. I played the guitar, drum and sang in the College choir and quartet, up to the Kenya National Television.

The guitar and lively services attracted a lot of young people, the elite teachers within and around Meru, etc. However, believe it or not, it also got me into a lot of trouble with the staunch, conservative, dominant diehards, elders and senior members of the church, especially those who belonged to the dominant Brethren Movement: The East African Revival Movement.

The initial protests brought to surface my diplomacy and negotiation skills. As a shepherd, following and endeavouring to emulate Jesus Christ, the Good Shepherd, I did not want to lose any of my 'sheep' – even one member.

On my visit to Germany, I had encountered stories of how Martin Luther the reformer blended in old and new, traditional and modern music to liven worship. Likewise, I was emulating him, but with a Kenya flavour, in the Kenyan context.

In colonial days in Kenya, guitar, band music, and all the good music including African traditional music, songs and tunes were attributed to the devil by the Missionary Churches. After my 'strange experience' and subsequent return to the church, I always felt that I must reclaim the good music, the beautiful tunes and instruments back for and to God, the rightful owner.

'Should we allow the devil to monopolise, hoard and stash all the good music,' I asked the elders. They all in unison answered: 'No! No!' Within a few months, most of the opposing members were soon convinced and were on my side. They had seen the light, the impact of lively music in the church and especially among the youth, the present and future church.

Modern music and lively services not only attracted the young and the youth, it also attracted non-church goers' grownups alike, to the church. The church in my area started becoming an exuberant church.

On 12 April 1975, I solemnised, and legally cemented my long-time relationship with Margaret Mebo. I met Margaret at Lavington United Church in 1969. Now I had company and a consort, someone to support me. Someone to turn to, amid my encounters and challenges. A real confidante.

To my surprise and the surprise of my members and congregations, The Methodist Annual Conference, of August 1975, transferred me from Meru. I was subsequently stationed at Charles New Methodist Church, in Jericho, Nairobi.

Charles New was the only real Methodist Church in Nairobi. Of course, there was Lavington United Church, the name says it all. There was also some Methodist partnership with The Presbyterian Church of East Africa (PCEA), at Bahati, in the East-lands, Nairobi.

The Methodist Church in Kenya was very much involved in the Bahati Community Centre and its outreach. In fact, the Warden, Mr Erastus Kirimania, was a Methodist. However, both Lavington United Church and Bahati Church, were not Methodist Churches.

Lavington United Church was ecumenical. Bahati Church was a predominantly Kikuyu, Presbyterian Church, with a few Meru Presbyterians, especially the Ameru from Chogoria area.

I was supposed to take up my new station on the New Year's Day, 01 January1976. My members in Meru were furious and vehemently protested, opposed and appealed against my transfer, but to no avail. Members vehemently opposing a transfer of a minister, was something unheard of and had never happened before, in the itinerant ministry of Kenyan Methodism. But it happened with me.

While in Meru, I sat for University of London GCE English and passed. For various reasons, when I was in Meru, I could not continue to focus a lot on my academic private non pastoral studies or pursuits.

First and foremost, I was a Probationer Minister, undertaking Probation Studies. Therefore, my time, day and week was full to the brim. Probation studies were prerequisite studies for the preparation and acceptance into Full Connexion and subsequent ordination.

In addition, I was a full-time rural minister, with over ten churches to look after, with a lot of church planting and missionary outreach. I, therefore, travelled extensively throughout my extended rural setting. In fact, in Meru, I was not able to access any public libraries. There were none.

Chapter Twenty-One: The Urban Jungle

In January 1976, I moved to Charles New Methodist Church, Nairobi. For a while, I worked directly under the mentorship and supervision of The Presiding Bishop, The Rev Lawi Imathiu, MP. Later, John Bowles, an Anglican clergy stationed at Lavington United Church, was appointed as my Superintend Minister.

This was unheard of in Kenyan Methodism, an Anglican priest being a Methodist Superintendent Minister. However, being a senior minister, having been born in Kenya, therefore a Kenyan citizen, with British ancestry and stationed at Lavington United Church, the arrangement was understandable and acceptable.

With John Bowles, I had a lot of opportunities to serve my former church, Lavington United Church. We exchanged pulpits quarterly. I was thrilled to regularly preach at my former church. My sermons at Lavington, were mainly, a reflection on the theme of reconciliation and our human interdependence.

The preaching at Lavington helped me, to completely put the painful experience and memories of the attempts to rescind my call to the ministry, behind and at the back of my mind. Positively, also, with John Bowles, we were able to compare notes, on our perception of Methodism and Anglicanism. We usually met weekly on Tuesdays, at the dawn of the day, just before the sunrise for about two hours including breakfast.

On several occasions, we delved into various subjects, pastoral issues, Anglicanism, etc. The Rev John Bowles was affiliated to Bible Churchmen's Missionary Society (BCMS), hence he acquainted me with very Low Anglicanism, almost poaching me to the Anglican ministry. Of course, I had encountered some Anglicanism at Lavington United Church, Nairobi and at St Paul's United Theological College, Limuru, respectively.

While at St Paul's United Theological College, in my final year, as I did not have 'O' levels and 'A' levels, I applied to Nairobi University - Mature Entrance Exams, into the BA and BEd degree programmes. I sat the exams and passed. However, Mature Entrance route was scrapped, with immediate effect. As it was just scrapped before my in-take and subsequent selection for the respective academic year, I was not lucky to be considered for admission.

Now, the only remaining route, into the only University in Kenya then, was 'A' Levels, for both mature and young applicants. Nairobi University advised me to take up 'O' levels and later 'A' levels, if I was still interested in any degree programmes and studies, at the University of Nairobi. Thus, I had to compete with the young candidates, straight from secondary schools, on the same par.

Being at Charles New Methodist Church, it felt as if I was in the jungle, not my familiar Tropical Rainforest jungle of Kakamega Forest, but the 'Urban Jungle.' I had moved with my family to Charles New, including my brother Japheth, whom I treated more like my son, than a brother.

While in Nairobi, I continued to support my siblings: Japheth V Shabaya, Ruth K Shabaya, now Mrs Mwachiro and Ages K Shabaya, now Mrs Masengo (both in secondary school) and my brother in-law Markland and sister in-law Joyce Kaddie.

My house in Nairobi was always full. My siblings always came with their friends during the vacations. By now Japheth was more interested in the Police Service.

I encouraged Japheth and exposed him to various security experiences, to intensify his experience, in preparation for Police Force intake and career. I managed to inspire him into the Kenya Police Force. On graduation, he was posted to the Airport Police, Jomo Kenyatta International Airport (JKIA), Nairobi.

While at (JKIA), Japhet had a paradigm shift. He developed great interest in teaching. With my passion for education, I encouraged and paid the Police Force Three months' pay in lieu of notice, for him to resign immediately and join teaching, initially as un-trained teacher. Later he joined Kagumo Teacher Training College and qualified as a Primary School Teacher (P1).

With extensive Police Force and Teaching experiences, Japheth was later appointed Senior Chief, Idakho Location. Now I was under my baby brother's jurisdiction.

While in Nairobi, I resumed re-tracking my path, my pursuit of further studies. As the university had discontinued and abandoned Mature Entrance Exams, I embarked on my preparation to meet Nairobi University's new entry requirements,

I attempted to register for the required 'A' Levels, but I was declined, for lack of KPE and EACE (KCSE) certificates. Determined, I requested St Paul's United Theological College and Nairobi University, Institute of Adult Studies Division, institutions that knew my capability, to write a recommendation letter to East African Examination Council (EAEC).

The East African Examinations Council, now Kenya National Examinations Council – KNEC, set out their requirements. As for St Paul's United Theological College, the respective letter should be on the college's letter headed paper. It should state that I had education equivalent to that of School Certificate.

The same was expected of Nairobi University, Institute of Adult Studies Division. In addition, Nairobi University had to state that I am continuing to pursue 'A' level studies through distance learning, which of course I was currently undertaking.

The two letters worked! The East African Examination Council accepted and registered me as an external and mature student for East African Advanced Certificate of Education (EAACE). Thus, I had made it to sit for academic exams, without the mythical KPE now KCPE and EACE, now KCSE credentials. My determination was rewarded.

I continued to study privately, mainly, in the evenings, late in the night, early in the mornings and on my off days, depending on my work schedule. In 1976, I sat the respective EAACE History, Divinity, Literature in English and Kiswahili exams and passed. In 1977, I took further University of London GCEs in Economics, Swahili, History and Religious Studies.

Joyfully, I approached Nairobi University, my application was acknowledged, as having the necessary requirements for a BA and BEd degree courses, fields of my great interest. I was therefore advised to patiently wait for the forthcoming admission. I was supposed to be admitted together with the school candidates in the following academic year.

To my disappointment, the rules changed again, just before my in-take. The 'goal posts' were moved again. The Nairobi University decided to take only straight entries of 'A' level young people, the Sixth Formers from secondary schools within the country.

There was now no more hope for mature students, even if they had the minimum requirements. Unlike nowadays, there were no private universities, no parallel option or intake and no distance graduate learning either. University was now for the esteemed privileged, a few young people, on full government scholarship. It was more like my days at Cambridge University in the 1980s, when the British Government gave full non-refundable grant, excluding overseas students, with immigration restrictions, required to pay overseas rate of fee.

The mature students' university entry embargo in Kenya was now on, until further notice. My hope of joining university was almost over and out for the unforeseeable future. Once again, I was locked out of the only university in Kenya and apparently, completely doomed. As far as the pursuit of university education in Kenya was concerned, that was it; that was the end of the story. It was, indeed, supposed to be the end of the journey for me. But me being me, with the immense determination that I had and belief in possibilities, I did not surrender or give up.

Chapter Twenty-Two: Look Elsewhere

Nairobi University, the only university in Kenya then, barred Mature students, bolted its gates and doors indefinitely, so that Mature students could not enter or get in. Therefore, inclusively and exclusively de facto, I was also locked out. Consequently, I started exploring other possibilities at hand and elsewhere.

Initially, I explored possibilities of admission into universities in West Africa, especially Ghana to no avail, due to financial constraints. I then applied to Cambridge University. I was advised that before any consideration and interview as a mature student, I had to demonstrate that I have a scholarship or the means and ability to pay the university, college fees and upkeep expenses. The figures were ridiculous amount of money for me. I approached the church to support my application and again, it declined.

As usual, I never gave up. I also applied to Bristol University, UK, for degree studies in Theology. I was informed, it would be possible with the support of the church to get admission as a mature student. I should therefore proceed with my application as I seek the support of the church. I approached the church, the church also declined to support my application.

A colleague, friend and classmate, Rev David Taati, who pursued same studies with me at Limuru, had applied for the same course at Bristol University. He was recommended, by the church and the church supported his application. He was accepted and secured a scholarship. However, for various reasons, David found Bristol academic rigour rather exigent and daunting. He abandoned the course and returned to Kenya, empty handed. Frustrated and disappointed, he decided to explore the American route and option.

As for me, based on my hobbies, the Methodist Church offered me a six months course in Church Music and Youth Work in Australia. I declined the offer. Of course, I had an interest in music and young people. However, I had no background in Music Studies, no knowledge of staff notations, no theory of music at all, not even 'The Sound of Music' tonic sol-fa. Therefore, in that sense I could not dare pursue music at an advanced level, even if I were offered a degree course.

I had been put off music by Mr. Lund, my former employer, the organist at Lavington United Church, Nairobi. On several occasions, I had approached him, requesting and pleading with him, to teach me some music e.g. staff notations, especially to play the piano and later the organ, but he declined. I loved the sound of the piano and organ, and I still do. However, he reckoned music, was too hard for someone like me to learn, grasp, comprehend and even appreciate. I wish he had given me a chance to try or tried me out!

I therefore just naturally, took to strumming the face of the guitar. Of course, I enjoyed making some harmonious noise, some sort of sound and singing. Playing, strumming a guitar, became my hobby.

Anyway, I was told that a Music degree course was not on the plate. Inadvertently, a degree in music was not on offer for me at that juncture. I would have appreciated a degree in an academic subject, related to working with young people, probably education or teaching. But even that, was not on offer for me.

Finally, I discovered University of London External Degrees. It admitted mature students and offered long distance learning programme. International students like me could also apply. I applied and I was admitted to study Bachelor of Divinity (BD) degree, on condition that I pass preliminary exams including a pass in Greek or Hebrew.

As I did not have opportunities to study Greek or Hebrew, prerequisite for the BD course, I enrolled with Wolsey Hall, Oxford, for preparation and coaching. I embarked on the long distance, international home-schooling programme. My Preliminary exams included Old Testament Hebrew and New Testament Greek. Furthermore, I also took introductory Biblical Studies. These included archaeological studies of Egypt and the Middle East.

I also pursued Early Ecclesiastical History: The Early Christian Thought - AD/CE 70 – 500. It was a befitting introduction to my theological and education passion, quest for truth, exploring probabilities and possibilities.

Books for such a specialised magnanimous course, were not easily available in the public libraries of the Nairobi urban jungle. When ordered, especially through the existing theological bookshops e.g., Catholic Book Shop, Keswick Bookshop, Church Army Bookshop, etc., they were very dear, a lot more expensive to buy and own. As a church minister on meagre stipend, I found purchasing most of the recommended books and resources, rather daunting and almost impossible.

However, Nairobi University, had a particularly good Department of Philosophy and Religious Studies. It was then chaired by Prof Stephen Neil, a renowned scholar and a Church of England bishop. In fact, some of his books were strongly recommended. They were a must to read by London University and later by Cambridge University. I embarked on networking.

In view of this, I went and introduced myself to Prof Stephen Neil, who in turn introduced me to other members of the Department. Most of the lecturers understood and empathised with my plight, challenges and demands of a degree course. They willingly, accepted and volunteered to help me with the course, at nil pay. With Prof. Stephen's recommendation, Nairobi University Library, gave me access and full membership, with borrowing rights. I was also accorded the same rights at Kenyatta College Library, by then, constituent college of Nairobi University.

Encouraged by Prof Neil's gesture, I also approached Kenyatta College, now Kenyatta University, by then a constituent college of Nairobi University, specialising in Bachelor of Education (B Ed), degree, designed especially to train Secondary School Teachers. The lecturers in History and Geography volunteered to help me with the Middle East Ancient History and Geography, relevant and vital for my course.

By the recommendation of The Rev David Philpot, I was enrolled as an external member of the St Paul's United Theological College Library. Most of the tutors were also willing to help me.

The Most Rev Gitari, later, the ACK Archbishop, and Rt Rev Horace Etemesi, Bishop Butere Diocese 1993-2003, had both pursued the same degree course while in UK. They were also willing to help me. Therefore, I received a lot of encouragement from within and without, in and around the urban jungle of Nairobi.

With the purchase of some basic textbooks, and the ensuing help, I was set. I embarked on my correspondence degree studies. With self-discipline, I ensured regular and prompt completion of my assignments. I forwarded my assignments to Wolsey Hall, Oxford, UK, by pre-paid return Airmail postage for marking and subsequent remarks.

Those were the days of my life, days of no on-line teaching or learning. The on-line teaching was yet to come. However, even though these were international distance studies, I was not new to correspondence, home learning studies. So, I was set, ready for the challenge, and I enjoyed it.

One year into my part-time degree course, I was again transferred to Kisii. It was a very new station, with no proper office or study area. The manse was at Ogembo Village, closer and nearer the boarder of Kisii County and Narok County, bordering the Masai of Kilgoris - Narok County. The area was prone to a lot of cattle rustling, resulting in sporadic violence, between the two tribes.

Kisii was a new Methodist outreach and Mission area. Most of the Methodist Church work in Kisii, was in the middle of nowhere. It was in the remote areas of Kisii. The predominant church was the Seventh Day Adventists (SDA), worshipping on Saturdays rather than Sundays.

There were only three tarmacked roads, both major roads, Kericho-Kisii, Kisii - Isebania- Tanzania and Kisii-Kisumu Roads. Therefore, the overall infrastructure was extremely poor. Literally, in most of the Methodist outreach areas, there were no roads, except foot paths through thickets. Again, effective means of transport in such an area was long wheelbase land-rover and walking on foot most of the time. As such I was very fit.

On several occasions, when at home I was the Volunteer Ambulance, ferrying emergencies from the village, to the nearest Kilgoris Catholic Mission Hospital and Tabaka Catholic Mission Hospital. Thus, the Kisii mission work was very demanding and indeed challenging, with scattered outreach posts, more scattered than my stint experience in Meru.

Furthermore, there were no libraries in the vicinity, no volunteer lecturers to help me with my degree studies. There was literally, nothing to help or encourage me with my academic pursuits. In fact, if anything at all, everything that there was made it exceedingly difficult to pursue intensive and extensive academic pursuits. The challenges were many, and rather enormous for me.

Committed to my church work, I deferred the pursuit of my London University degree course. I embarked on learning Eke-gusii, the local language, to enhance communication and effectiveness of my ministry. Having been a translator myself, I understood the challenges of translation. I noted sometimes the distortion of my message, through bad translation or literal rendering of the message by the interpreter. I did not want to rely on translators or interpreters indefinitely. Some of my translators were not very conversant with English or Kiswahili, for that matter, their rendering of my messages was very unreliable.

After three years of grounding myself in Kisii in Western Kenya, I was transferred back to Charles New Methodist Church, Nairobi. I immediately resumed my degree studies. By the time I returned to Nairobi, I was no longer, the loner, 'Mr Accident' in the Methodist Church in Kenya. In fact, by then the Methodist Church had extended to Western Kenya, especially in Kisii County, where I had just been.

Additionally, Lydiah Nyawade had by now been recruited in The Methodist Conference Office, Nairobi. Later, she became the Presiding Bishop's Secretary and Personal Assistant (PA), thus manning the Conference Office. She became a great confidante and a colleague.

She encouraged me in my pursuits of higher learning and in many ways, supported me extensively. In return, I volunteered to help her with proofreading, including minutes and other vital materials, of the Annual Methodist Conference, various committees, District Synods, etc.

Likewise, she volunteered to provided me with remarkably high specialised standards of meticulous services. She was my voluntary Personal Assistant (PA) in her free time. In fact, I used her more, and she became a real blessing indeed. Without her support and conscientious services, I do not know where I would be now? Probably, I would not have made it to Cambridge University, with my remarkably busy schedule.

I also personally, picked up from her, a lot of administration, organisational and interpersonal skills, vital for my busy schedule, and in my entire career. I am therefore grateful to Lydiah. I am greatly indebted to her and I owe her a great deal.

With a short stint back at Charles New Methodist Church, Nairobi, I was seconded to the Kenya Armed Forces, now Kenya Defence Forces (KDF) as a chaplain. My in-take and initial completion of cadets training was delayed due to 1982 coup attempt in Kenya. After the fateful coup attempt was quashed, I joined Armed Forces Training College (AFTC), for military training at Lanet, Nakuru County.

Chapter Twenty-Three: The Cambridge Attraction

My interest in studying at Cambridge University never dwindled, especially once I was challenged to find a scholarship. However, while at AFTC, I had no option but to defer anything and everything academic, including Cambridge pursuits.

Of course, on entry, at AFTC, I surrendered everything including myself, even my identity. This was literally symbolised in the surrender of my personal civilian Identity Card (ID). I never saw my civilian ID, until many years later, when I resigned my commission and left KDF, back into civilian life.

While in KDF, I was fully kitted, including underwear. My personal belongings and clothing were therefore not necessary, to be worn or used only when I got a 'pass,' time off, etc.

On arrival at AFTC, Lanet, once I passed the entrance gate, I was shouted at and screamed at. I was screamed at, together with the other recruits, cadets and officers to be. No body referred to us, as officer cadets.

The welcoming trainers, especially the drill Sergeant screamed at us all the time, with a shrieking voice: *'weka satifiketi na digri zenu kwa kit-baga, na msahau kabisa, sahau kabisa mambo ya masomo.* Simply paraphrased, 'put your certificates and your degrees in the kitbag, store them away and completely forget that you ever went to school, forget your academic achievements.

The welcoming introductory and motivation shrieking speech and words were astonishing, as the voice itself. Initially, the Senior Non-commissioned Officer's (SNCO) shrieking voice was not funny at all, especially when Commissioned Officers, passed nearby. He had this serious stone face look. Later, it became a real amusement and amazement to remark on whenever we were on our own....

Commissioned Officers, Senior Cadets, and Non-commissioned Officers (NCOs) nearby seemed not bothered. They just carried on with their business and duties, as duty called and as if it were normal. Families, especially kids in the nearby Married Quatres (MQ) just stood by, mesmerised and watching us, screamed at. They watched our bitter initiation with great amusement.

The Senior Sergeant continued, *'mimi ndio mwalimu hapa.'* which translates, 'I am the only one who is the teacher here. Of course, my team was a combined group of specialists, most already qualified in various disciplines, except the military. Some of us, were university Graduates, qualified graduate teachers, padres, nurses, doctors, accountants, mechanical engineers, chefs, etc.

The Senior Sergeant screamed again, this time at the top of his voice as if beckoning deaf people or audience miles away. I never comprehended what he said.

Shocked, some Nurses in my in-take, burst into tears. The Senior Sergeant, posed, with his eyes twitching, he looked straight into our faces and direct into our eyes. Imperatively, he commanded, ordered and screamed at us, at the top of his voice as if we were all deaf or something: '*Atis*! *Ajua*!' stand at ease! As you were!

We all obeyed and immediately stood 'atis' (stood at ease). This time, in a different tone as if he cared less about the crying nurses, he sarcastically commanded us,'*simameni kabisa,* '*kaaeni chini, kila mtu kaa chini,*' stop, everyone stop, sit down, everyone sit down.' Sarcastically, he asked and remarked, once again in a funny tone and accent of Kiswahili, as if 'taking the mic': *'kwa hivyo watu wanataka kulia! Na kama watu wanataka kulia, na watu walie sasa.'* Literally, 'so people want to cry! And if people want to cry, now let the people cry now.'

Ashamed, the crying nurses immediately stopped crying, wiped their tears. Once more, the Senior Sergeant screamed and shouted, 'attention!' Once we were at attention, now at a much higher pitch, the Sergeant screamed again: *'Wewe ni kurutu, na kurutu ni chombo cha kazi, mali ya serikali.* Again, literally: 'You're recruits, and recruits are vessels for work, weapons to do the job, to be put to work. As vessels, weapons, you are now the property of the government.

The rest is history. A few months later, it was my Passing-out Parade (Graduation Ceremony) at AFTC. Afterwards, I was posted to Nairobi. When I returned to Nairobi, I immediately returned to my part-time academic pursuits, amidst the demands of my new military job.

My appetite for the quest for truth was once again rekindled. It was enhanced by my encounter with Military top cream, top echelon and Senior Officers. Many had been overseas, trained at various Military Academies, institutions of higher learning, including Sandhurst, elite military institute, in UK, universities and Military Academies in Europe, USA, Pakistan, etc.

Most of the officers had been exposed militarily, academically, existentially, experientially and asked perceptive questions, in their apparent quest for truth. They needed a fellow officer, a chaplain who can walk with them along the path of the quest for truth. They needed an officer-chaplain who would wrestle with and endeavour to respond to their ultimate questions.

This rekindled, fuelled and fired my academic pursuits and further quest for truth. I wanted to explore, get the tools and have the answers, especially for Padre Hour classes, discussions and question times.

My surname was a great amusement and a ridicule. Lt. Malaya, sounded funny, but more so derogatory and abusive. *Malaya* in Kiswahili means, a harlot, a prostitute, a sex worker. To be addressed Lt Harlot/Prostitute was not a musing. In view of this, my Commander advised me to change my surname.

Henceforth, I agreed to change my name. The Legal Officer (SO1 Legal), a Lieutenant Colonel was instructed to take the necessary legal action, to get my name changed. By the end of 1983, my name changed by deed poll and was gazetted accordingly in Kenya Gazette from John Shabaya Malaya, to John Lisamula Shabaya. Thus, I took my father's middle name as my family/surname and my siblings have followed suit.

Just after my name change to Capt (Rev) John L Shabaya

I revived my never dying interest in Cambridge University. I forwarded my application again to Fitzwilliam College, via Wesley House, Cambridge. I was given a conditional offer, if successful to start in October 1984.

I applied for a Kenya Government scholarship and funding through the Department of Defence, via the Office of the President, to the British Council. My application was declined. Reason, it was time barred. Departmental budgets, including further training had been forwarded.

As I had been admitted at Fitzwilliam College, Cambridge University, I was therefore advised to defer my admission to the following year. I was assured verbally that my course will be included in the Training Budget 1985/1986.

My parents, especially my mother, were very proud of my achievement and promotion to Major (Rev) John L Shabaya In Kenya Defence Forces. A dream come true.

Chapter Twenty-Four: Why Cambridge?

My interest in studying at Cambridge never dwindle away, especially once I was challenged to find a scholarship. However, while at AFTC, I had no minute to spare, therefore, no option but to defer anything and everything academic.

While in Nairobi, especially at Kahawa Garrison Barracks, I made the best of our former military facilities, surrendered to the Ministry of Education, now Kenyatta University. My daughters attended Kenyatta Primary School, mixing and rubbing shoulders with the children of academicians. It paid dividends.

Unlike me, my daughters, Rose Shabaya, Rehana Shabaya and Sagina Shabaya, now Mrs Koloko, are all university graduates. They have superseded my expectations. I am glad, for their sake, I stayed on in 1995 to the extent of being fired and sacked by The Methodist Church in Kenya. They have been all over the world, visited more countries than I have visited. Indeed, I passed on to my children, my passion for travel.

I also used Kenyatta University library facilities and various lecturers, particularly Prof Sifuna, helped me with my academic work. My morning and evening runs and jogging through Kenyatta University College cavernous grounds were unrestrained. This was vital for my own personal edifice and a military fitness requirement. Indeed, I cannot emphasise enough, the significance of fitness in the military.

Both physical fitness and spiritual fitness, especially the inner power, peace and motivation, the will power and the will to go on regardless, is an essential morale requirement in KDF and permeates the military service.

To be in Kenya Defence Forces, and forces worldwide, I had to be fit, or else I wouldl not have lasted long there. No short cut, no circumnavigating fitness. I just had to be fit and I was as fit as a fiddle.

My interest in Cambridge, was developed over an exceedingly long period. Initially, through longing to sit for Cambridge Secondary School exams that were set and marked by Cambridge University Examination Syndicate.

All secondary school exams in Kenya, for a long time, were set, printed, distributed and marked by University of Cambridge Local Examination Syndicate (UCLES), now Cambridge Assessment (CA). Cambridge Examinations were esteemed highly, respected for their rigour and high standards academic cogency.

Secondly, most of the outstanding good scholars, a must to read, on most of my theological encounters, were Cambridge dons. I really wanted to sit at their feet. Thirdly, A few of my St Paul's United Theological College tutors, were alumni of Cambridge University, including Dr John Newton, my mentor. They were Brobdingnagian academics; demonstrated, displayed vast, literally 'massive' excellent in-depth knowledge and scholarly learning, with a vast grasp of facts, skills and mastery of their subject.

Finally, a lot of the outstanding African scholars then, were from Cambridge University. For me, these included Prof Bolaji Idowu, University of Ibadan, Nigeria and Prof John S Mbiti, Kenyan scholar and Director, Bossey Institute, Geneva, Switzerland, to name but a few.

In fact, it was my face to face encounter with Prof Mbiti at Bossey, Geneva, Switzerland in Summer 1974, that was the grand push and inspiration for me to head to Cambridge. I thought, imagined myself walking in the moccasins of Cambridge, long pedantic, outstanding history and tradition.

I always believed that at Cambridge, I would experience and wear academic moccasins of great and renowned scholars. I would also walk in the footsteps of not only great scholars, but pioneers in many fields, even great and extra-ordinary people. Cambridge has impacted and significantly contributed to the world in many ways.

There was the famous Isaac Newton, a mathematician, physicist, astronomer, theologian and author. He was especially renowned for his laws of gravitation and universal motion. Charles Darwin: Theory of Evolution. CMS roots 1799 can be traced to Cambridge alumni. The discovery of DNA structure in 1953 by Francis Crick, were just some of Cambridge University innovations and contributions.

In 1984, I was fortunate enough to be selected to attend a Military Officers Conference in Seoul, South Korea, via UK, Dubai and Taiwan. En route, I had a brief stint at Sandhurst elite Military College in UK. I also used my stop-over and lay-by in UK very well. I got the opportunity to attend in person the subsequent conditional offer interview at Fitzwilliam College, Cambridge University.

I interviewed well, and my conditional offer was thereby confirmed. My admission was amicably deferred to Autumn 1985, as I had requested earlier. Nevertheless, the admission was still subject to my undertaking one ancient - dead language.

I had to take Summer Language course either in Greek, Hebrew, Latin or Sanskrit, at Peter House College, Cambridge, prior to Autumn (The Fall) Matriculation – Cambridge University admission ceremony. The most probable time at this juncture was the Summer of 1985.

By matriculation date, I also had to demonstrate that I have read extensively, scholarly publications from the given reading list, by The Faculty of Divinity. The bibliography, the reading list, was undauntedly long. Thank God, it included my friend Prof Stephen Neil's publications, which I was already familiar with in my academic pursuits then.

I proceeded to Taiwan and South Korea, via the Middle East. The experience was amazing. I met and rubbed shoulders with top echelons like the CEO of Hyundai, worldwide Senior Officers, including four-star Generals and most decorated officers from all over the World. I experienced Taiwanese and Korean hospitality and delicacies. This was another eye-opening experience, that enhanced my appetite to explore other beliefs, at an academic level, including Buddhism.

Back in Kenya, I had limited time to go through my reading list, ensure prompt application for a Government scholarship in time for 1985 matriculation. With the help of Lydiah, I embarked on the process. It was tedious, time consuming, with a lot of paperwork, trips between the Department of Defence (DOD) and the Personnel Department, Office of The President and Methodist Conference Office.

There was also a lot of paperwork and correspondence, including phone calls to Cambridge. Amidst my demanding military busy schedule, I also made several errands to The Methodist Church Conference Office, the Headquarters of my sponsor to be.

By Easter 1985, I had secured accommodation at Wesley House, Cambridge. My Kenya Government scholarship had been tentatively approved and I was authorised to embark on the necessary preparations for my long-awaited Incredible Journey to Cambridge.

By this time, I had a family of three daughters, youngest about to turn two years. I also had customarily fostered two of my brothers Shem and Josiah, who were studying at Starehe Boys Centre, Nairobi. Additionally, I was still supporting my mother and my other two siblings Patrick M Shabaya and Solomon V Shabaya, back in the village in Western Kenya, including paying my siblings' secondary school fees.

Towards the end of June 1985, I was cleared to travel to UK to undertake my Summer Course studies in preparation for Autumn matriculation. I randomly chose Greek among the mandatory ancient languages. I had encountered a bit of Greek in my London University Preliminary preparations.

At a personal level, I was assured by my Commander that my family was safe. I was guaranteed and assured of accommodation for my family, at my current Officers Married Quarters, until they join me, in Cambridge once my scholarship is ratified and I matriculate.

Fires have been significant in my life. Prior to my departure to UK, there was the usual power cut in Nairobi. I sent my daughter Rehema aged 5 years to our bedroom to fetch her goodbye gift I had hidden in the wardrobe. Splash! the candle she was using to light her path set fire to the hanging clothes in the wardrobe. Within minutes, the room was engulfed in fire. Thank God we had fire extinguishers in the Officers' Quarters. I managed to extinguish the fire promptly. Careless fires are taken very seriously in the military. Another fire incident that almost cancelled my trip to my education pursuit.

I arrived at London Heathrow Airport on 04 July 1985. As per military protocol, I reported to the Defence Attaché at The Kenya High Commission, London. He cleared me to embark on my Summer Course at Peter House College, Cambridge University.

After a few days into my Summer Course, I was summoned by The Defence Attaché at The Kenya High Commission, London. He informed me that he had received instructions that my scholarship was not ratified. Therefore, I should prepare to abandon the course and return to my post and station in Kenya.

I enquired of the Defence Attaché and asked, 'Afande, Sir! is this a command?' He replied, 'now, certainly not, but I will confer and consult with DOD for further instructions and details.' He spoke as if to conclude, 'I will keep you posted.' He paused and with a calm tone and said, 'meanwhile, continue with your course until the final command and last details.' Once again, as the story of my life goes, I carried on without knowing 'what next?'

Chapter Twenty-Five: Money to Cambridge

I am often asked: How did you raise money to come to Cambridge? This question is not only asked in my taxi or cab, but whenever questions about how I came to be in UK arise. It became more poignant during my teaching career, in a predominantly middle class white rural England. In most cases, I normally say, 'it's a long story.'

One day, one of my esteemed clients, just frankly rejoined, 'today you'll cut the long story short and tell me a bit about it!' He continued, 'I would like to hear this story. I may have a similar story. Maybe not a replica or exactly like yours. It is nice to share.'

I always try to avoid this question, because it always reminds me of my Summer experience in 1985, and subsequent years, that followed thereafter. It metaphorically goes back deep into my 'veins and blood', back to my struggles and financial constraints that extensively impacted, dictated and directed my education path.

In Summer 1985, a few weeks, into my Summer Course at Cambridge, prerequisite for my matriculation, The Kenya Defence Attaché summoned me again. This time, I was informed that communication from Kenya had been received with further clearer details.

The details were almost, what is referred to in military terms as 'last details,' in other words 'last orders.' These were specific instructions from DOD. The Defence Attaché noted that in view of my course not having been ratified, DOD had given instructions for arrangements to be made for my return to my post in Kenya, with immediate effect. Apparently, the instructions reflected a lot of care and concern for me. For example, the military did not want me to be penniless, languish and suffer in a foreign land.

For me, those were very disheartening and dispiriting news to receive at that juncture and at such a critical point in time, in my education endeavour and pursuit. I beseeched and implored the Defence Attaché for leave of absence without pay, while I explore fund raising alternatives. My request was forwarded to Kenya. Unfortunately, it was declined.

I was therefore advised to return to Kenya promptly or else, resign my commission. I was pleased, at least I had gracefully been granted an option to resign. Moreover, if I opt to resign my commission, I should refund any funds paid to me and received by me so far, including warm clothing allowance and the one-way air ticket from Kenya to UK.

Sadly, regrettably, I could not visualize in my mind any other option. I opted to resign my commission and requested to be discharged from my military duties. On top of that, I pleaded for a waiver for payments received so far. In addendum, I remarked, 'I came to Cambridge with the understanding that I had been granted a scholarship.' I, therefore, entreat, appeal, request and beg DOD for clemency.'

In due course, my resignation was accepted. I returned my Officers' ID. Reciprocally, my Kenyan civilian ID and the Kenya Armed Forces Certificate of Service for Officers were forwarded to me via The Defence Attaché at Kenya High Commission, London. Thank God there was no further mention of refunds. I assumed; my plea had been heard by KDF. The deed was done, back to civilian life, this time, in a foreign country. I was on my own again.

With my resignation, my family had no choice but to vacate the Married Officer's Quarters (MQ). I moved my family to Fort Jesus, Kibera, Nairobi. One would say, 'I was back to square one, with no scholarship and my family in the shanty part of 'Kibera!' This was reminiscent of my time in Gatina slum. However, as for my family, luckily, it was not Kibera Line Saba, the massive squalor area of Kibera.

Meanwhile, I took my school age daughters to different schools: Rose – Eregi Roman Catholic Primary Boarding School, Western Kenya. She was approaching her grand finale exams, KCPE formerly KPE, that mythically catapults learners into the great future, the one I had failed. I registered Rehema at the best slum school in Kibera, Olympic Primary School, Nairobi, Kenya, visited by the former Prime Minister Gordon Brown in 2005. Sagina was a toddler, too young a girl, to be bothered about school.

Once my family was settled, I embarked on fundraising for my survival at Cambridge University. Thank God, at least, I did not have to worry about winter clothes. The Military had given me money for warm clothing and had gone silent on the refund. Therefore, I had no worries for the approaching Autumn (The Fall) and Winter.

I talked to Dr Graham Davies, Director of Theology and Religious Studies, Fitzwilliam College, Dr Ivor H Jones, Principal, Wesley House and Beryl Green, The Bursar, Wesley House about my plight. They agreed with me that it was wise to continue with the course, rather than quit. Of course, I was known not to be a quitter and I have never been known to quit.

I therefore started fund-raising for the course. The trio agreed to support me along and all the way, throughout my course and stay at Cambridge. Being assured of such support I had the motivation and the will power to carry on. Being over thirty, it was more ambitious, trying to get a full undergraduate scholarship.

On my behalf, the trio requested the University to give me grace and let me continue with the course, while I endeavour to raise funds for the course. They also entreated Fitzwilliam College and Cambridge University, to allow me to pay fees and expenses, in instalments as funds became available.

Being a Commonwealth Officer, I had no restrictions on my entry in UK. On arrival, I was granted indefinite leave to remain in UK with no restrictions. Therefore, I had no worries about visa renewals. Even my recourse to public funds was allowed. However, having been an officer, I was too proud to go for State Benefits. Instead, in view of this, I requested Cambridge University to waive off overseas fees, a rate Prime Minister Margaret Thatcher had recently introduced.

I set myself a target to raise funds in manageable instalments, quarterly, based on the academic year up to the grand total of the whole academic year. Beryl Gardner, Bursar at Wesley House, volunteered to be my accountant. Money raised was to be forward to her. She was to make all payments on my behalf, to Fitzwilliam College, Cambridge University and other relevant Departments etc. We further agreed that she pays me upkeep money as necessary and when funds were available.

Dr Graham Davies, Dr Ivor Jones and Beryl Green, the three of them, also agreed to be my referees when necessary. References were very vital, indeed essential and were the normal expectations. All the charitable organisations, grant giving institutions and individuals alike, required, requested for and insisted on a lot of references.

We agreed that, as a mature student, I should reside at Wesley House, rather than Fitzwilliam College. Wesley House was in the City Centre, in the old part of Cambridge. Being right in the city centre, it was close to essential services and places in Cambridge, therefore very convenient for me.

I could walk, and I walked almost to anywhere and everywhere within Cambridge, before I acquired a derelict, ramshackle of a bicycle. Moreover, the bicycle was and is the Cambridge transport, best vehicle around and in Cambridge, almost, the celebrated Cambridge City transport, a must for Cambridge students and residents.

For instance, Wesley House was awfully close, about five minutes' walk to The Divinity School, which was on St John's Street, opposite St John's College. That is where most of my lectures, tutorials and seminars were held.

Apart from my three subjects' tutors, most of my tutorials, commonly held in the tutors' residential study rooms, were within the precincts of the city centre. The Faculty of Divinity has since moved from the city centre, to West Road, to the area, commonly known as 'The Backs.' Indeed, it is at the backs of the senior, old and famous colleges.

While pursuing my Greek Summer Course and a little bit of Hebrew, I embarked on fund-raising mission. I spent a lot of time in the University Library (UL), researching various grant giving organisations, their necessary requirements and criteria. I managed to narrow to about two hundred that I thought might be sympathetic to my case, plight and support my course. Most were willing to give me small donations, ranging between £20 to £500. A few were able to pay lump-sums of over £1,000 or more.

Others were able to support the purchase of books, travel, especially to places with extended academic interest like Israel and Egypt. Others paid grants directly to bookshops like Heffers Bookshop, Trinity Street and stationary shops like Ryman, Sydney Street, for me to acquire the required and necessary books, stationery, etc.

Once I collected the relevant information, I embarked on applying for the grants and scholarships. These were the days of handwritten letters and typewriting, unlike the luxury of word processing and saving on computers or digital devices nowadays, to be reused later. Initially, I wrote over two hundred (200) handwritten letters to Charitable Organisations and about one hundred (100) to individuals or family foundations, a total of over three hundred (300) handwritten letters.

About one hundred (100) in total, individuals and organisations inclusive, responded and acknowledged my request. Forty out the one hundred who had acknowledged, for various reasons, declined. Initially, sixty applications were favourable.

Some organisations declined after seeking further enquiry, several more exchanges of correspondences, and clarifications. This went on, term after term, year after year, throughout the entire duration of my three-year course at Cambridge. Thus, my time at Cambridge was permeated with a lot of uncertainty, never knowing if I will make it and where the next penny will come from.

I got my first good news of significant funding and scholarships from Fitzwilliam College itself, initially for one year, later extended to two years and finally rolled into my third and final year. I also got a lot of support from Cambridge University itself, in the form of scholarships, grants, including travel grants.

Through the initiative of Susan Barr, The Methodist Church Overseas Division (MCOD) also supported and helped me throughout the course. I also got a lot of support from The Methodist Church Social Responsibility Department (MCSRD). Through Bishop Lawi Imathiu, The Methodist Church in Kenya agreed to chipp in.

Several Charitable Organisations, including The Diocese of Bristol, also agreed to help. I received various donations, some annually, from Foundations, Trusts, several philanthropic organisations and generous individuals, that I had written to. Some requested to remain anonymous. Their wishes were honoured and remained so. Therefore, with such help, I was encouraged and set to carry on with my studies at Cambridge.

Thus, with great faith, hope and sheer determination, I was able to raise enough funds annually, to see me through Cambridge University. Moreover, in summer 1986, at the beginning of my second year, I was able to move my family from the shanty Kibera, Nairobi to Cambridge.

Furthermore, my secondary school age daughters, Rose and Rehema were also awarded prestigious Boarding School scholarships for their secondary school education at Culford Independent school in Suffolk County, UK. Another milestone achievement.

I am therefore ever indebted to and grateful to Fitzwilliam College and Cambridge University, for the encouragement, support and various extensive scholarships, they endowed me. Likewise, I am also indebted to Wesley House, the Methodist church, various other churches, including the Diocese of Bristol, Church of England, charitable organisations, family foundations and individuals, out there, known and unknown to me, who made it possible for me to study at the University of Cambridge.

Without such support for myself and my family, I would never have made it to Cambridge. I would never have stayed at Cambridge with my family and realised my dream, ambition, pursuit, pursuit and quest for truth of such high quality. I was able to access precocious and progressive education at Cambridge University.

I also owe so much to the individuals who also supported me, financially. And for those, to those who enhanced my morale with personal encouragement, faith, hope and love, thank you so much. Without such concerted effort and support, I would never have made it to Cambridge. I would never be who I am now. I am and I will remain ever so grateful.

Chapter Twenty-Six: At Cambridge

In the 1980's and 1990s, there were very few black students at Cambridge University. In fact, in 1985 Fitzwilliam College Matriculation (admission), we were only 4 black students. One of the 4 of us, a lady, has returned to Cambridge, as a Master of a University College.

My future and time at Cambridge hinged on my first academic year (1985-1986). The withdrawal of my scholarship had ushered in the unforeseeable challenges of an imaginable magnitude of subsequent fund-raising marathon.

Determined, and focused on moving forward, I was not deterred by these challenges that I encountered. My experiences and my time at Cambridge, affirmed my faith, hope, my optimistic attitude to life and commitment to pursuing my dreams, no matter what.

I successfully completed the Summer Greek course. I successfully raised the necessary funds to study at Cambridge, at least for one year. A year later, I successfully completed the First Year Part I Tripos course. I passed the mandatory first year exams, including the dreaded Greek.

The dreaded Greek that I skipped in my Makerere University Diploma in Theology back in Kenya, that I thought would come to haunt me, became a blessing in disguise. In fact, if I had the required basic Greek or Classics qualifications like Latin, which I also skipped at Makerere, I would never have set foot in Cambridge, except for the interview, that I had already undertaken in 1984.

This is due to fact that matriculation is normally in Autumn and my scholarship was withdrawn in Summer. In retrospect, thank God, lucky me, blessed me, my scholarship was withdrawn, at least, when I was already in Cambridge, on the Greek Summer course, prior to Matriculation. That was 'simply the best' timing.

My time and years at Cambridge went by fast. I was steeped in long history and tradition, going back over 800 years. I discovered, students were not allowed to bring in cars unless they got special permission and granted exemption by the University of Cambridge Praelector.

I had plenty of time to explore Cambridge University and the various colleges, dotted around Cambridge, discovering their character and history. I discovered that most Cambridge colleges had distinct characters and traditions.

However, there were some common practices, like most colleges still said grace, a prayer before meals, in Latin. Students, graduates and fellows wore gowns to formal dinners, at their respective colleges. Formal dinners meant it is time to dress up smartly and wear your gown, unless you are a guest. In fact, even guests had to be properly, formally dressed up. Students had to sign in at the beginning of each term and at the end of each term.

Strangely, 'May Balls,' were not celebrated in May, but in June, after end of year examinations and impending summer graduations. 'May Ball' dress was strictly formal, a black tie or white tie, depending on the college. Only the invited guests were allowed in the respective college's 'May Balls.' The tickets were very dear, ridiculously priced, remarkably high and indeed very costly, in fact, highly priced.

'May Ball' nights, were colourful nights. They were something to reminiscent over, for many years to come. Nevertheless, there are a few constituent colleges of Cambridge University that hold 'Winter Balls', in Michaelmas and Lent Terms, instead of Summer Term 'May Balls' in June.

While at Cambridge, I encountered and met great and famous people. I sat under and by the feet of great scholars, like The Most Rev Dr Rowan Williams, former Archbishop of Canterbury and Master of Magdalene College, a poet and a theologian. He taught me Ecclesiastical History, particularly, Patristics, within Early Christian Thought. I rubbed shoulders with some of the best brains in the world, both students, visiting scholars, fellows, lecturers and professors.

At Cambridge, I also rubbed elbows with the famous and the mighty. I rubbed shoulders, met and shook hands with various celebrities, dignitaries, VIPs, leaders of the world like the first and former President of Zambia, Kenneth Kaunda, Nobel Peace Prize Laureate Archbishop Desmond Tutu, the South African theologian and vehement opponent of apartheid and many others.

At Cambridge, I pursued Theology and Religious Studies Tripos 1985-1988. After a short stint in Kenya 1989-1991, I returned to Cambridge. I intended to pursue a PhD I had embarked on in 1989, registered at Westminster College, Oxford and supervised at Cambridge. I was exploring 'The Development of Education in Kenya 1944-1964: An Ecumenical Perspective.'

Due to financial constraints, I abandoned my PhD in 1991. Instead, in the same, year, I applied and got a grant to pursue Post Graduate Certificate in Education (PGCE), with Secondary School Teaching option, at

Homerton College, Cambridge University. While I studied at Homerton for my Postgraduate Certificate in Education, I remained a member of Fitzwilliam College, retained my Fitzwilliam College membership and graduated as such.

As a student at Cambridge in the 1980's and 1990s, unlike nowadays, gates and doors were open for me to attend any lecture in any Department or Faculty. I grabbed the opportunity and the advantage. I, therefore, attended lectures in as many subjects as I could, including lectures delivered by Stephen Hawking, Theoretical Physicist, etc.

In the second year, Part II Tripos, undergraduates could change and pursue any subject of their choice. Hence, most Cambridge undergraduates, graduate with Bachelor of Arts degree (BA), irrespective of the subject studied or their major subject. As for me, I had already made up my mind. As such, I preferred and focussed on in-depth study of Theology for the entire three years of my undergraduate programme.

My college, Fitzwilliam College, had a spacious site. It had moved out and away from the squashed and congested city centre, to Huntingdon Road, in the suburbs of Cambridge. Now, however, the main entrance and The Porter's Lodge is situated on Storeys Way.

Perhaps Storeys Way makes it look closer to the city, proximity to other colleges and Senate House than the former Huntingdon Road entrance. The other two out of town colleges are Homerton and Girton. The latter, Girton College, was initially and is formerly a female only college.

Cambridge University itself, is a myth. It has thirty-one constituent colleges. Each College has a library.

Cambridge is dotted with many libraries, all over. It has various libraries, including Public Libraries.

There are also various Theological Colleges, each with a library and over one hundred Faculties/Departments, each has a specialised library, coupled with the grand University Library (UL) on West Road. These provided me with the most conducive environment, for my pursuit of the quest for truth and later, education and pedagogy course.

The tutorials and especially mandatory small group teaching, sometimes even, one to one teaching, if necessary, for me, is the 'hall mark of Cambridge University.' This attracted me to Cambridge, particularly impressed me and impacted me considerably.

The Cambridge style of teaching and learning was my 'cup of tea,' and style of learning. I had the best I could ever have had. I used to be lost in the 'jungle and forest' of overcrowded classes, where sometimes I was just a name on the register or even just a number, hence my ever-burning desire to study at Cambridge.

My tutors and supervisors at Cambridge knew me by my name and face. Overall, they were positively critical, analytical, required evidential support and justification for every explanation or word I uttered by mouth and every sentence I scribbled and wrote in my essays. Even the smallest minute detail, had to be considered, scrutinised, even the 'iota,' the Greek 'dot.'

Cambridge emphasised originality, student's own work, with proper acknowledgement of others work, that was well referenced. Plagiarism was loathed. Foremost, Cambridge encouraged independent learning, my sort of 'cup of tea.' For a self-made learner and student like me, Cambridge just brought out the best in me and out of me.

Most tutors were meticulous, paying attention to detail. For such tutors, even the smallest 'iota,' dot in the assignments, could not pass unrecognised. They insisted on the use of proper English vocabulary, spelling, punctuation and grammar (SPAG) in essays, research, etc. This was significant for me, as English was not my first language, and I had learned most of my English the hard way.

Therefore, Cambridge University enhanced my command of English language and helped me to home in my language skills. It enhanced my cogency, logical thinking, presentation of my ideas, other persuasions and thoughts as well.

Through small travel grants from Fitzwilliam College and various Cambridge University grants, I was able to travel extensively, especially to areas of educational interests, including Israel, Egypt, Germany, The Netherlands and even Kenya. This exposed me beyond belief.

Knowing me and knowing where I came from, where I had been, I learned a great deal at Cambridge. Being organised in small family like groups, encompassing the tutor and students from other disciplines, e.g. if you are a theologian, the family Tutor would be a scientist, one student per subject, up to about five students, therefore five disciplines. This exposed me to a great deal to other disciplines. I also learned and experienced the etiquette and decorum for life.

With my humble background, being just a poor boy, from a mud hut in Western Kenya, it was a great honour for me to have been at Cambridge University. Apart from the warm clothing allowance, I embarked on my course at

Cambridge penniless, but I survived, with the support of Fitzwilliam College and Cambridge University itself.

I can vouchsafe that Cambridge University and most colleges, like Fitzwilliam College, have a caring environment. In fact, most colleges, Fitzwilliam College, being exceptionally high on my list, have a commitment, to all students, poor and rich alike. The University and respective colleges ensure that, a student who is able and admitted to Cambridge, does not drop out, drop off or even fall out, just because of coming from a poor background and subsequent lack of funds.

Cambridge University enhanced my self-esteem and confidence. After Cambridge, I could face anything, I could face the world head on, like a 'bull fighter' from Idakho, Western Kenya. I also realised, I could survive anywhere and everywhere, in the world, no matter where and what. Proverbially, I developed the 'heart of stone' and 'the body of steel' at Cambridge, 'I had seen it all!'

Chapter Twenty-Seven: Does Teaching Matter?

When I tell people that I am a retired teacher, they often ask me, 'does teaching matter?' Very few people, like me, live to achieve, attain, realise and even surpass their own dreams in their lifetime, leave alone fulfilling their family dreams. My mother just dreamed and wanted me to be basically and merely literate. She just wanted me to be able to read and write.

Mama just wanted me to be able to read letters for her. She wanted me to read the Bible for her. She just wanted me to decipher hymns from the *Vasomi* – learners, readers – Mission Churches hymnals, into vernacular; hymnals of churches like Quakers (Friends), Church of God, and Anglicans.

My mother was notoriously religious. She was deeply involved in her indigenous church. Being illiterate, unlike her peers and fellow adherents of her indigenous church, mama loved singing. She enjoyed Christian songs and hymns of all denominations. She often recited Psalms and creeds. Being notoriously religious, my mother was also a woman of prayer.

Consequently, my interest in education, was instilled in me at an incredibly early age. It must have sunk so deep, up to and even into my subconscious, the inner me. Later, it just permeated my life. It became the driving force in many aspects of my life.

However, the paradigm shift towards pedagogy and subsequent teaching, came about, the hard way, through my struggles and pursuit of education. It became much clearer in my mind, well over, after my fateful day of failing my basic Primary School Exams (KPE) in 1966.

My late encounter with inspiring teachers, mentors, tutors, and lecturers just did it. I wanted to become a teacher. I wanted to be one of them. I wanted to be like them and one with them. I wanted to be a helper of others.

Having walked the long road, the difficult journey, into education, if possible, I did not want others, to walk the same difficult journey like me. I did not want others to walk the long path unaided, along the route of education, so late in life, as me.

Of course, everything and even life itself hinges on education, including learning to be human, even socialising into any society, in the respective human communities and cultures. I believe human beings are perpetual students, perpetual learners, from cradle to their destination and destiny, whatever that may be, hence teaching matters, in fact it matters a lot.

Moreover, I believe a teacher is constantly a learner, but not a selfish learner, who stashes, hogs and hoards knowledge just for oneself. A teacher is a learner who acquires knowledge and is willing to share the acquired knowledge.

A teacher enjoys leading others to drink from the bosom, the well or the fountain he drank from, and drew knowledge from. Figuratively, a teacher draws or pumps the water – knowledge, to the learners. The teacher brings knowledge and learning nearer and closer to the 'hearts' and 'minds' of learners. A teacher enables them to have convenient access and drink knowledge and education to the full, and achieve their full potential.

Like everything else in my life, even getting into teaching was not an easy walk. It was not even an easy ride or an effortless journey. First, my primary school teachers put me off teaching absolutely. They almost, also completely put me off education per se, education and all it entails. Thank God 'bad teachers,' if I may call them so, did not own education or even have the monopoly of education.

Failing my primary school exams, almost sealed my interest in education. It almost locked the doors and the gates of education for me. Metaphorically, it almost threw the key to the doors, to the gates of education and my access to it into sheol, the underworld, hades, abyss, in the depth of the deepest and fathomless ocean. In view of this, such a key would have supposedly, never been trodden upon. It would have never been stumbled on, or even found by me, save for my parents, my grandma's unwavering encouragement, determination and faith in me.

My initial attempts to get into teaching in Kenya, were futile and were all in vain. Then I was beckoned by a higher call. With my theological pursuits, the idea of teaching per se, especially in the secular context, dwindled and went 'through the roof,' just for some time.

Of course, I comforted myself that as a Minister of Religion, a pastor and a preacher, I was a teacher in many ways, more so in my services and particularly as a clergy. Of course, teaching percolates priesthood and pastoral care. Homiletics, preaching, though not entirely or in its totality teaching, in many aspects, it is teaching.

Pastoral Care itself is teaching, without the vocabulary, jargon or pedagogy of teaching. Pastoral care is being with people at their highest points in time and life. It is also being with people, at peak moments in their lives, including their lowest times and moments, particularly when they hit the 'rock bottom.'

When everything else people thought they knew, or even held on as dear and true, has failed, evaporated, for many that is the time to call on the Ultimate Being - God, that is the time to call on the pastor - God's ambassadeur. Indeed, most people, that call on God, call on the pastor, the shepherd of the sheep, at such times, they discover comfort, hope and strength to carry on.

In fact, any liberation experience, freeing people from shackles of domination is education. Offering hope in times of desperation, ignorance, and even from perpetual poverty in its many aspects, the paradigm shift, for me, that is education, that is teaching.

In Pastoral Care, in most cases, you meet people when they have sunk into the abyss. In most cases, you meet people, when they have hit the rock bottom. Pastoral care lifts them up and teaches them how to emerge from the abyss, from dust, ashes, from the rock bottom and live. Consequently, good pastoral care teaches one how to emerge from dust and ashes and live again.

Therefore, I view pastoral care as teaching, and indeed it is teaching. As such, if it is teaching, it is teaching at the higher level of the spectrum. As such, it is teaching at its absolute best, when is needed most.

In view of this, then I was already a teacher for an awfully long time. Even before I became a teacher, a trained teacher in England of age 11 -18, in fact I was already a teacher. Of course, a good teacher. I started by teaching myself, as I am 'self-taught' and 'self-educated'. As a good teacher, I have tasted my own 'honey', my own 'wine.' And behold it was tasty and nice! Of course, as self-made as I am, I had to teach myself, and I really taught myself a great deal. Most of my education was Do it yourself (DIY) education.

For me, teaching also is just saying nothing, nothing at all. Just being there with the learner and for the learner, letting the learner learn, letting the learner explore and discover the truth. Teaching is enhancing the learner's quest for truth. It is being there for the learner and with the learner in case the learner needs somebody to help.

Therefore, figuratively, a teacher is somebody 'to lean on' and a 'shoulder to cry on,' indeed, somebody to 'lean on when you are not strong.' Yes sometimes, there are a lot of 'tears' shed in learning. But also somebody to rejoice and celebrate with.

Teaching is therefore motivating and offering the learner hope, the opportunity to ask questions, explore, find, get answers and clarification. It is an opportunity for the learner to even share their discoveries and shout out their own 'eureka!' I have found it!

For me, teaching is being there, to encourage and support the learner. Teaching is not viewing the learner as an empty vessel, in which to pour in the superior knowledge of the teacher. For me, the learner is a human being, a thinking and feeling human being.

Therefore, teaching is acknowledging that the learner is coming from somewhere, has been somewhere in life, on pilgrimage. The learner having been somewhere at a specific point in time, hence, is going somewhere, or wants to go somewhere. Consequently, teaching helps and points the learner in the right direction. I have often been asked, 'How do you do that?' For me, the 'how you do that', is teaching.

Sometimes, in the process of teaching and learning, learners find themselves at crossroads, intersections of life, intersections of education, etc. Sometimes learning itself, takes one into the intersection.

In such a situation, the need of 'nodding' and the need of 'affirmation' to go on the main path or take an alternative path, is necessary and paramount. Acknowledging the learner's ability at that point in time and pointing the possible direction that leads somewhere... to their possible and potential destiny to be constantly reviewed along the way, is real teaching.

Teaching means, help direct the learner with possible redirection, on the map of life. As we are in the digital era, of paperless maps, the metaphor I can use for teaching is the SatNav. As a SatNav, I believe, teaching helps learners realise, they are lost. They should review their expectations, experiences, and encounters. In other circumstances it just affirms they themselves are on the right and appropriate path of education.

If lost, such is the time for recalculating. Even if the SatNav of teaching is muted, you still see the 'witting on the wall,' *recalculating* the route. Yes, sometimes learning can go on, even when teaching and even the teacher is muted. In this context, teaching may go on quietly. Teaching may be just going on quietly, in the background and even in the subconscious.

Reflecting on my own learning experiences, I believe, in teaching, it is the learner that matters, it is the learner that is at the centre. It is the learner that needs several recalculations. Whether more able or less able, with Special Education Needs (SEN), whether lost or stuck at the crossroads, intersections, etc.

In this context, teaching becomes a redirection on and to the right path. When the learner is at what I call the crossroad, intersection, that is when the learner needs recalculating and the teacher needs to help with the recalculation. Then the teacher points the leaner in the right direction.

I cannot emphasise enough that teaching matters. As such, as a teacher, there is no need to 'get mad' or get 'worked up' at the learner or to 'be mad' with the learner, especially when the learner is lost or is at the crossroads, at the intersections of education, particularly, when learning seems to have hit 'dead end'. That is exactly, the time the learner needs teaching most, especially encouragement.

In the real world, this may sound like utopia, 'easy said than done.' But for me, that is what teaching and learning is all about. It is a lifelong experience, 'until death do us part.' It requires a lot of patience, for both the learner and more so the teacher. This is my thinking and approach to teaching and learning.

With that at the back of my mind, in 1991, I embarked on a teaching per se career. I had achieved most of the other dreams I longed for and dreamed about in my life. However, teaching per se, was not yet. Getting into teaching in UK was another formidable uphill journey.

Actually, and overall, getting into teaching in UK, was an accident.... Apart from being nicknamed 'Foolish John,' in my primary school, at St Paul's United Theological College, Limuru, Kenya, I was nick-named 'Mr. Accident.'

Not only was this relevant at Limuru, but even so at Homerton College, Cambridge, it was real. At Homerton College, I was the odd one out in many ways and aspects. My determination to get into teaching, even then, underlined my belief in teaching and that, indeed, 'teaching matters.'

Chapter Twenty-Eight: The Pedagogy

In 1991, I resigned my commission again, thus in total, I resigned my commission, not once but twice. This time I resigned my commission to complete my PhD in Ecclesiastical History. My research was hinging on missionaries' contribution to education in Kenya.

Of course, prior to independence, African education in Kenya, was missionary education. African schools were mission schools. That time Missionaries and Christianity permeated the entire African education in Kenya, apart from a few DEBs secular schools. Therefore, my PhD encapsulated my interest in History, Education and Theology, three in one, endeavouring to hit the 'three with one stone': the PhD.

On arrival in UK, just after I had resigned my commission in Kenya, the job I had come to do, to work and study part-time fell through. I had been offered and promised a job at Papworth Cardiac Hospital, now Royal Papworth Hospital, Cambridge, as a Chaplain.

This job guaranteed funding for my PhD that was part time research degree: The Missionary Movements and Development of Education in Kenya: An Ecumenical Perspective 1944-1964. I was registered at Westminster College, Oxford, resident in Cambridge, supervised by Dr John Lonsdale, Trinity College, Cambridge.

Dr John Lonsdale is a specialist in African History, particularly, Kenyan History. Moreover, we shared interest in missionary history, education and especially the work and contribution of Archbishop Leonard James Beecher.

I had greater interest in the 1944 Beecher Education Commission. The Beecher Commission focused on colonial African education and 1964 Otiende

Commission, focused on Post Independence education, preceding 8-4-4 education in Kenya, now 2-6-3-3-3. Therefore, Dr Lonsdale was looking forward to my study, as much as I was.

For some reason, when I returned to Cambridge, this job mysteriously disappeared from the 'radar' of the offer. The offer was no longer on offer or 'on the plate,' as they often say. There was no mention of it at all. There was no explanation either. It was just dead silence. The job was no more. It was gone, just like that.

To make the matter worse, I had resigned my commission, with the understanding that I had a job to come back to and it will pay and support my PhD pursuit. Furthermore, I had returned with my family. Therefore, unlike 1985, when I first came over on my own, this time I had to put food on the table, not just for myself, but for the entire family. I also had bills to pay. I had used up my Short-Term Commission gratuity and benefits to pay for travel expenses to Cambridge. I was again impecunious.

Furthermore, I was turning forty and nobody was willing to give a Post Graduate scholarship to an over thirty-five years old geriatric, whose chronological light was fading towards fifty. I could not compete with the young bright graduates, with many years ahead of them to offer more to the world of knowledge, than a senescent, like me, left with a few years before retirement.

My life at that point in time, seemed and appeared to contradict the famous saying: 'Life starts at forty.' My life then was not starting at forty but seemed to be ending and collapsing at forty. Furthermore, I was exhausted from fund-raising every year, for the preceded three years undergraduate programme. I would not dare do it again.

Thank God I had returned to UK before two years elapsed, which could have invalidated my indefinite leave to remain in UK. By this time, I was still holding on my Kenyan nationality. I had not taken up my British citizenship or nationality, which I was entitled to, based on my residency status, then.

With indefinite leave to remain, I had no option but to stoop low, to sign on at the Job Centre. My name was inscribed on the unemployment roll call, written in the unemployment register. I was on dole.

My parents, particularly my mother were very proud of my achievement and realisation of my dream to join the army, up to the prestigious rank of Major. In fact, If I had stayed on in the KDF, I was destined for even greater things, to be promoted to the rank of Lt Colonel. I would have succeeded my boss Lt Col S K Mwambire, to become the next Staff Officer One (SO1). In due course, I would also have been promoted to full Colonel, as the Chaplaincy Corps was set to expand.

Being on dole, was therefore a great humiliation. Imagine, from an Officer and a Gentleman, to a pauper on dole. I had decided to 'bite the dust,' 'throw in the towel' and recourse to public funds as a last resort. For a while, I survived on State Benefits. I really appreciated the British welfare system.

As I was on dole, I received unemployment benefits based on my family circumstance, the immemorial time, before the 'Universal Credit,' was ushered in. Payments were based on weekly calculations and paid weekly in cash at the local Post Office. My children were entitled to free school dinners and several financial exemptions.

The dole helped me to put food on the table and clothing for my family. My rent of a bedsitter flat was paid. As we were perceived overcrowded, in the bedsitter flat, for health and safety reasons, I was visited by Cambridge City Council Health and Safety Officer.

After the visit from Cambridge City Council Health and Safety Officer, I was advised to apply for a bigger house, and move out of the student accommodation. Moreover, I was not a student anymore. I got a house with Cambridge Housing Society – social housing. This was a three-bedroom house, spacious enough for my family of three kids then and later my brother Patrick.

I applied for several jobs advertised at the Job Centre, just to be turned down for being overqualified. That was very frustrating. Then I remembered, my long-term interest in education. I also remembered, when I graduated in 1988, the last note and letter in my Faculty of Divinity pigeonhole, was a flyer about Teaching, pedagogy, training to be a teacher.

This was a Postgraduate Certificate in Education (PGCE), to teach Religious Education (RE) also known as Religious Studies (RS). This was mandatory in state secondary schools in England and Wales (age 11-18). However, parents could get exemption for their kids, from the subject. I had applied for the PGCE course. De facto, in effect, I was offered a place at the Department of Education, Cambridge University.

As I was returning to Kenya Defence Forces (KDF), I did not take up the offer. Desperate now, I remembered the offer. I contacted the Department of Education. I informed the Department that this time, I was interested in teaching two subjects, rather than a single subject. In that case, I was directed and advised to apply to Homerton College, a constituent college of Cambridge University.

I applied for the course at Homerton College. By the time I applied, the requirements and criteria were now different. Homerton College by then was mainly offering Bachelor of Education (BEd) degree, extinct nowadays, focussing on Primary School Education and teaching. However, it was now also offering PGCE, mainly focused on secondary school teacher training (11- 18 age group). Most of the applicants were not Homerton students. My application was declined.

The reasons why my application was declined did not make sense to me. When I inquired further, I was notified that, I did not meet all the basic requirements and criteria for teaching in secondary schools - state schools in England and Wales. The basic requirements were a degree in a subject taught in state secondary schools in England and Wales. In addition, at least a 'C' and above at GCSE level in Mathematics and English.

I met two of the requirements. I had an academic degree in Theology and Religious Studies, a subject taught in secondary schools in England and Wales. I had a 'C' and above in English Language, London University GCE. However, I did not have Mathematics 'C' and above at GCSE level.

It looked and sounded ridiculous, but that was the reality. Again, me being me, I appealed against and petitioned the decision. Of course, I did not have a certificate, a piece of paper showing I had a 'C' in Mathematics at 'O' level. But with my experience and educational pursuits, I had picked up a lot of numeracy skills, well over and above, or even beyond GCSE level.

Among my GCE pursuits, I had pursued, London University GCE Commerce and Economics. They included, involved numeracy and logical Mathematical skills. The only thing I lacked, was documents to that effect or a piece of paper to support and prove that I have a 'C' in Mathematics at GCSE level.

Furthermore, I was a mature student, passionate about education and well over and beyond the time, when that criterion was introduced, set in and 'written in stone.' My petition was acknowledged. I was given an equivalent GCSE mathematics exam promptly. I sat and passed the Special Mature Candidates Mathematics GCSE equivalent exam, well and above grade 'C' level.

There was no more valid reason to deny me a place on the pedagogy opportunity - teaching course and a career in teaching. I was offered a place at Homerton College, again to start the course early, with classroom observation in a primary school around Cambridge. I had never been in a British school or classroom, except for parents' consultations for my kids and taking School Assemblies.

I was awarded a British Government grant, and a supplement loan. I was also awarded an incentive allowance of £700 as a teacher trainee, of a shortage subject of teachers – RE/RS & PSHE, on par with mathematics and science, other staff shortage subjects.

At the end of Summer 1991, I signed off from unemployment statistics at the Job Centre. I was gladly off the dole. I took up my last resort at that time and joined Homerton College, Cambridge University, to train as RE/RS and PSHE Teacher, the subjects I really loved.

My generosity had not ceased. I still had responsibilities for my siblings back in Kenya. I therefore invited my brother Patrick M Shabaya, now a lecture at Strathmore University, Nairobi, to come and pursue BSc degree in Software Engineering, at Anglia Ruskin University, Cambridge. I undertook this single handed, without any fund raising or Harambee.

During my teacher training, I was attached to schools in Cambridgeshire and neighbouring counties. With a family, I could have a car in Cambridge. This became helpful for commuting to far places to my attachment and teaching experience schools.

I was attached to schools such as Hinchingbrooke Secondary School, Impington Village College, Netherhall, St Bede's Ecumenical School, and Swavesey Village College in Cambridgeshire and Thurston Upper School, near Bury St Edmunds, Suffolk County.

While at Homerton, I got a travel grant to research and develop Religious Studies resources and materials. I developed slides focusing on age 11-18 (secondary school) Christianity, Islam, Judaism, Hinduism and Sikhism. I had easy access to these vibrant communities and religions in Kenya, with fixed places of worship and outreach, especially in Nairobi, the Capital city.

In 1992, I had two graduations at Cambridge University in absentia. On 25 January 1992, I was admitted to the Degree of Master of Arts (MA) and on 18th August 1992, I was awarded the Post Graduate Certificate in Education (PGCE).

Prior to that, I had been through one Cambridge University graduation in person. On 25 June 1988, I was admitted to the Degree of Bachelor of Arts (BA). Unlike the grand open-air graduations of Kenyan universities and colleges, Cambridge University graduation ceremony dates to over 800 years ago.

The Cambridge University graduation ceremony is a pomp ceremony. Strictly, for the invited by ticket only guests to witness the actual ceremony. However, Cambridge graduates in gowns are welcome. We assembled at Fitzwilliam College. After initial checks, especially to ensure, we were appropriately attired for the occasion, we were then escorted to the Senate House, guided by The Master, College Fellows and The Praelector.

On a summer day, this is a grand open parade, march and historical procession. It originates from each graduands' college. For me, it started at Fitzwilliam College, downhill from Fitzwilliam College, through the beautiful mature gardens at The Backs, across the river, into Senate House grounds. The Graduation Ceremony congregation itself, is normally small. It is indoors, a small congregation in the tiny, the small and historical Senate House.

As graduands of Fitzwilliam College, we lined up in the order of the seniority of our degrees and alphabetical order in accordance with our surnames. Of course, each college is timetabled to present its candidates, one at a time. We walked to the dais in a group of five, each graduand holding one of the five fingers of the Praelector.

The Praelector presented us to the Vice-Chancellor. Everyone was individually conferred the degree by the Vice-Chancellor. I remember kneeling at the feet of the Vice-Chancellor and the degree was conferred to me in Latin. The deed was done.

When I looked at the English translation of the Latin formula, being a Theologian, I noticed the Trinitarian formula, ... in the name of God, the Father and the Son and the Holy Spirit, was used by the Vice-Chancellor, after saying my name. However, the Trinitarian formula can be omitted at the request of the graduand if she/he so wished.

I vividly still remember my graduation in summer, on 25 June 1988. It was on a gorgeous sunny summer day. It did not rain at all on that day. While it always rains, rains and rains, 'rains cats and dogs' in most cases without any notice, it was a one of the rare moments in UK. There was no rain on that day.

Moreover, it was just after 'summer solstice,' the longest day in the year, in the northern hemisphere, UK included. It occurs between 20 - 23 June. The sun rises incredibly early, by 04:30 (4.30am) in the morning and sets past 21:30 (9.30pm) at night. This is when the tilt of Earth's axis is inclined more towards the sun and directly above the tropic of Cancer.

For some strange reason, I can remember the first person to congratulate me, was a tramp, a homeless person. I vividly remember his words, ' young-man be proud of your hard work and achievement.' He stammered, 'it is not easy to get to Cambridge. Well done my boy.'

I wondered how and why on earth he had gotten onto Senate House grounds, but there he was! I also wondered how he knew my struggles and challenges to get where I had reached. I looked at him again, filled with great joy, I just smiled brightly nodded in appreciation and reciprocated: Thank you. I was now a graduate of the University of Cambridge. Back into the real world.

Chapter Twenty-Nine: Teaching in England

My teaching experiences have been varied, spanning over twenty years and over two continents: Africa and Europe; two countries, Kenya, mainly voluntary untrained teacher and England, UK, professional trained teacher. As untrained teacher, I never had proper experience of classroom teaching in Kenya, until very recently, in my own school, Atsinafa Education Centre. Most of my professional classroom teaching experiences have been in England, UK.

Teaching in England was my third career. My first career was unskilled labour, as a young man, up to about twenty-one years old. It was followed by my second career, 'the higher call.' This spanned from 21 years of age, until I turned forty years. It included ordained ministry in The Methodist Church in Kenya and Chaplaincy work in Kenya Defence Forces, plus pursuits of higher education.

I started building my third career at forty plus (40+). Perhaps I embarked on building my third career rather late, when my individual faculties had deteriorated. However, it has been said that 'you're only as old as you feel or think.'

Having joined teaching at forty plus, I can guarantee that age is real, and it runs out fast. Postgraduate PhD Scholarships organisations declined my attempts to secure a research scholarship, based on my age, contradicting the ' life starts at forty' admonition. Contrastingly, on the other hand, my teaching career reaffirmed that 'life starts at forty.' Additionally, the taxi business has asserted that life goes on beyond sixty-five.

My first teaching job was Humanities and Sociology Teacher, at Ely College, Ely, Cambridgeshire (Secondary

Age 11-18). Humanities included: Geography, History, Religious Studies (RS/RE), Sociology and General Studies. Moreover, RS/RE also included Hinduism, Buddhism, Judaism, Christianity, Islam and Sikhism, with some reflections on Agnosticism and Atheism. Additionally, every teacher taught Personal Social and Health Education (PSHE).

Moreover, for over eight years that I was at Ely College, I was the only black teacher. Within that period, my timetable was full. I was promoted and rose to Head of Religious Studies, i.e., Subject Leader. I must have been extraordinarily strong and resilient, to have survived the pressure and challenges of being the only black teacher and a Tibetan colleague Sanjay, teaching in a predominantly white school and locality.

After about eight years of a full timetable, I decided to take time off to pursue MA in Judaism and Christianity at Wesley House, Cambridge. I was planning and hoping to join The World Council of Churches (WCC) in Geneva, Switzerland, focusing on Interfaith Relationship. The MA degree pursuit fell through, once again because of financial constraints.

I took up free-lance teaching (Supply Teacher) all over Bedfordshire, Cambridgeshire, Hertfordshire, Norfolk and Suffolk Counties. Whenever any teacher was off, for various reasons, I was there. I was ever ready and henceforth, exposed to all subjects and all ages, including Reception and Primary School Classes.

After a while, I again took up a full-time job at Chalkstone Middle School, Haverhill, Suffolk County, as a Teacher of English and Humanities. I later moved to Long Road Sixth Form College, Cambridge, Cambridgeshire, where I taught Religious Studies and Sociology.

Later, I resigned, from full time teaching to focus on returning into the church ministry. I also wanted to realise one of my long-time dream: visit Australia. I had read about Australia as part of World Geography and World History courses, while undertaking self-taught courses in Nairobi and later at St Paul's United Theological College, Limuru, Kenya.

Therefore, prior to embarking on returning to full time ministry within the Church of England, I took time off, to travel to Australia, to visit my Australian brother Josiah Shabaya and his family. I was given a VIP treatment by Josiah and his wife Veronica, including my niece and nephew, Theo and Jonathan, respectively. Thus, my Australian tour was awesome!

As mentioned earlier, I took Josiah in my wings, after his primary school education and KPE exams at Ivonda Primary School, our village school. From the village, I brought him to Nairobi. He resided in my home at Kahawa Garrison Barracks, Nairobi, just like my son, rather than my brother. He lived with me and Shem, until I left for UK in June 1985. When I left Kenya, my sister Ruth Shabaya, now Mrs Mwachiro took over.

On homecoming from Australia, my return to full time ministry within the Church of England did not materialise. I continued with freelance teaching and embarked on an SFPE Introduction Course in Editing and Proofreading.

Afterwards, I embarked on freelance Proofreading and translation services (Kiswahili - English). Remembering my own struggles, I also volunteered to help 'A' level, undergraduate and postgraduate students, with study skills, essay writing, research craft and dexterity.

Through teaching in England, and having been a Minister of Religion, I perceived and recognised that real pedagogy, education and theology is in the field, with the people. It is with the learners, the recipients. It is where the learners and people are; as real farming, is on the land, with actual tilling and cultivation of the land.

I never had the opportunity to teach in Public schools in England, except taking Assemblies at schools like: The Perse, Leys Schools in Cambridge, and Culford School, in Suffolk County.

Being a teacher, with a passion for words, I know jargon and terminology matters. Certain words mean certain things and even different things to different people, in different cultures, places and contexts. For example, Public school in UK, is the antonym of state school in USA. In UK, it is, mostly, high cost, private fee-paying school, with boarding facilities.

While in the USA, Public school is just as it sounds: Public. A public school in USA is a school that is funded and supported by public funds; what would be known as state school in UK. Thus, complete opposite, in terms and meaning.

In UK, an Academy is a state school, mostly a former failing school, funded by the Department of Education, but independent from the Local Authority. Therefore, it is a non-profit making school, run by the community or a charitable organisation. While in Kenya, an Academy is a high cost fee paying Private School.

Teaching in England, being the only black teacher, in state schools, I encountered a few shocks, that required significant shock absorbers, in many aspects. In some state schools, teaching was as if I was again, back in 'combat' zone, although, not using real guns, tanks, torpedoes, etc. I was stunned, astounded and even flabbergasted by the sheer number of disinterested and disgruntled learners.

Some learners came from poor families that did not value education. They just saw education as something they had to do till, they could legally leave school. A quite different attitude from that of the kids in Kenya, who value education extensively.

Moreover, there were also a few disgruntled teachers. In response to the learners' disenchantment, they did not bother, care an inch, or even care less for that matter, about quality teaching and learning.

Initially, I thought it was the subject, Humanities, RE, that the learners were disinterested in, because they could not envisage its immediate returns and value in 'real life.' On the contrary, oh no! No! Not so! Not at all! It was not just Humanities and RE/RS related problem. As I covered lessons in other subject areas, I discovered, it was a cross the board.

In fact, it was worse in Mathematics, Science and Modern Languages (French, German and Spanish) lessons and classrooms. As education in UK is mandatory for ages 5-16, most learners were focused on just turning sixteen (16) and getting out of school.

Some schools grouped learners in ability groups. This had its own repercussions, that I may not discuss here in details, the pros and cons of banding and mixed ability teaching. I remember while I was a free-lance teacher, I encountered a lot of the so called, bottom groups, the sunken groups, the kids who had given up on education, but had to remain in school until they clock age sixteen (16). Most teachers had also given up on such groups.

I remember covering lessons for such groups, that had stressed teachers almost into nervous breakdown. I remember teaching such a group science in Suffolk County, initially for one week, using various anecdotes, that most of them started paying attention and learning something. They talked highly of me to the Headteacher. She offered me a Science teacher full time post, based on my rapport with the group and their subsequent achievement just to discover I am RE/PSHE teacher, and not a Science teacher as such.

In another school, as I managed a group that was unmanageable, and most teachers loathed, one Headteacher desperately offered me a special teaching post for two terms, six months appointment of Temporary Part-Time Teaching Staff, the circumnavigating title of my post. I taught the 'sunken' group GSCE Science, English, Mathematics, especially Numeracy, Religious Studies, Humanities and Life Skills, until the end of the academic year, the end of their mandatory education.

Through my efforts, the 'written off' group remained in school, improved their attitude and behaviour, up to the end of the academic year, rather than being excluded. Most of them got reasonable GCSE grades, rather than being un-graded. We were all happy. I got several Thank You Teacher cards and gifts from the learners. I wished them well in Post 16 education.

When I was about to finish my PGCE, I was supposed to hand in my potential Curriculum Vitae (CV) – 'Resume,' to my respective tutor for approval, before I embark on applications for teaching jobs all over the country. Initially, coming from Kenya, I assumed, I will just be posted into a school after completion of my course and 'carry on with it' – again, cultural differences and practices.

In view of this, I hesitated to hand in my CV. The tutor noticed and summoned me to her office for a 'one to one talk.' I told her about my Kenyan experience and reasons for my apparent indifference, especially teaching in England, UK. I also remarked, 'my CV is not good enough. It lacks primary school, secondary school certificates and respective grades. It reflects a lot of my struggles in my pursuit of education, that no school in England would be interested in me. Hence, I am contemplating exploring other alternatives.'

My tutor replied and commented that in fact my story, if highlighted and outlined in my CV, would be one of the best. It would be a strong CV. She advised me to emphasise the so called 'struggles' and show how I can use them to help learners, to motivate learners and turn learners around, to achieve their full potential.

Initially I did not understand what she meant. But I did just that. With my esteemed CV, I applied for teaching jobs in Suffolk and Cambridgeshire counties. I discovered I was in high demand and spoiled for choice. I got two offers, one in Suffolk County and the other in Cambridgeshire. I took up the teaching job in a state school, nearer to my home in Cambridgeshire. Indeed, later, my struggles in the pursuit of education, became my strength in many ways.

Chapter Thirty: Anecdotes

Teaching in England, in state schools was not always 'a bed of roses.' It often reminded me; even beautiful roses have thorns that can prick. Likewise, some learners had their moments. Some learners were just completely switched off, needed a lot of rekindling their education light, fire and will power, to go on, including self-esteem.

Having worked the land and having been employed as a gardener before, I had a lot of anecdotes at hand. Through my past varied experiences, I had learned to focus on the potential, opportunities and possibilities, rather than the 'straight jacket' expectations. Gardening had made me more aware that even the beautiful roses, in the garden, with nice lovely colours, with beautiful flowers and scent, must have been cultivated, watered, etc. As roses must be cultivated, into exotic plants and gardens, likewise disgruntled learners, also must be turned around, moulded into 'civilised' citizen and human beings.

Based on my own experience, interests, struggles and sacrifices in my pursuit of education, I was dumbfounded, dismayed by the miserable, piteous, unfortunate, pathetic attitude of some of the disinterested and disenchanted learners.

Here were learners, in state schools, with almost everything conferred and presented to them on a 'silver plate.' Here they were throwing it back 'into my face.' Free education! Free resources! Almost Free everything! 'How can one not grab this or such an opportunity?' I would ask myself. 'How can learners not snap such an opportunity and pursue education to the utmost?' I marvelled, with great astonishment.

When I was a newly qualified teacher, fifteen minutes of my lessons or even more would be gone, just trying and endeavouring to settle the class down to serious work. Most of the protesting and distracting elements and statements were interestingly pathetic. For example, 'I am only in school because the government has forced me to be here, even my parents are not bothered about my education.'

Bold ones would say, 'I am here just waiting to get to age sixteen, then I don't have to be forced to come to school and take this c... b.' Some would scream, 'Sir, you're doing my head in with this s..t, you call education! Education for what?'

Holding their heads, blocking their ears, endeavouring to block, shut me out, completely out of their system. They would shriek, 'education does my head in!' I would reply, whatever that means, I am here to teach you.'

As I was the adult here, I would calmly remind the respective learners, to calm down, mind their language, lest they get into more trouble. Bad language, 'mouthfuls,' were unacceptable to me and in most of schools' Behaviour Policies. Of course, corporal punishment was illegal and considered serious child abuse. It was more so in in UK, and in agreement with my deep beliefs.

Most learners were aware of their respective School Behaviour Policies. Such learners co-operated and refrained from using unacceptable language. With no corporal punishment option, I dealt with the villainy accordingly, not necessarily threateningly or violently.

In most cases, my look, my eye, the gaze into my eye said it all. Disproof was written all over my face and most of my students had the skills to read it and co-operate according or even instantly, like instant 'Kenyan coffee.' Body language, though not vocal, was loud and clear.

Others would say 'I am waiting to get to age sixteen (16).' I would sincerely ask, 'then do what?' In most cases, muttering and unsure of what to say, they would retort back, 'then I can get married!' Then I would remark, 'of course yes, with your parents' consent, if you are aged sixteen years, you can get married.'

I would continue, 'hurry up then, get on with your work, before you instantly and magically turn sixteen and leave school and get married.' I would add, 'better be married with some good quality education, skills, etiquette and behaviour.' They would quickly answer, 'get real Sir! I do not need all that .... Ah..., my parents can't stop me either, getting married at sixteen!'

Indeed, two of my students cohabited (married) at sixteen, with dismayed and frustrated parents. With my encouragement, they continued to come to school to complete their GCSE. Parents frustrated, approached the police, but the police seemed not excited, at their approach, leave alone bothered, to get involved.

Accordingly, the young couple had consented to elope and cohabit, therefore not really married legally. They were perceived as just friends, living together. Even though they themselves, viewed their relationship as marriage. In addition, each had a National Insurance (NI) number, entitling them to work, therefore employable and independent.

In African culture, such relationship, would also have been viewed as marriage. Living together in most African cultures and traditions, equals to marriage. There is no such thing as boyfriend and girlfriend, when cohabiting for more than one month, leave a lone six months.

On several occasions, some learners would retort, 'I want to get out of this prison soon, then go get a real job, not like you teacher. Teaching is c..b, it is s..t, education is c..b, s...t, excuse my French, ops!... Excuse my language!'

Initially, innocently, I would ask, 'and can you get a job, retain a real job without good quality education and qualifications?' I would remark and say, 'you need good quality education and qualifications, to get a job, a good job, a real job.'

One student once said 'Sir who needs a job, a good job anyway? Who needs this s..t. Who needs qualifications? Education is for snobs! I will go and work on bin collection! Another said, 'I will go and work the land, drive a tractor. At sixteen (16), I can drive a tractor legally. You see, I don't need education.'

I answered, 'yes you do, you need education, in fact quality education in life and for life. There is nothing in life you can do without education. Therefore, the more education you get, the better life you get.' Then, from nowhere, another one budged in, 'Sir, when I get older, I will go on dole. And another one said, 'my parents are on dole, even my Nana is on dole. Who cares?'

I replied, 'I have been on dole, even for dole, you need education. The class was surprised, with gob smacked faces. When they discovered my extensive experience, most calmed down and focused on the work, activities and the learning tasks at hand.

On another occasion, I used the same 'carrot' to enhance interest in education and hammer the point that education is for life, not just limited to getting a job.

Amidst all the apparent grief and disillusionment, there was hope, there was joy. My efforts were not all in vain. Thus, most of my learners started realising and appreciating that indeed 'education is for life.'

In life and even for 'dole,' you need to research, find out and get information about whatever you are looking for, and whatever you want. In fact, you are better off if you can read, write and do some calculations.

Moreover, if you can write, beyond just scribbling or signing on and work out if you are eligible, if you are receiving your rightful dues, and so forth,' you stand a better chance in life. I continued, 'you see, education is vital, it is helpful.' I rattled on to hammer the significance of education, since 'with education, you are much more better off, we have mandatory education up to age sixteen.'

One day, in a changed, almost charged and an apparent threatening tone, for no apparent reason, from nowhere, one learner retorted, 'leave me alone sir! If you do not, I will frame you for child abuse. Everybody will believe me.'

I again calmly said, 'I have a lot of witnesses around here, they will confirm I am the innocent one.' Sir I am the child here, the leaner replied. 'Police will believe me and not you Sir.'

The learner continued, 'everything I say and tell them, they will believe me. Oh no! No sir not you!... These are my mates, and not your mates, sir, they will definitely support me.' I answered, 'No, they'll say the truth! And if they do not? I continued, 'then the truth, the truth will set me free!'

The learner then, murmured, almost through the nose, 'Are you Martin Luther King Sir? If you are, then the truth will set you free ... 'Others joined in: 'Free, Free at last ...' Smiling and actually with a beaming face, rather than getting worked up, I asked, 'And who told you about Martin Luther King Jr?' The learner replied, 'You Sir, you taught us! That's it!' I continued to smile.

The learner then changed the aggressive tone, in a calmer voice, 'On a serious note Sir, when I grow up, I want to work hard as an Englishman, to make sure all people live together in harmony. Is that the word, 'harmony" yeah?' seeking my assurance. I nodded. 'I will try to do my bit', he continued.

'We all feel pain, don't we? .... yeah, we do,' he answered himself. 'We all have same red blood, it's just the cover, the colour of my skin! Ya man!' imitating the Desmond's 1980 classic British sitcom, TV Soap, set in Peckham, London and Bob Marley.

'Sir you see we are learning; we are getting something to think about... Something to use in my other life .... life after school,' then faces of other learners beamed, ready to get on with the business of the day, and for the day. Thereafter, lessons of the day took their course and went on very well.

I realised that learners, are best teachers to themselves and to others. The saying that when the student is ready, the teacher is found or is available' rang a bell in my mind.

Learners find out and pass on the discoveries, information and share knowledge. I discovered whatever I encountered and counteracted with one class or group of learners, even a justified individual reprimand, circulated fast.

In view of the challenges I encountered, I drew on my vast past experiences. I developed and constantly reviewed, various survival strategies. I focused on time management, good teaching and learning strategies. I also tried to utilise differentiation, Individual Education Programmes (IEP), etc., to manage and minimise time wasting distractions and sometimes unnecessary debates, etc. I endeavoured to enhance teaching and learning, that encouraged individual learners to achieve their potential.

Overshadowed by their distracting peers and very vocal characters, one would have thought and concluded that all under sixteen (16) were all disillusioned with education. But in most cases, that was not one hundred percent (100%) true.

Of course, not all learners were disenchanted with education, disinterested in education or even disillusioned with education and about education. There were many, who were very keen. This was evidenced and demonstrated in many ways. Apart from attitude, classroom work, etc., the kindness and significant gestures said it all.

Teaching in England, I received a lot of inner satisfaction. I also received many symbols of appreciation. These included, thank you cards, Christmas cards, chocolates of various kinds/types, seasons and genuine small gifts, extended to the teacher, both from learners, guardians and parents alike.

Henceforth, I made up my mind, to ensure those interested, are getting on with their learning, while I engage the 'combatants' and disenchanted, endeavouring to turn them round. I attempted to engross, occupy and motivate them. I tried to 'combat' them, in most cases, by turning their weapons, their negative ideas, vibes, language and attitude 'into ploughshares.'

Teaching eleven plus (11+), I was constantly aware that some were bound to be just driven over the wall, by adolescent, explosive hormones of their age. Others may have come from dysfunctional families and unsupportive domestic environments. Indeed, there were those who just had learning disabilities, Special Education Needs (SEN), while others were gifted, creative, being stifled by the education system.

In view of this, I adopted a more positive attitude and willingness to encourage students to learn, within their ability, always to attempt to try, do their level best and pursue excellence. Some learners had extremely low self-esteem, living-out their self-fulfilling prophecies and stereo types, vicious family cycles, that needed breaking, that needed turning round and subsequent about-turns. The use of persuasion, diplomacy and non-aggressive approach, worked.

However, I had to continually remember OFSTED. It was always on my back; it was on my neck. OFSTED had a 'straight jacket' to fit in. League tables too, were on my shoulders and that mattered a lot for the respective schools. My approach had to reflect and deliver OFSTED inspection expectations and league table scores, or else I would have no job.

The hierarchy of subjects did not help either. Maths and Sciences, English, Modern Languages and at the bottom of the scale were Humanities, General Studies and Religious Studies. I was always on 'my feet' trying hard to satisfy the OFSTED, while I endeavoured to get good grades for league tables.

I also ensured that I don't give up the 'battle' and 'fighting' for my corner, my own survival, in the classroom, in the poorly resourced Subject Department, the threats and impending extinction of my subjects from the National Curriculum and so forth.

I also was on my heels, attempting and putting in a lot of effort, to outrun, outshine, outsmart the disillusioned and the villainy. In fact, I personally had a notebook for the villainy, the **Red Book**. For 'street credit' and evidence of misdemeanour, most learners never wanted to be inscribed at the back of the **Red Book**. The front side was reserved for those outstanding characters and achievements. Believe it or not, they were many.

My **Red Book,** included details of the misdemeanour and subsequent appropriate sanctions, including communication with parents, especially during consultations. It was fair and square, as most of my students reckoned. Surprisingly, it worked. It reduced misbehaviour and distraction, extensively.

Henceforth, I could get on with my business of teaching.

Furthermore, I celebrated learners' achievements, sometimes the ignored ones, those that goes and passes by unnoticed, yet wonderful students, motivated and determined, putting up with a lot of disruptions and 'put downs.'

Teaching in England, I was always on my feet, thinking fast, what to do or say next. As a teacher, one had to be street wise or 'smart' as Americans would say. I was always on my tenterhooks, on the look-out for any surprises that might be suddenly, sprung on me, bang!

I assessed and prepared accordingly. Of course, most of this was in advance, and not in 'contact time.' It was in my own precious time, even when on holidays.

If had been attracted to teaching by apparent long holidays, I would have been extremely disappointed. I worked throughout weekends and holidays, day and night. I incorporated in my teaching, schemes of work, lesson plans, classroom management, activities that would enhance and focus on teaching and learning.

I kept reviewing strategies that did not work and those that worked. I adopted those that encouraged learners to learn, rather than wait to be spoon-fed. There was a lot of marking and assessments as well.

There was also a lot of paperwork, writing reports, unnumbered meetings, both planned and unplanned, as need arose. Responsive interventions, name them, all were part of my teaching career.

In all the schools I have been to and taught in England, there were clear policies. As Head of a Subject/Department, I was also involved in writing some policies for my department, later incorporated in the whole school policy document. Swearing and racism were not tolerated. Racism and swearing, especially to or at a teacher, was equal to immediate suspension and subsequent exclusion. Racism was thus not a misdemeanour, or something to stomach, or be tolerated.

I remember one incident of great hostility to learning and education. One learner decided to use bad language towards Religious Education and education overall, referring to education as s—t, in attempts to wind me up and distract the whole lesson, and make it impossible for me to teach. With agricultural background and teaching in rural England, I decided to 'grab the bull by the horns' or 'take the bull by the horns,' as the saying goes, instead of being worked up and irritated.

I asked the learner if he eats carrots or vegetables and for that matter farm produce. I asked him if he ever admires nice gardens, parks, etc.? Finally, I asked the learner to think of any better synonym to use now and in future, instead of the bad language he was using. 'What is synonym Sir,' he retorted. 'Sir, speak English! For God's sake we are in England, he rattled on.'

I replied, 'synonym is actually an English word. It is a vocabulary, borrowed from Ancient Greek.' You can check up the details, etymology and meaning in the English dictionary or lexicon at your own time, or calm down and get the etymology and meaning from your teacher in England, actually standing in-front of you, ready to teach you.' I waved, and said, 'can you see me clearly now, can everyone see me clearly. One learner answered, 'yes sir we see clearly now the rain is gone!'

One of the keen learners budged in, 'yes we can see you sir! It is an English word, tell him Sir.' Another learner said, 'It just means similar word, another word with the same meaning. Think of a better word, as the teacher has requested, than a swear word.' I remarked, 'correct.'

I said, 'Thank you!' 'in that case, a similar and a better word is manure.' The leaner continued to attempt to distract me again or maybe he was genuine and retorted, 'Never heard of that Sir, is that an English word?'

'Yes,' I replied, trying to turn him around. 'It is animal dung, used to fertilise farms and garden. I continued, 'it is organic compost, organic fertiliser. In fact, it is muck, it could be horses or cattle dung, waste of course...,'.

Manure, muck and compost, though real waste, when used well, helps plants to grow better. I continued, 'a lot of what you enjoy eating, a lot of beautiful exotic gardens, a lot of what makes you strong and healthy, is grown with manure, fertiliser.

A lot of gardens and farms have been helped by manure, smelly waste, that was discarded, thrown away. We get electricity, biogas and fuel from waste, from fossils, compost, etc.'

I remarked in conclusion, 'here is my free word of advice, instead of always swearing at teachers, swearing at education and school, with a lot of hate, please love education! Love education with all your mind, heart, soul and even your body....

Education is like manure for you... It will make you a better person now and in days to come. It is intended to make you a better person, and as such, it will make you a better person. I can't emphasise, or stress it home more than this now,' I paused and continued.

'You want to get good produce, use manure. You want to be a better learner, a better person use education, get real, get educated. Grab the opportunity education offers.'

I remarked, 'use well the chance the government has bestowed upon you – given to you freely, freely have you been given, please freely receive.' Surprisingly, he was listening calmly. In view of that, I seized the moment and continued, 'kindly and thankfully, not just by words, but by actions, show your appreciation. Remember the adage, the maxim, the proverb, 'actions speak louder than words.'

This education is your manure. You need education for life, just as agriculture and gardening needs compost, manure, and fertiliser, etc.'

I continued, 'likewise, as machines, vehicles, etc., require energy, biogas, fossil fuel, solar power, you require education. Enjoy education! No human being can survive without education.'

Believe it or not, that short snap of education homily, turned round, not only the apparent 'nasty piece of work' as most teachers referred to him, but the entire group. The whole class was transformed, just by a simple counteracting anecdote.

Manure, muck, became the catch word, the motivating word in my lessons. When I entered any classroom or learners came into my classroom. They would say, let us get down to it, let us get down to work, let us make use of our 'manure.'

Even when I covered Physical Education (PE) lessons, another mandatory subject, in the absence of the regular PE teacher, the talk was 'manure, manure for Mr Shabaya. Learners said to one another, 'let us stop mucking around and get on with our work.' The word spread around, especially among the disgruntled. It worked! The anecdote worked.

Another incident was when I was teaching English. One day, one learner exclaimed, 'You can't teach me English Sir! I am English. What have you come to do here? How can a black man from Kenya teach me English?'

My General knowledge in many subjects, including some other languages and English itself, gave me an upper edge. I asked the learner, 'What makes one English? Is English pure as a language, and not dynamic, not enriched by borrowing from other people's languages, cultures, etc.?

I continued, 'haven't you heard of the saying, 'no human being is an island? Do you know your origins, the origins of English language, the English people in England? I calmly and sincerely asked the learner, 'what qualifies you and makes you think that you know English more than I do, that I can't teach you English?'

Then I turned to myself, and asked myself, 'is this just logical rhetoric and debate, philosophical question into play here, or is this pure, nasty attitude, or mere racism by the learner?'

While pondering this question in my mind and how to respond further without demolishing the leaner, the learner sincerely retorted, 'I was born in England. I don't know much about its history, or the history of my family, and ancestors and English language.'

I thoughtfully suspended the question in my mind. I said to myself, 'my pronunciation and accent may be an issue here, but even then, there are varied accents and pronunciations, within Britain and England for that matter. As for spoken and written English there is standard formal English and there is also informal English, so which English?

I picked my courage, that had almost been shaken, and remarked, 'as you are under sixteen, I have actually been in England longer than you.' I continued, 'before you were born, before you were here in England, I was here, in England, learning, listening, hearing, speaking, reading and writing English, for that matter, at a very high standard.

I starred at the learner, the attentive class, starred at me in return, waiting for the 'hammer to fall,' with heavy sanctions and punishment, I was about to unleash or dish out.

Surprisingly, I just continued, 'I have spoken English, I have read English and spent more time learning and teaching English than you have been alive. I, therefore, qualify to teach you English and I will teach you English. I will teach the whole class English and Humanities as it is timetabled.

I announced to the whole class, I am your new English and Humanities teacher and I will be your teacher for some time. If my pronunciation is not clear, I will write on the board, I will spell the respective word and vocabulary. I calmly and confidently asserted myself.

'We will start with spelling, reading and finally writing, using connectives, to make our writing interesting. Thereafter, there were more perceptive genuine inquisitive questions, from my learners. I responded accordingly and enjoyed teaching the class English and Humanities. That was it.

Chapter Thirty-One: What Are My Interests?

While Theology has been obviously central and at the heart of my interests, my life is not just theology. My life, while permeated with theology, it is also more than theology.

I have a lot of various interests. Since my childhood, most of my interests, have kept me going. They have helped me maintain my sanity; amidst the challenges I have encountered en route my Incredible Journey.

Some of the challenges I encountered, would have been incredibly stressful, without my interests. My interests enhanced my stress management, knowingly, and in most cases, unaware or just unconsciously.

As a child, apart from playing with my peers and having great fun, in the tropical weather, in the spacious vast villages and rural setting of Western Kenya, I helped my mother with manual farmland jobs. These included digging, tilling, weeding and working on other 'better off' villagers *shamba,* land, farms or gardens

Such an interest not only kept me 'out of mischief', but of course, brought in the more and most desperately needed family income. When working on 'better off' villagers land, sometimes I was paid in kind, with items like food, clothing, etc. However, this had an impact on me, the enjoyment of working and doing other things in my free time, rather than just schoolwork. Consequently, my interest and approach to gardening, pared and turned, the supposed work into fun-like activity.

Through self-reliance attempts, as an interest, I had a kitchen garden, in my childhood. I never wanted to be idle, and even now I do not like being idle. In most cases, I am never idle. From school, and out of school, I have tended a garden, whether mine or other people's gardens.

Of course, doing what I enjoy is relaxation. Even if it is apparently hard work, or hard labour undertaken after a long day, a long week, or working hard at something, particularly in my free time, is not hard work as such. Even when I am undertaking heavy duty work like 'Doing It Yourself (DIY) stuff, I always feel, it is not heavy, it's just my interest. Consequently, relaxation, even when doing nothing is not idleness.

In my childhood 'kitchen' garden, I planted vegetables like onions, tomatoes, kale, local greens such as *likhubi* - cowpeas, *murenda* – okra.

I also reared some chicken and goats, that were bestowed on me as a young boy, by my uncles, aunts, grandpa and grandma, after my initiation into adulthood. Thus, although I was significantly stooped in my traditional African culture of the 1960s, however, unlike most of my peers in the village, I had significant interests.

Most of my kitchen garden produce, was for domestic consumption. However, I also exchanged some of the produce from my small garden, for some pocket money. I also shared some of the apparent income with my mother. She bought the necessary domestic essentials for our family.

I personally used some of the income from my hobby on my school resources, like pencils, pens, exercise books, etc. Thus, self-reliance was significant for me even at an early age. Nowadays, I just endeavour to keep a tinny garden wherever I am, and whenever I can, just for my aesthetic great satisfaction and joy.

From childhood, I loved running. I wish I had known running can be more than just a hobby. It can be a career that can generate such great wealth and catapult someone into an international celebrity. I would have gone for it, especially on my fateful day in 1966. I would have run, and ran all over, long distances, marathons and so forth. I would be a star, a shining star.

During my childhood, as I enjoyed running, I literally ran to almost everywhere I went. When my mother or anybody sent me on errands, I joyfully went running. I often pretended to be the fastest vehicle or animal in the village. Even now, I still enjoy some jogging, sometimes, just faster strides or faster walking.

Even in my retirement, I still enjoy outdoor activities. Of course, I love outdoor activities and exercises, rather than indoor activities in enclosed locked up gyms, running on the spot. Nowadays, I am beginning to find outdoor activities rather difficult in winter times particularly in the UK cold winter weather. Being as senescent as I am, I fear and feel discouraged from outdoor activities in freezing winter weather. However, come Spring, Summer and Autumn (The Fall), you will find me out there.

For long time, I collected postage stamps from all over the world. In fact, I was surprised to discover in 1985, I shared a hobby with one of my lecturers and tutor John Snaith, from the Department of Oriental Studies, now **Faculty of Asian and Middle Eastern Studies,** Cambridge University. He supervised and taught me the Old Testament, especially the Poetic Books, like Proverbs, Psalms and the Inter-testament, deuteron-canonical books and respective period. He was a passionate stamp collector.

John Snaith bequeathed me a variety of commemorative stamps of many different countries and areas. Likewise, when I became overwhelmed with my various pursuits, I passed the same to my eldest daughter, who had shown a lot of interest in the same hobby: stamps collection. However, currently in the age of digital communication, postage stamps hobby, may be extinct, if not yet, it will soon be extinct.

Reading has been my pursuit and interest for an exceedingly long time. If I had not approached reading as an interest, then I would not be who I am. I would not have come from where I have come from and where I have been, except for reading.

I would not have been to some places where I have been, except for reading. I would still be stuck, with who I was on the fateful day of my life in 1966, with no hope at all, if I had not loved reading.

My interest in reading, inspired me to take up a lot of challenges, head-on, more recently, proofreading. As a free-lance proof-reader, I can be paid for reading: proofreading, other people's work, providing a 'third eye,' a critical eye, and attention to detail.

Reading up to now, is still one of my greatest interests. For that reason, I therefore, on several occasions do not charge some of my needy clients for proofreading, especially, if it is academic proofreading like PhD thesis.

My parents, particularly my mother were very proud of my achievement and realisation of my dream to join the army, up to the prestigious rank of Major. In fact, If I had stayed on in the KDF, I was destined for even greater things, to be promoted to the rank of Lt Colonel. I would have succeeded my boss Lt Col S K Mwambire, to become the next Staff Officer One (SO1). In due course, I would also have been promoted to full Colonel, as the Chaplaincy Corps was set to expand.

Being on dole, was therefore a great humiliation. Imagine, from an Officer and a Gentleman, to a pauper on dole. I had decided to 'bite the dust,' 'throw in the towel' and recourse to public funds as a last resort. For a while, I survived on State Benefits. I really appreciated the British welfare system.

As I was on dole, I received unemployment benefits based on my family circumstance, the immemorial time, before the 'Universal Credit,' was ushered in. Payments were based on weekly calculations and paid weekly in cash at the local Post Office. My children were entitled to free school dinners and several financial exemptions.

The dole helped me to put food on the table and clothing for my family. My rent of a bedsitter flat was paid. As we were perceived overcrowded, in the bedsitter flat, for health and safety reasons, I was visited by Cambridge City Council Health and Safety Officer.

After the visit from Cambridge City Council Health and Safety Officer, I was advised to apply for a bigger house, and move out of the student accommodation. Moreover, I was not a student anymore. I got a house with Cambridge Housing Society – social housing. This was a three-bedroom house, spacious enough for my family of three kids then and later my brother Patrick.

I applied for several jobs advertised at the Job Centre, just to be turned down for being overqualified. That was very frustrating. Then I remembered, my long-term interest in education. I also remembered, when I graduated in 1988, the last note and letter in my Faculty of Divinity pigeonhole, was a flyer about Teaching, pedagogy training to be a teacher.

This was a Postgraduate Certificate in Education (PGCE), to teach Religious Education (RE) also known as Religious Studies (RS). This was mandatory in state secondary schools in England and Wales (age 11-18). However, parents could get exemption for their kids, from the subject. I had applied for the PGCE course. De facto, in effect, I was offered a place at the Department of Education, Cambridge University.

As I was returning to Kenya Defence Forces (KDF), I did not take up the offer. Desperate now, I remembered the offer. I contacted the Department of Education. I informed the Department that this time, I was interested in teaching two subjects, rather than a single subject. In that case, I was directed and advised to apply to Homerton College, a constituent college of Cambridge University.

I applied for the course at Homerton College. By the time I applied, the requirements and criteria were now different. Homerton College by then was mainly offering Bachelor of Education (BEd) degree, extinct nowadays, focussing on Primary School Education and teaching. However, it was now also offering PGCE, mainly focused on secondary school teacher training (11- 18 age group). Most of the applicants were not Homerton students. My application was declined.

The reasons why my application was declined did not make sense to me. When I inquired further, I was notified that, I did not meet all the basic requirements and criteria for teaching in secondary schools - state schools in England and Wales. The basic requirements were a degree in a subject taught in state secondary schools in England and Wales. In addition, at least a 'C' and above at GCSE level in Mathematics and English.

I met two of the requirements. I had an academic degree in Theology and Religious Studies, a subject taught in secondary schools in England and Wales. I had a 'C' and above in English Language, London University GCE. However, I did not have Mathematics 'C' and above at GCSE level.

It looked and sounded ridiculous, but that was the reality. Again, me being me, I appealed against and petitioned the decision. Of course, I did not have a certificate, a piece of paper showing I had a 'C' in Mathematics at '0' level. But with my experience and educational pursuits, I had picked up a lot of numeracy skills, well over and above, or even beyond GCSE level.

Among my GCE pursuits, I had pursued, London University GCE Commerce and Economics. They included, involved numeracy and logical Mathematical skills. The only thing I lacked, was documents to that effect or a piece of paper to support and prove that I have a 'C' in Mathematics at GCSE level.

Furthermore, I was a mature student, passionate about education and well over and beyond the time, when that criterion was introduced, set in and 'written in stone.' My petition was acknowledged. I was given an equivalent GCSE mathematics exam promptly. I sat and passed the Special Mature Candidates Mathematics GCSE equivalent exam, well and above grade 'C' level.

There was no more valid reason to deny me a place on the pedagogy opportunity - teaching course and a career in teaching. I was offered a place at Homerton College, again to start the course early, with classroom observation in a primary school around Cambridge. I had never been in a British school or classroom, except for parents' consultations for my kids and taking School Assemblies.

I was awarded a British Government grant, and a supplement loan. I was also awarded an incentive allowance of £700 as a teacher trainee, of a shortage subject of teachers – RE/RS & PSHE, on par with mathematics and science, other staff shortage subjects.

At the end of Summer 1991, I signed off from unemployment statistics at the Job Centre. I was gladly off the dole. I took up my last resort at that time and joined Homerton College, Cambridge University, to train as RE/RS and PSHE Teacher, the subjects I really loved.

My generosity had not ceased. I still had responsibilities for my siblings back in Kenya. I therefore invited my brother Patrick M Shabaya, now a lecture at Strathmore University, Nairobi, to come and pursue BSc degree in Software Engineering, at Anglia Ruskin University, Cambridge. I undertook this single handed, without any fund raising or Harambee.

During my teacher training, I was attached to schools in Cambridgeshire and neighbouring counties. With a family, I could have a car in Cambridge. This became helpful for commuting to far places to my attachment and teaching experience schools.

I was attached to schools such as Hinchingbrooke Secondary School, Impington Village College, Netherhall, St Bede's Ecumenical School, and Swavesey Village College in Cambridgeshire and Thurston Upper School, near Bury St Edmunds, Suffolk County.

While at Homerton, I got a travel grant to research and develop Religious Studies resources and materials. I developed slides focusing on age 11-18 (secondary school) Christianity, Islam, Judaism, Hinduism and Sikhism. I had easy access to these vibrant communities and religions in Kenya, with fixed places of worship and outreach, especially in Nairobi, the Capital city.

In 1992, I had two graduations at Cambridge University in absentia. On 25 January 1992, I was admitted to the Degree of Master of Arts (MA) and on 18th August 1992, I was awarded the Post Graduate Certificate in Education (PGCE).

Prior to that, I had been through one Cambridge University graduation in person. On 25 June 1988, I was admitted to the Degree of Bachelor of Arts (BA). Unlike the grand open-air graduations of Kenyan universities and colleges, Cambridge University graduation ceremony dates to over 800 years ago.

The Cambridge University graduation ceremony is a pomp ceremony. Strictly, for the invited by ticket only guests to witness the actual ceremony. However, Cambridge graduates in gowns are welcome. We assembled at Fitzwilliam College. After initial checks, especially to ensure, we were appropriately attired for the occasion, we were then escorted to the Senate House, guided by The Master, College Fellows and The Praelector.

On a summer day, this is a grand open parade, march and historical procession. It originates from each graduands' college. For me, it started at Fitzwilliam College, downhill from Fitzwilliam College, through the beautiful mature gardens at The Backs, across the river, into Senate House grounds. The Graduation Ceremony congregation itself, is normally small. It is indoors, a small congregation in the tiny, the small and historical Senate House.

As graduands of Fitzwilliam College, we lined up in the order of the seniority of our degrees and alphabetical order in accordance with our surnames. Of course, each college is timetabled to present its candidates, one at a time. We walked to the dais in a group of five, each graduand holding one of the five fingers of the Praelector.

The Praelector presented us to the Vice-Chancellor. Everyone was individually conferred the degree by the Vice-Chancellor. I remember kneeling at the feet of the Vice-Chancellor and the degree was conferred to me in Latin. The deed was done.

When I looked at the English translation of the Latin formula, being a Theologian, I noticed the Trinitarian formula, ... in the name of God, the Father and the Son and the Holy Spirit, was used by the Vice-Chancellor, after saying my name. However, the Trinitarian formula can be omitted at the request of the graduand if she/he so wished.

I vividly still remember my graduation in summer, on 25 June 1988. It was on a gorgeous sunny summer day. It did not rain at all on that day. While it always rains, rains and rains, 'rains cats and dogs' in most cases without any notice, it was a one of the rare moments in UK. There was no rain on that day.

Moreover, it was just after 'summer solstice,' the longest day in the year, in the northern hemisphere, UK included. It occurs between 20 - 23 June. The sun rises incredibly early, by 04:30 (4.30am) in the morning and sets past 21:30 (9.30pm) at night. This is when the tilt of Earth's axis is inclined more towards the sun and directly above the tropic of Cancer.

For some strange reason, I can remember the first person to congratulate me, was a **tramp**, a homeless person. I vividly remember his words, ' young-man be proud of your hard work and achievement.' He stammered, 'it is not easy to get to Cambridge. Well done my boy.'

I wondered how and why on earth he had gotten onto Senate House grounds, but there he was! I also wondered how he knew my struggles and challenges to get where I had reached. I looked at him again, filled with great joy, I just smiled brightly nodded in appreciation and reciprocated: Thank you. I was now a graduate of the University of Cambridge. Back into the real world.

Chapter Thirty-Two: Taxi!

I am not the first minister or the only clergy to be involved in the Transport Industry. There has been at least a Methodist Minister; Jack Burton, who preceded me. He opted to become a full-time bus driver in Norwich City, Norfolk County, UK, as 'ministry with the real people in the community.' He wrote his story in a book called: 'Transport of Delight,' published by SCM, 1976.

What on earth are you doing in a taxi? is a typical question that I encounter almost on daily basis. For some passengers, it emerges after several other questions, already raised and discussed, sometimes, without their full comprehension.

I have no idea, how I present myself, when taxing or cabbing, to generate such many questions. I get, a lot of questions from a lot of my fares – passengers. Some even go further and inquire, is taxing and cabbing your only job?

Some customers even remark, 'you do not look like a typical taxi driver.' I wonder, 'how does a typical taxi driver look like? I have never dared ask my customers this question.

I have just pondered and kept it to myself. This only and often, just lingers in my mind, as a thoughtful reflection and probable response to theirs, lest I offend my clients, whom I depend on.

My immediate response is remarkably, reflected in the prompt answers I give. 'I am in the taxi to meet nice people 'like you.' After a short pause, and a smile, I normally continue, 'I am in a taxi for various reasons: 'It has flexibility, it is my hobby, as such it helps me to maintain and retain my sanity.'

I enjoy reading and writing, I get the opportunity to read and write in between jobs in a taxi, that I would not easily get in another job. To some, I reply, 'I taxi for charity, mainly to raise funds for my charity Room2Excel.'

For the clergy and religious people, I normally reply, I am 'working like the rest of us.' All these and many other reasons, are why on earth I am in a taxi. Bottom line it is by choice, that I am in a taxi, cabbing whenever I can, mostly for charity.

Unlike some clergy, whom I have met at my various stations, who felt the urge and call into priesthood while at school, college, university, etc., then offered for priesthood, I had worked before. I had worked hard jobs. Unlike some priests I had worked like 'the rest of us.'

My training at Limuru, also exposed me extensively, to how the 'the rest of us' work and go about their daily lives, their business and duties. Some theological colleges curriculum lack that encounter with the world, especially, current curriculums.

I encountered the book 'Working Like the Rest of Us, SCM, 1979' by Richard Syms, early on in 1979 while on my persistent theological pursuits. In my Ecclesiastical History, I also read about the Roman Catholic working priests.

This movement was started in France in the 1940s and spread to other parts of Europe. Such Priests, tried to get to the people where they were, in industries, factories and so forth. They experienced the life of the 'working-class' people in factories.

I also encountered 'Working like the rest of us' in the Bible too, epitomised by St Paul's characteristic 'tent making ministry (Acts 18:3-4, 20:33-34).' By the time I got interested in tent making ministry, it was still being debated in Methodism in Kenya and most former Missionary Churches.

However, such ministry was not allowed. Nowadays it is more common in Kenya, especially in the Anglican Church. Most of non-stipendiary clergy are in respectable jobs like teaching.

In retrospect, I am in the taxi, doing what I like. Building on my secular teaching career, I am taxing/cabbing to obviously affirm that my life is not just theology. My life is more than theology.

Moreover, for me, for that matter, the ministry is not just limited to the parish ministry, circuit ministry or purely to the pulpit.

In 1994, while I was teaching in UK, in view of my kids being at a critical stage in their education, I applied to The Methodist Church in Kenya, to allow me to reside abroad. This was for the sake of my children to complete the impending critical stage in their education, while I continue to work as a teacher. It was to be for a limited time.

My request was viewed as disobedience and my application was declined. According to The Methodist Church in Kenya, my failure to return promptly to be stationed in Kenya by January 1996, was disobedience. Accordingly, I therefore deserved summarily dismissal without any benefits.

Surprisingly and shockingly, this became the premise of the end of my ministry in The Methodist Church. I was sacked and fired from the Methodist Church in Kenya in August 1995, confirmed by the Presiding Bishop's letter of April 1996. I was fired and **sacked**, just like that.

The concluding paragraph of the letter that sacked me stated that, 'we continue to pray for you during this difficult time and hope that your call would be strengthened despite this set back,' signed for The Presiding Bishop, Dr Zablon Nthamburi. Indeed, personally, my ministry has been strengthened more and more since then; and grown from strength to strength.

From there on, like John Wesley himself, I felt, and I still feel, 'the whole world is my parish.' The schools where I taught were my parish. Likewise, my taxi is my parish. To the question What on earth are you doing in a taxi? My answer is 'I am, engaged in real education, charity and doing real theology, working with real people.'

In the taxi, I am in the field with people and where the people are, going about their daily lives, their daily business and duties. The taxi like other jobs, is as real as farming or tilling the land.

Doing theology in such an environment, shows that theology should therefore not only be limited to the luxury of lecture rooms, theological colleges, scholarly journals and nice Cathedrals or wonderful church structures.

To my clients and anybody who asks me that type of question, I normally remark. 'do not get me wrong. I love the feel of a serene Cathedral and a nice church atmosphere. I love the church. It is my mother.

But that is not the only, ἐκκλησία *ekklēsia* – '*ecclesia* – an assembly, a congregation of the people. Ecclesia, of course, in Ancient Greece involved buildings. However, I believe, the real *ecclesia* is the people, the people of God, hence the Biblical saying, 'where two or three are gathered in my name, there I am in their middle' (Mat 18:20).

For me, even without exegesis, where there is 'one', there is the *ecclesia*, because there's the encounter, that encounter with the ubiquitous, Omnipresent God, therefore there is the ecclesia there, even with only one with God.

Indeed, corona virus pandemic (COVID-19) lock-down has brought this question to surface. The future of *ecclesia*, the church is bright. I wait to hear stories how the clergy diversified and adjusted to the corona virus COVID-19 lock-down, the ban on congregating for over three months.

It feels different not going to church, citadels, to the mosque, to gurdwaras, synagogues and temples. The church, the ecclesia, the religions of the world that had become complacent, with their places of worship, have to come up with a strategy for the way forward.

I am in the taxi sharing knowledge, and acknowledging, life is 'holistic' not necessarily dichotomised. I am therefore in the taxi ministering. I am serving the people of the World, the people of God. I serve even the atheists and agnostics, the children and people of God.

As such, children may decide to divorce themselves from their parents, however, they cannot cease to be their parents' children. Of course, they have the free will to maintain the relationship or sever the relationship, but the fact remains their DNA belongs to their parents, whatever, wherever and whoever they may be.

For me, anything and everything I do, I do it for God. Once I had the 'strange experience,' I discovered my purpose in life is to serve God through others.

To serve 'others' is ultimately, to serve God. So, I serve God in others. Each one of us in our shared common humanity, must think of and explore his or her own beliefs. Each one of us has a purpose, a destiny and a pursuit.

Through taxi-night, I have met, both 'The Great' and 'small.' I have met people rejoicing, celebrating, and rejoiced and celebrated with them. Being in Cambridge, a university city, I have met people hurting, students on the verge of giving up, being discontinued from their courses, failing their exams, their PhD proposals being rejected. I have helped such students to pick up the pieces and they have carried on to graduation.

I have met people grieving, bereaving for their loved ones, for their beloved pets and empathised with them. Some just longing for someone to pray with. As I happen to be there, in my taxi, at their 'opportune time,' just when they needed prayer most, I have prayed with them and for them.

Through the taxi, I have shaken hands with great people, authors, celebrities and so forth. Through the taxi I met the family of The Great Girl and shook hands with The Great Girl herself, in person and face to face, not once but more than twice: The Girl from Pakistan.

Like me, she has great passion for education, that almost cost her, her own life. I met her family through taxing. I was able to get into her home and talk with her and share our passion for education. I had a few minutes to share with her our passion for Philosophy and Religious Studies, which she was taking for her 'A' levels, in preparation for Oxford University, reservedly not Cambridge University.

The Girl who stood up for Education and was shot by the Taliban, in Pakistan, The Nobel Prize Laureate, imagine, she gave me her book, her own book. Through taxi, I humbly received her autographed book: 'I AM MALALA!' with remarks............

'To John Shabaya,

Thank you for your great work and helping children get education.

You are an inspiration.

Best wishes,

Malala 30 NOVEMBER 2016'

The Cambridge May Ball often has the most and varied clients for taxi drivers. They come from within Cambridge and from far and wide. Some will go to the extent of clogging over a lot of money on the metre, going round in circles to various address within Cambridge, dozing off in between, not recalling their address or house, and so forth.

Simply, May Ball is an overnight grand finale event and celebration. Taxi drivers within and around Cambridge, would rather not miss the 'May Ball nights.' One college at a time, one college per night, clients in their pomp dress and attire, demanding taxis promptly.

Most taxi drivers would wish that the 'May Balls' go on almost forever, Unfortunately, they, just last for about a week, timetabled by the university, well in advance. Each college endeavours to outdo or beat the preceding college, all with final grand fireworks display that lights the skyline of Cambridge.

My classic fare was one lad I picked from a 'May Ball' at about 02:30 hours. We went round and round in circles, he kept directing me to various places that were apparently not his home address. After more than one hour, I gently told him, 'sir, enough is enough, you will have to pay the fare on the metre and disembark or I take you to Cambridge Police Station.'

At this juncture, he remembered his mother. He told me his mother is the only one who can rescue him and direct him home. In a drunkenness tone, he remarked 'please not my girlfriend.' He added, 'I will be in a lot of trouble, in fact 'hot soup,' if you contact my girlfriend at such an hour of the night.

Furthermore, she was supposed to be with me now and she is not! Where is she? Of course, nowhere.' he asked the questions and answered himself.

He then requested me to scroll down his phone for 'Mum' and call his mother late in the night about 03:30, almost in the morning. His phone had no credit, so I called his mother on my cell phone. In shock, the mother picked up the phone.

In a calm and soft tone, I explained to his mother that I am a taxi driver in Cambridge; her son is on board my taxi and has refused to disembark. In addition, he does not want me to take him to the police station to forcefully remove him from my cab. He has the money in cash for the fare. However, he has refused to pay me until he finds his way home. He desperately needs direction home, to his own apartment in Cambridge.

The mother nicely checked her contacts book and gave me the respective address. I safely took the 'gentleman' home. On arrival at his address, he exclaimed in a drunken voice, 'mothers are great! Mothers are the best. See, we can't do without them.'

In a breath of sigh, I remarked, 'indeed!' He stammered, 'thank you Mr. Taxi man.' He continued, 'you are a genuinely nice man, the AA man, the Alpha man.' I thought to myself, 'what a complement? He paid the fare on the metre plus a nice tip for what he reckoned to be 'my patience' and 'my kindness.'

In taxing and cabbing, I have also met various, not necessarily genuinely nice characters, but they have been in the minority. I have met some young and abusive clients, especially when they have had what may be called, 'one too many.' Some call it a 'nice day' or a 'nice night out,' mostly, Friday and Saturday' nights.'

Twice, I have had customers who have declined to pay the fare and run off into the woods, some through the alleys. I have had a few so drunk that could not be bothered to pay their taxi fare or even disembark.

With some, I have ended up taking them to the police station and collected the fare next day from the police station when they had sobered. Some have gone 'scotch free,' without paying the fare,

On two occasions, I have encountered characters who took me to remote places, in the Cambridgeshire Fenlands, farms and bushes, woods, almost in the middle of nowhere. While and when I feared for my life, I have been requested to stop the car immediately, as if they want to be sick, vomit or dash for a short call.

To my surprise and relief, the clients have then run off without paying the fare. Unlike other taxi driver, as my life was spared and left intact, I did not chase after them to pay. Here I am, continuing with the job.

Those are some of the joys and confessions of a Cambridge Taxi Driver; the joys I have personally encountered. Some people would say I have been incredibly lucky!

I have never been robbed or threatened to death, at a knife point, or with a cricket bat in summer, leave a lone at gun point in the cold, dark miserable winter weather. Overall, my taxing and cabbing experience, has been and is still a wonderful experience.

There are a lot of genuinely nice people out there, about and around. A lot of genuinely nice people are sometimes overshadowed by the baddies. But I can affirm that genuinely nice people are still there, left in the world, our Global World, here and now.

The morning Assembly and Parade at Atsinafa Education Centre, Western Kenya.

Chapter Thirty-Three: Not Tired

When I tell my customers, I retired in December 2011, some are incredibly surprised. Some even go further and ask, 'what did retire mean to you?' Others are more concerned with the present and just ask, 'what does retire mean to you now.'

Early on in my life, when I was young, if there was anything that I was afraid of, that I feared and that really scared me, it was retirement. However, nowadays, retiring for me is like standing on a hill, or standing on high grounds, admiring what I see near and yonder.

Retirement is like standing on even a higher mountain, higher than a hill, looking down on the valleys, looking down on the plains of life, those nicely cultivated and those not yet-cultivated, the land of life, life gone, life past, life now and life to come...... Lo! and behold all is well!

When I was young, living in Ishanji Village, in Western Kenya, life expectancy in my village, was between fifty to sixty years old. I used to see my uncles aged between fifty and sixty years old, look so old and really 'ancient'. Most never made it to sixty-five, retirement age in Kenya nowadays. Believe it or not, in my youth, retirement age in Kenya was forty-five.

Encountering the significant experience, the 'strange feeling' in Nairobi Central Park, in the nineteen-sixties, subsequently, changed all that. With that paradigm shift, I changed my outlook to life and even retirement. Of course, my motto became: 'All for God.' Therefore, in retirement, I had something to live for and look forward to.

Then I became a Pastor and a Preacher. Being a pastor and a preacher, the fear of the old age and retirement disappeared. I rubbed shoulders, with both the youth and the elderly. I, thereafter, looked at life differently. As such, I saw and even now, still view life as a gift, indeed a gift, endowed to me by the Ultimate Being – God.

My interest in the and study of other religions, such as Hinduism, Buddhism, Judaism, Islam, Sikhism and African Traditional Religion (ATR), exposed me to a variety of positive attitudes to our shared view to old age. Ecclesiastical History and Christian Thought, throughout the ages, exposed me further to issues concerning old age and retirement.

I read about great Christian men and women. I also read with great interest, about saints, who retired, but 'were not tired' of doing good and carried on working in retirement, regardless of their age. Some never retired, until death.

In my theological quest and personal interest, I read about saints like St Francis of Assisi (circa1181-1226), Mother Teresa of Calcutta (1910-1997), to name but a few, who viewed life differently.

Indeed, Mother Teresa of Calcutta is among those who kept going on. She kept going on with her mission, even in her retirement. She even became greater and more famous, apparently in her retirement, if there was any. She was given Order of Australia 1982 aged 72, Order of Merit (UK) in 1983 aged 73, USA Presidential Medal of Freedom by President Ronald Reagan in 1985 aged 75 and USA honorary citizenship in 1996 aged 86.

So, for me, retirement brings to surface realisation that life is not only about material or just the physical. There is more to life. Life itself is a gift, a gift I have freely received. Indeed, I as *John L Shabaya*, I have received a lot in my life, as my story narrates and celebrates.

For me, therefore, as life is a journey, as such, retirement is part of that journey. Probably, using motoring imagery, retirement is a services area, resting area, a stopover, on my Incredible Journey. Retirement offered and offers me opportunity to reciprocate, what life has bestowed upon me.

Additionally, my retirement has enlightened me that, life does not stop and end with retirement or at retirement. Retirement is therefore an opportunity for me to grow old and age gracefully. In fact, for me, retirement is just another new life, a new beginning.

The Western view generally diminishes and apparently discriminates against the ageing. For me, with my African background, steeped in the African philosophy and culture, 'the older I get, the wiser I become.' In fact, the older I get, 'the more respect I win and get.'

In view of this, I have been able and am able to do a lot in retirement. I have done and I am engaged in a lot of what I have wanted to do, and always wanted to do, but could not do while in full time employment.

In my quest for truth, I encountered and spent a bit of time studying Eschatology. I therefore explored, thought and reflected about the last things, the end. As a pastor and a preacher, I also preached several *hotuba*, sermons particularly during Lent. I preached on the imminent Kingdom of God, the Kingdom of God imminent here and now, here on earth, yet also to come, to come in the life to come, at the end of life and at the end of time.

As an ordained minister, I was also realistic. Retirement, senescent, old age is real and comes by without ringing a bell, without a *'ding, dong, ding, dong'*, hooting, honking, or screaming, 'here I come!' Ageing just comes. It comes gradually, gracefully, yet fast.... Of course, many people, especially the youth, do not like to think about retirement, leave a lone to talk about it.

In view of this, while in Kenya, I contributed to a pension scheme, likewise the church also contributed a certain percentage as well, to the same pension scheme. The money was invested, to help me in my old age. Likewise, while in the military, my pension was catered for, so long as I served the Kenya Defence Forces (KDF), at least for a minimum of ten (10) years of continuous service. That is at least two Short Term Commissions, or more, of five years each.

As I resigned my Short-Term Commission twice, I did not complete my minimum ten-year continuous service requirement. I therefore receive no pension from KDF. I only got Military Gratuity, in 1991, which I used to immigrate with my family to UK. Since I was also fired and sacked from The Methodist Church in Kenya in 1995, I lost my pension and gratuity, including my own contributions, hence an appreciation, why, in vain, I feared and dreaded retirement.

Now I am no longer afraid, scared or even have any tinkling of fear of my retirement. I am on my retirement. Bold, I approach my retirement, without the fear of the here and now or the future a head and the life to come. Henceforth, I am enjoying my retirement.

Chapter Thirty-Four: Atsinafa Education Centre

Having benefited from education, travelled extensively, taught for over nineteen (19) years in UK, I have been very keen to give back to the community. My greatest joy is to be able to help rural children identify, develop their talents and improve their lives through access to quality education. This is what makes me tick.

Since my deceased illiterate mother Atsinafa Muhadia Shabaya spent most of her life in the rural villages, in Western Kenya, my Retirement Project is to focus my efforts on rural kids in Western Kenya. As my mother was instrumental and encouraged me in my educational determination, I am committed to supporting girls to access education as well as boys.

As a young man and mature student, having also benefited a lot from public libraries, I am committed to setting up a Resource Centre too. I believe it will help children and adults, to improve their literacy skills and education.

I also believe and concur with UNESCO that "Education is a prerequisite to national development...... It is an indispensable means of unlocking and protecting human rights, since it provides the environment required for securing good health, liberty, security, economic well-being and participation in social and political activities" (UNESCO, 2003).

Often, I am asked, 'how did it all start?' To reciprocate, generosity I have received in life, for a long period, I had dreamt of setting up an educational project in my retirement. The project that would support disadvantaged children access higher education.

I had hoped to invest in some property in Cambridge, to generate the necessary resources. Unfortunately, when my divorce ensued in 1996, it was impossible to implement this idea. I therefore shelved the project and the idea. I had literally to 'keep my head above the water.' Like me, I did not give up. When I retired, I decided to set up something closer, even without sustainable foreseeable funds: the leap of faith.

Atsinafa Education Centre is a 'dream' come true. I started Atsinafa Education Centre in January 2013, approximately, two years after my retirement from teaching. This is a legacy to my deceased illiterate mother. Hence, I have named the school Atsinafa after my mother's first name.

I kicked off, with scarce resources and nil capital, just with one sterling pound (£1) to start with. This was donated by an un-known elderly lady in my taxi, for what she reckoned as my 'exemplary service' that she had never received before from a taxi driver.

Furthermore, she commended me for an incredibly clean taxi, with classical music in the background. She was also impressed with The Story of My Life. Thereafter, I also got a lot of help and encouragement from my dear friend Judith Wyss, whom I met while I volunteered at Ely Cathedral.

Judy has continued to support Atsinafa Education Centre, tirelessly. In fact, she has made a personal visit and taught Art to the kids, which has enthused and fascinated the kids since her visit.

My wife, then Pamellah Shabaya and other family members, particularly my sister Agnes, joined me, with encouraging informative and instrumental ideas. This encouraged me exceedingly.

Later many friends joined hands to support me particularly, my long-time friends, Edwin Panford-Quainoo and Dr Jeremiah Ngondi. Other friends included Nathan Tama (Information Technology), Mendi Tama, Winfrida Ashiono, Mary Kamuyu, Angela Kamuyu (donations, architectural advice and ideas) and John Raynham (Director, Panther Taxis, donation towards the Staff Room).

Ely Cathedral and St Mary's Church, Ely, also supported and donated to the school through Room2Excel Educational Charity.

I started Room2Excel Educational Charity, to raise funds for the school. This has not been easy. I have encountered a lot of challenges since its inaugural. In fact, several charities have witnessed a big drop in donations over the past years, so, Room2Excel is no exception.

What was the driving force and impetus for such a venture? As usual, I was driven by the 'leap of faith,' passion and commitment to improving children's lives through quality education. One of my daughters, calls it, 'emotional impetus and strategy.' She feels that I am driven by my dreams, emotional strategic planning, rather than realistic, sustainable strategic planning.

For example, she often asks me, 'what would happen, if you suddenly dropped dead? Will the project, the school be sustainable?' I normally jokingly reply, 'I hope I won't just drop dead now, and if I did, so be it now!' Then I normally pause and remark, 'I hope God will give me a few more years to complete setting up the school and leave it standing at least, on its own feet, rather than perpetually relying and depending on me to raise funds for it. I hope, then, it will be able to go on.'

I normally finish by saying, 'However, if it doesn't, and I suddenly drop dead now or later, at least I did my best, I tried.' Hopefully, someone will pick up the pieces, to ensure, the school goes on and my mum's legacy also goes on.

As I write, the school has been progressing one step at a time, one day, one week, one month, one year, a year after a year. In the 2020, the school made a lot of strides, celebrated significant seven years.

I started with a Pre – School, Early Child Development Education (ECDE. This included Nursery education, initially, by the name of JOPA. The Pre-school started, in the Living Room (Lounge) of our Kenya holiday home, by then, in a small semi-permanent house. It had limited space, just enough room to squeeze in and accommodate less than ten (10) children.

Later I moved the school to the adjacent, rather and a little bit spacious maize/corn store, though unacceptable for Health and Safety of the kids. The number rose to thirty (30) children within a month. After three months, the Pre-school had over thirty-four (34) smiling faces of children, eager to learn, and who were a real joy to watch and teach.

In January 2014, in view of the high demand, for the Pre-School (Nursery/Reception ages 3-5), I moved the school from the maize/corn store to the family's incomplete house. I also started a Primary School, Class one to five - ages six to twelve years old, concurrently.

I then changed the name of the school from JOPA to Safina ACK School; incorporating Anglican Church of

Kenya (ACK), to help with management of the school. The school was run by the Board of Management (BOM), while I remained the Director and Sponsor of the school.

On 30th July 2015, in view of my impending divorce, from Pamellah Shabaya, my second wife respectively, The Anglican Church of Kenya (ACK) representatives resigned from the Board of Management. By their resignation from the Board of Management, they withdrew ACK support for Safina ACK School. St Mary's Church, Ely, UK, also withdrew its support.

Instead of closing the school and completely shutting it down, I decided to run the school single handed. I now dedicated the school entirely to my late mother. On 01 August 2016 in honour of my late mother, I changed the acronym. ACK in full, became Atsinafa Centre of Ken (ACK).

I moved the school to a new site, a piece of land given to my wife Everlyne by his father, John Wafula. I dedicated the new Campus to the late Major Wafula, my father-in law, the school's great benefactor. The kids were initially taught under the canopy of trees, while I constructed temporary classrooms.

In October 2017, the school had ten temporary classrooms, an Administrative block of two rooms, one staff quarter/house, store and a kitchen. I confidently changed the name to Atsinafa Education Centre, Major Wafula Campus. It was granted Full Registration by The Ministry of Education. The Kenya National Examinations Council (KNEC), also registered and recognised it as an examination centre.

Atsinafa Education Centre is registered as a private school, although it is a non-profit making school.

Currently, I am the sole Director, supported by my wife Everlyne Shabaya and my son Wickliffe Lisamula. The school uses The Kenya National Curriculum design, currently 8-4-4-system, and started piloting the New Curriculum design 2-6-6-3 from 2018.

Children from Safina Village, the surrounding neighbourhood, with siblings in the school are given priority during admission and registration. The school normally admits children aged between 3 years and 14 years, respectively. However, over 14s are also accepted, especially if they are illiterate.

The school endeavours to help the rural children access quality education within the village, rural environment and its neighbourhood. It also endeavours to help children to avoid circum-navigating, many kilometres to get to school.

Children with various abilities and talents are encouraged to develop and realize their potential, celebrate their achievement and improve their lives. Teachers are continually monitored, encouraged and trained to enhance quality education, encourage child centred learning and differentiated teaching.

At Atsinafa Education Centre, Life Education is viewed as an important and integral part of the curriculum. Therefore, the curriculum is permeated by, Life Skills, Personal, Social and Health Education (PSHE), and Global Dimension Education.

My dream is to set up a Resource Centre. Once established, it will be used by Safina Villagers, children and adults alike, to enhance their education, reduce illiteracy, encourage talent development and improve lives.

The Resource Centre (when established) will provide space (room) conducive for 'fun education.' It will have a laboratory to encourage science and technology, especially investigation and innovative thinking at an early age, rather than waiting until children get to secondary school, to access a laboratory. I missed that.

I envisage and hope to include a reading room in the Resource Centre, with materials for learners to benefit from extended work, extend their learning and research skills. I also hope to have an Arts and Drama, room to nurture artistic talent, a Computer and Information Technology (IT) suite, to enhance IT skills.

I would love to encourage and encompass Extra-Curricular Activities, Clubs, outdoor activities, sports, like athletics, football (soccer) and many others. As land is awfully expensive in the area, this may not happen in the near foreseeable future. I am therefore hoping to explore, an alternative option, that will enhance and encourage children and people in the neighbourhood, to develop sustainable and practical skills like farming, entrepreneurship, sports and so forth.

Overall, Atsinafa Education Centre aims and endeavours to provide the necessary support and facilities, within its means, to enable rural children excel: 'reach for the stars.' The Resource Centre while initially, is mainly for the school, when more funds are available, and it is established, full and running, it should include Community Outreach.

The school depends on my fund-raising efforts. My major source of finance is currently driving a taxi/cab in Cambridge. I also endeavour to raise funds through Room2Excel Charity. However, in the current economic environment, charity fundraising has become exceedingly difficult and almost impossible.

In view of this, I am encouraging parents and guardians to contribute towards fees, meals and uniform of their children. Majority of the parents are very disadvantaged, on meagre incomes from peasant, subsistence farming. Most therefore, cannot afford much.

These payments and any donations or funds I raise and any funds I receive, from friends like Judith Wyss, Aliya Khalid, are used to endow the school with resources, text books, stationary, meals, pay and train teachers to endeavour to provide quality education. These efforts support, equips, empowers, inspires and improves children's lives.

As for meals, the school provides porridge and lunch to the kids. For some kids, that is the only meal they get in a day.

Likewise, as for the operations and internal organizational structure, the school is managed voluntarily by me John L Shabaya. I am the Director, helped by the Manager Mrs. Everlyne M Shabaya, Assistant Manager Wycliffe Lisamula, Administrator, Head Teacher, Deputy Head Teacher, Senior Teacher and the Teachers' Council, Parents Association and the Learners Council.

The name of the village is significant. It connects very well with the mission of the school. The school is in Safina Village, a Kiswahili word, which literally means a vessel, a boat or an ark, to row a cross a flooded river, lake or even the sea, reminiscent of Noah's Ark in the Bible (Gen Chapters 6-9).

The school is therefore symbolically, a vessel. It takes learners safely into deep waters of education, to fish and cross safely to the other better side, improved and healthier. Subsequently, as the learners develop, likewise, later they will contribute significantly to development, both near and yonder,

Therefore, symbolically, Atsinafa Education Centre encapsulates the symbolism of Safina, as a vessel. Therefore, Atsinafa Education Centre rows children across the floods of ignorance and poverty and takes them into deep waters of education that improves their lives and livelihood, now and beyond, into the future.

Atsinafa Education Centre is located and situated off Muliro – Duka Moja Road in Safina Village, Muliro Location, Tongaren Sub-County, Bungoma County. It is nearer Kitale town, on the slopes of Mt Elgon, on the border of Bungoma and Trans-Nzoia Counties, in Western Kenya, almost bordering Uganda.

The school aims to equip children with quality education and life skills that will enable them to identify, develop their talents, improve their lives and contribute significantly to the local community, their country and the world at large.

It was my dream and it is my dream that Atsinafa Education Centre, responds to the dire need for a caring and friendly school, and endeavour to provide quality education. Therefore, the school's purpose is to endeavour to help the rural children access quality education within the village and rural environment. It also attempts to help children to avoid circum-navigating, many kilometres to get to school.

It is also my dream that Atsinafa Education Centre will compare favourably and contribute significantly to providing quality education. With inclusive education, commitment to quality education and Life Education (Life Skills), it will develop to a remarkably high standard of education, to become a beacon, model school and one of the best schools in rural Kenya. Thankfully, that is my dream.

I continue to dream, dream, dream, that one day, the school will be able to support itself, in turn, support more disadvantaged children, orphans, children of deprived single parents, and therefore under-privileged. I hope one day, it will have more funds to help children from poor backgrounds with fees and learning materials. I also believe, having boarding school facilities, will help children from far, orphans and others from difficult or dysfunctional families a great deal.

I believe learner centred learning, embeds knowledge better. However, it requires increased resources, better administration block, including office facilities and space that enhances quality education. I realise that better trained staff, committed and who share the vision of the school, are the key to the implementation of the envisaged vision and provision of quality education.

I am therefore committed to encouraging the entire staff to continue to improve their education and skills. I intend to inspire the staff to embed, share my vision, mission of the school, to become the best and overall be the best. In effect, and as a result, make Atsinafa Education Centre the best. That is my dream for now. When implemented, it will be my dream come true!

I continue to dream of having furniture conducive to quality learning, classrooms design, environment and effective classroom management, conducive to quality learning. I dream, one day, the school will have a superb

Day Care Centre, playground facilities and Resource Centre that enhance learner centred enquiry.

I also dream that one day the Resource Centre, will have library facilities, resources, research facilities, IT Room with computers, printers, sufficient furniture: desks, tables, chairs and cupboards, play equipment and so forth. It is my prayer that there will also be sufficient textbooks, exercise books, children's writing equipment, stationary, conducive to quality learning, teaching and overall education.

The establishment of a Secondary School (age 14-18), will epitomise my dreams. Health and safety issues and requirements like modern kitchen, running water, sufficient sanitary facilities are indeed also my long-term dreams.

I am often asked, 'How can I get involved? The common answer I give is, become a friend of Atsinafa Education Centre, sponsor or educate a child, contribute resources or just volunteer if you can. Help organize talent development activities. If you can just fund raise, as an individual, a community, as a school, or even at your workplace, if you are employed. Just raise what you can, to educate and improve a life of a child at Atsinafa Education Centre or even elsewhere.

Atsinafa Education Centre Mission Statement

Our Motto

Together we can, together we will

Our Vision

We pursue excellence.

Our Mission

We endeavour to improve our lives through education.

Our Philosophy

Education is the key to life. Given quality education, we can all excel.

Our beliefs

Every child matters and should have quality Education.

Our values

We are a caring and friendly school.

Benefits Matrix:

Challenges	Benefits
Long walk to school.	A school in the village/nearby, boarding facilities.
Children have no library/ IT facilities.	Set up library and IT facilities.
Children with no space at home, etc.	Offer space for Extended Work and Clubs
Traumatised/Abused children.	Children to access pastoral care/ quality education
Children, Orphans, etc.	Protected through provision of education and secure environment (Children's Rights).
Under-privileged Children.	Give them access to an inclusive quality education.

leap of faith in the right direction. Atsinafa Education, Centre, Western Kenya, Early Years Class in action, February 2019.

Chapter Thirty-Five: A Pastor and A Preacher

From 1968, all my struggles and pursuits, even educational pursuits, were geared to and would have been branded, 'all for God'. This was epitomised in becoming, being a pastor and a preacher. I have been 'a man of the cloth' for awfully long time. Most men of the cloth never really retire, they never rest or stop until they rest and stop in The Paradise.

Being clergy in the Methodist Church, I have worked in various capacities, diverse places, several locations, and at least in two continents. I have fallen severally and risen again, respectively. I have been elevated, and I have also been humbled and even humiliated.

I have also worked in and with a variety of congregations, both denominationally and in ecumenical contexts. In the varied congregations, I encountered people of multifaceted backgrounds and almost people from all walks of life, except direct contact with the royals.

However, in 1988, I attended a service at Westminster Abbey, London, UK and the Queen was in attendance. It was 250th celebration and commemoration of John Wesley's conversion and subsequent establishment of Methodism. I represented The Methodist Church in Kenya.

I have also preached a lot of homilies, a lot of sermons, especially on a variety of themes and subjects. My favourite themes were faith, hope and love. For me, the most fascinating and the greatest is love. Life is about Love and Love is about life.

Through it all, in my ministry and life, faith gave me hope, and hope gave me love, and love kept me going. Hence, for me, love is the greatest, indeed it is rich in meaning, encompassing fathomless exploration.

Ancient Greek reflects the depth of love, with the variety of the synonyms of the word love. It had several words for love, used accordingly, depending on the context of 'love,' unlike the English, mixed sense of one single word, representing and evoking, enormous different feelings and experiences.

For example, in Ancient Greek, Πράγμά – pragma referred to long standing mature and practical love, pragmatic love. However, I have no idea of the etymology of 'pragma' in computing, computer language and programming, or how it is related to pragma love.

In Ancient Greek Ἔρως - Eros is the sexual, passionate, romantic love, the 'falling madly in love'. Eros is the motivational love. Στοργή – Storge is deep friendship, thoughtful loyalty and the parental love. When referring to brotherly and sisterly love, Ancient Greek used φιλία philia for affectionate brotherly and sisterly love and love between friends. Φιλαυτια was used for love of self, egoistic, conceitedness, love.

My favourite aspect and characteristic of love, the love for everyone, selfless, self-giving, sacrificial love, is άγπη - agape. The Christian Bible, the New Testament uses agape a lot for love of God, and the love for God.

Agape can also be used for the selfless love between couples. It is irrational love, love that loves even enemies. It is love in action. It is the love that does 'most loving thing' to do, sometimes challenging the status quo or even shaking the foundations of the accepted norms. Agape is the most 'loving thing' to give. It is the strategy for acting towards others and for the benefit of others, not just based on our feelings.

So, when I preached about LOVE as the greatest, in English, I had to go to the Greek etymology. I would also compare love in other languages that I know. This helped me to explore and bring out the deep meaning of the word LOVE.

This was my joy, to really endeavour to help my audience to fathom, comprehend and understand the depth and weight of what was conveyed by the word love. I liked engaging the congregation in my sermons, to reduce dozing and snoring especially on a hot or nice warm sunny day.

If I had not studied the extinct, obsolete old Greek language, initially through distance learning at London University and later at Cambridge University, I would have really missed to appreciate the depth of such a word, like love and the depth of many other words and ideas.

Thus, even little things make such a big difference in life and even in homilies, sermons and so forth. With this glimpse I leave you to imagine what my sermons at weddings and St Valentine's Day were like... On several occasions, I have been asked, 'were my sermons hilarious, did they leave the audience in stitches? Of course, sometimes they did...., and sometimes, they left my audience and congregations, asking more perceptive deep ultimate questions. Some were just left in owe and wonder. It just depended on the occasion and place.

Glimpsed so far, my sermons were also exploratory expositions, more teaching, learning about and learning from the respective theme, text, topic and occasion.
 Most of my sermons were based and were inspired by

the Church Calendar or the occasion itself. Some of my sermon ideas came to me by night. Some were inspirations of the sixth sense gift, intuition and vision. Sometimes my sermons just came in my dreams.

Others came to me when I was just idle, relaxing, a sleep or while travelling. I therefore always had a pencil/pen, a notebook or just a piece of paper, at hand, or next to my pillow, when asleep. I would wake up, scribble and jot down ideas that came to me in my sleep, in my bed, or else, the ideas disappeared and evaporated by morning.

For I had learned from the Israelites experience, with manna in the wilderness, the desert experience. The manna was supposed to be collected and used by the 'use by date.' The manna went bad if not used by the same, 'best used by date.'

If hogged, the manna went bad next day. Likewise, my ideas and inspiration, if not jotted down, would evaporate and disappear into the oblivion, the following day or even later in the same night or day, never to be remembered. I also discovered; best ideas came when I was relaxed. I, therefore, developed a habit of keeping a pencil and a notebook with me nearby, most of the time. May be in this digital era, I will have to 'change tack.'

Some of my sermons came from the media, daily newspapers, my experiences, other people's experiences and voices. Likewise, some came from my passion for studies, observations, and so forth. My sermons emerged from anything and almost everything, around me, beyond and everywhere. Sometimes, and on most occasions, I just felt like I was an instrument of God, for God, in God hands, to be used by God.

Most of my homilies were from, daily, weekly, monthly and over a long period, or just periodical reflections.

Some emerged from my journeys, extensive travel and exposure. Sometimes, I would spend hours days and weeks on sermon preparation, write out, edit my sermon. When I am just about to step in the pulpit, to deliver it, an inner voice, would override me.

In such circumstances or situation, I would put aside the long well-prepared sermon and script, then just speak verbatim, impromptu, like most Quakers and charismatics preachers. I would surrender, and let the spirit take over and guide me.

Surprisingly, I got very encouraging feedbacks on my sermons. Sometimes I just preached loudly to myself as I preached to the audience. At the end of the service, someone would come to me and say, 'that sermon was just for me,' I would also sincerely remark, 'same to me.'

Some would narrate how the sermon reflected their experiences. Others would especially reflect on where the sermon just touched most, helped them to respond to a need, struggle, dilemma, a 'thorn in the flesh.' In this context, unlike the 'better than thou' approach, the 'the thorn in the flesh,' the struggle that was just mine, was indeed a shared human experience.

In most cases I used to audio record most of my sermons, especially impromptu sermons, hoping to literally grieve over them later, and review for next time. Believe me, I always hoped there will always be a next time, for myself and the congregations to reflect, to improve.

Some sermons were a great inspiration, reflection, showing that amid my challenges, amid my ups and downs, the Ultimate Being – God was there... and indeed life is worth living and celebrating.

I loved preaching and using symbols. Indeed symbols, especially based on the calendar of the year, both religious and secular, have fathomless deep meanings. I remember I once had to preach at a Retirement Service. Being a young minister, it was exceedingly difficult to prepare the sermon, but I had to.

The Christian calendar helped on this occasion. I compared retirement to Advent, a season and time set aside for preparation and reflection for Christians. It is a time set aside for reflection on faith and final destiny, shared by all, young and old alike. It is also a time of great expectation and the joy of anticipated New Birth, the coming Christmas celebration.

In the context of retirement, positively, the expectation is 'one foot in the grave.' It is also the inevitable, impending end. The **END,** that is also the beginning of new life, in the future, life to come. Retirement is thus, having plenty of time, to look back retrospectively, a reflection on life, vital and constant for our shared and final destiny.

I have also used Lent – *Saum* (*Saumu*), to preach at an Inauguration Services of Youth and Young People's Club. I contrasted Youth and Young Life with Lent, another season in the Christian calendar. Lent is time of reflection and repentance, reflecting on the sacrificial love of God - ἀγάπη – the *agape* love. It is also a time to think about our life, temptations, trials and tribulations, uphill and down hills of life.

As the explosive nature of human life is epitomised in the youth and youthful life, so likewise, Lent does help, Lent helps people to reflect on the explosive joys, sometimes, turned upside down, and inside out. Lent is therefore about trials, temptations, and tribulations, particularly those which brings people down, the falling and rising again of human life and the human destiny.

Comparatively, Lent is helpful. It reminds the youth and even the elderly with what they can and what they should endeavour to do when still young and when they get to retirement. Lent reminds me that Life should be celebrated, especially when we are young.

We should rejoice over and over, even more so, as we await the final that we are heading towards and really coming over us and will come. Like the Easter celebrations that finally come for Christians and *idd ul fitr* finally comes for Muslims, after the holy month of Ramadan, likewise there is the END. Life is therefore a celebration and a foretaste of life to come.

For sure, as a matter of fact, I am who I am, because I endeavoured to be an educated Pastor, Preacher, a Minister of Religion, Priest and a Padre. I believe I am, and I have been ONE of them! I Pursued excellence and endeavoured to give the best I could.

Chapter Thirty-Six: Lost and Found

The writing of my story was delayed for over a year. Mainly, it was because I lost my precious vital records, for writing the story of my Incredible Journey. Gone were my diaries, in which I had meticulous entered a lot of detailed information, daily, weekly, monthly, annually, including events and entries, preserved and kept over many years.

Regrettably, the audio recorded conversations, speeches and sermons, even the digital word processed ones, that I had also kept for many years were not destroyed accidentally by fire, but were lost, when my laptop crushed, beyond repair, while in Kenya. Moreover, pen drives and portable back up hard disks with the vital and necessary information, were just stolen, not borrowed.

To make the matter worse, back in UK, I also lost hard copies that I was transferring digitally, daily in between taxi fares, while waiting for customers. Finally, on the same day, I embarked on endeavouring to continue to write my story, I also lost the drafts.

My car was and has been my office for an exceptionally long time. In view of this, for many years, I have been incredibly careful with my car and my valuable contents. Since I was that careful, I stopped contents insurance. Moreover, contents insurance, could not replace some of my valuables. For example, if I lost, items particularly, those closer to my heart, those of tender value, and more so, of sentimental attachment, would insurance replace such? No, not at all.

I never, ever left anything precious in my car. I always carried my valuables with me, whenever I left the car. In addition, over the years, Cambridgeshire Police had sent messages, warning taxi drivers, not to leave valuables in their cars, especially their earnings in cash. The message also warned that even when vehicles are locked, thieves have devices like metal detectors to detect valuables hidden or left in vehicles.

Even though I had been incredibly careful over the years, one night, while preparing to travel to Kenya, I went to collect a parcel from a friend, to be specific, my friend's mother's medication. I was supposed to take this precious medication with me to Kenya, to my friend's mother in the village in Western Kenya. It was in a place considered to be safe. The friend beckoned me for a meal. After a day's shift, running into the late Winter's night, I was very hungry, as hungry as a horse.

Like a vulture, diving on a chick or hare, I just dived into the warm house. I forgot I had left everything I was carrying on me on the front passenger seat of my car, including the laptop, bags, several valuables and my weekly earnings, to be banked the following day. This is the day and the week, I had forgotten to adhere to the adage, 'Never put all your eggs in one basket.'

The day I just forgot to take my valuables with me, out of my car, while visiting a friend, my car was broken into, the passenger side window was smashed. When I came back to the car, I was met and welcomed with pieces of glass all over. For a moment, I was dumbstruck. I just screamed and wailed. I was in total shock.

I lost almost everything and anything I really valued; name it, it was gone; bank cards, library cards, etc. I even lost hard copies of diary entries that I had kept for many years. The burglar, the opportunist thief, must have celebrated his or her luck, whatever gender? I never like remembering it, or even thinking about it.

My apparent ignorance and carelessness were his or her blessing. My loss was his or her find, I really do not know and could not tell, whether the thief was female or male, and I cared less for his or her respective gender. I reported the matter to the Cambridgeshire Police. All I wanted, to hear, was my lost dear personal effects, would be found. That was a few years ago, and nothing was ever found. I therefore lost my dear personal effects. The Police just recorded the report and my statement. That was it.

I was devastated to the verge of breaking down. Apart from feeling being violated, I regretted and bitterly blamed myself for such sheer carelessness. I lost some items, with invaluable sentimental value and attachment, especially my documents. I remembered and really appreciated my late dear mother's oral traditional mnemonics.

How I wished, at least she had imparted on me in some ways, some of her handy, oral traditional mnemonics. Thus, at least, whatever I had in the form of documents and recordings, would not have been lost forever. Like an *Hafizi*, a preserver, especially by memory, I would have memorised my important writings and regurgitated, recollected and recalled my stories one day, one by one, as necessary, from my precious memory and subsequent writing of my story.

Later, if necessary, I would scribble my story, I would write it, to share with generations to come. Such an exercise would not have been that difficult, or so daunting, as it has been. Nevertheless, I had lost what was so dear to me and too close to my heart. For an exceedingly long time, I grieved and mourned, as if I had lost a loved one, a dear one, gone forever.

This experience brought to surface and reminded me my growing and becoming senior in age. As I have grown older, I have lost so much en route my Incredible Journey and the pilgrimage of my life, through life. Some of what I have lost, I will never ever find again.

As a result, I have learnt to carry on regardless. I have learnt to explore and discover new options, new friends, new alternatives and new opportunities. In that case, and for that matter, whatever I have lost, likewise, I have found. I have often found what I lost, not necessarily an exact or replica replacement, but in most cases, an even better replacement. Indeed, life is all about that, losing and finding, indeed, 'Lost and Found.'

Two of my friends one from the United States of American and the other one from Fiji, in the Pacific Ocean, really encouraged and comforted me. The American One, bless her heart, told me, whenever she loses her documents, she has no choice but to sit down and write another one. She often and always feels and finds that, the one she later writes, is always much better than the one she lost earlier. In fact, accordingly, it supersedes the lost one.

The other one from Fiji said, 'when something is stolen from me, or lost, I always try never to mourn, never to 'spend sleepless' nights over the loss or even suffer over it.' He said, it is like 'weeping over spilt milk.' He reiterated, 'in fact, I often, if not, always find, receive, get, or buy something even much better, than what I had lost.' Having an Engineering and Mathematics background, he elaborated with equations: 'Lost equals to found, lost plus found equals to Lost and Found.'

Indeed recently, when clearing my shed, after thirteen years, I stumbled upon and found some precious documents, photographs, that I thought I had lost forever. I also stumbled onto some sermons, especially, one I preached on Christmas Eve 24 December 1995, St George's Church, Chesterton, Cambridge, where The Most Rev Dr Rowan D Williams, was a Curate 1980-1983.

In October 2016, I went to my General Practitioner's (GP) surgery, I went to my doctor for a normal regular, the usual visits, and routine check-up. To my surprise, I was diagnosed with Type 2 diabetes. For a few days I felt lost. In fact, I thought the doctor had made a big mistake. Further tests were conducted, nothing changed, it was confirmed, I am diabetic.

The GP recommended and immediately put me on more regular visits to the clinic. At least, I am reviewed every six months, the diabetes reviews. The reviews include regular blood tests, blood pressure check-ups and annual diabetes eye screening, that examines the back of my eyes for diabetic retinopathy. The doctor also prescribed life long and life changing oral medication, tablets to be taken twice daily, with meals, 'till death do us part.' I lost the old John, I found a new John, living with diabetes!

I have come to realise, in life, sometimes the things we worry so much about are not real threats as such. In fact, a lot of what we often worry about never materialise, they never happen in accordance with our worries. What we thought we had lost, is found elsewhere, or like a seed, it probably falls on apparent fertile ground and grows into a better plant, better life.

Chapter Thirty-Seven: Where I Have Been

Wherever I have been, places I have been to, that still linger in my mind, archived in my subconscious, have inspired me a great deal. Likewise, the congregations I served and preached to, have also left indelible marks on me and on my life. Geographically, mentally, emotionally and spiritually, I have been all over.

While in Kenya, I had opportunities, to work with different ethnic groups and tribes, especially the Masai. While on voluntary work experience, with Presbyterian Church of East Africa (PCEA), I worked at Ong'ata Rongai, Kiserian, Olorgesaillie and Lake Magadi (Salt Lake), in the great Rift Valley, now in Kajiado County, Kenya.

At Olorgesaillie, there is a significant archaeological site, the Masai pre-historic site, rich with fossils of the Masai ancient existence and culture. This area is the home of several ancient remains of the earliest Masai tools, and significant archaeological discoveries by The Leakey family.

The places I have been to all over Kenya, left a mark on my life. I went to the coast region, along the Indian Ocean. My visits and encounters there, culminated in visits to places like Mombasa, Kilifi, Malindi, Kwale, Tana River Counties, covering most of the former Coast Province.

Indeed, the expanse, massive and vast Kenyan Indian Ocean coastline is a beautiful coastline, with white sand beaches, and blue clear warm ocean. Doted along the Kenyan side of the Indian coast are varied cultures. Thus, the coast is a real holiday paradise.

The coastal Kenya has interacted globally, for what I personally call time immemorial. Some of these interactions, go back to as early as seventh (7th) century. Be it Asians, Arabs, Chinese and Europeans, the Portuguese, Spaniards (Spanish), Germans, Italians, British, they have all set a foot on the Kenyan coastline. Most, endeavouring to trade or to conquer it or just enjoy the holiday of a lifetime.

In fact, places I have been to in Kenya, taught me a lot. Kenya is a vast country, approximately, over twice the size of Great Britain (GB), with contrasting beautiful scenery. It has the beautiful coastline, dotted with beautiful beaches and whispering palm trees, cashew-nuts, baobab trees, etc. Up on the high grounds, the highlands, the scenery changes and the temperature too changes. The higher you go the cooler it become, epitomised by Mt Kenya right on the Great Equator, Latitude 0°.

Most of the Game Reserves and National Parks are upcountry, with great wildlife and safari. I have been fortunate to have been on Safari and visited a few, such as Tsavo, Amboseli, Meru and Nairobi. Almost in the middle of Kenya, there is the Great Rift Valley home of the great Masai Mara, renowned for its breath-taking safaris and wildlife, particularly the seasonal migration of the wilder-beasts.

There are also a lot of lakes in the Rift Valley. I have visited Lakes: Naivasha, Elementaita, Nakuru, and Baringo. They all have wonderful wildlife, including lions, flamingo birds and other wonderful species.

In the plains, there is the Lake Victoria, the freshwater lake shared by three East African countries: Kenya, Uganda and Tanzania, the source of River Nile, lifeline of Egypt. Kenya has also the vast semi-arid North and North Eastern Areas. Such places still linger in my psyche.

Whenever I walk 'down the memory lane,' I am cheered up, fired up to go on. Recently, my memory was triggered, by one of my friends. I was reminded of some of my congregations and places where I have been. I recollected how each of the congregation I served, received me so well, that I was constantly humbled by their generosity.

I am indebted and incredibly grateful. Of course, the respective congregations were varied in attendance and membership. For example, in Meru, I worked mainly among and within the agricultural community of subsistence farmers. Therefore, my sermons, examples, anecdotes and illustrations, were hence varied.

My speeches, messages, sermons, examples and illustrations; were principally based, on the respective congregation, members background, my extended reading and exposure. Most of the places where I have been, have been so special to me and remained so, impacting my ministry and my entire life.

In fact, to ameliorate my sermons and messages, in the villages and rural settings, I used a lot of oral traditional stories, significant in African informal education and culture. Most of African cultures and traditions, relied heavily on oral tradition and teaching. A lot of teaching was and is through stories.

In urban and town churches or environment, I adjusted and used, down to earth illustrations, with urban connotations and implications. Wherever, I went, wherever I was, I adjusted to the environment, accordingly.

While in Nairobi, I was involved in broadcasting some Religious Programmes, on the Voice Kenya (VoK), now Kenya Broadcasting Corporation (KBC), a National

Television and Radio Broadcasting Network. Later in UK, I also had more opportunities to reach many, through BBC World Service, particularly the radio broadcast, especially beamed to East Africa.

Eventually, my mother could often hear the voice of her son, the apparent 1966 'failure' and the 'foolish John,' beamed from far and yonder, in the days before digital communication and mobile communication.

I also attended several International Conferences in Nairobi, for example World Council of Churches Conference (1975), Methodist World Council Conference (1986). In Nairobi, I also exchanged pulpits, not only with Lavington United Church, but other denominations, especially, the Anglican and Presbyterian Churches. Likewise, building on my guitar playing hobby, I formed a singing group of five (6) lads, known as 'The Fountains.'

The Fountains comprised mainly of the slum boys, except two. Four of us were from Gatina and Kawangware areas, respectively. We were from different tribes and denominations, an ecumenical group: Myself, Luhya (I had lived in Gatina), Jimmy Kariuki, Kikuyu (Gatina), Simba Mboroge, Kisii (Kawangware), Bernard Ovukuluku, Luhya (East lands) and George Omondi, Luo (East-lands).

With the Fountains, I initially focused on the youth and schools' outreach, around Nairobi and the surrounding suburbs. Later, as the demand increased, I extended the outreach. We started reaching out to schools and youth meetings, conferences, far and beyond Nairobi, including Youth Camps all over Kenya, particularly during the holidays or school vacations.

The Fountains and outreach missions were well received and had significant impact on young people and among the youth. With my military duties, extensive travels and responsibilities that ensued, I surrendered my leadership and active participation in The Fountains. I let The Fountains go on and flourish without me. In addition, I eventually left Kenya for further studies at Cambridge.

While at Cambridge, in view of my background, I was privileged to participate and contribute to various courses, organised by The Federation of Cambridge Theological Colleges. I also presided at various Eucharist Services, etc.

I regularly took a lot of Sunday Services in the rural Circuits and villages in places like Attleborough and Wyndham, Norfolk, Aylesbury, Buckinghamshire and the surrounding churches in Bedfordshire, Cambridgeshire, Hertfordshire, London, Norfolk, Suffolk, etc. That was my voluntary itinerant ministry and preaching in England.

I believe I contributed significantly, especially, helping some of the rural congregations encounter an African at a closer range, in fact, face to face. I helped demystify some of the rather negative and distorted media images of Africa, and Kenya in particular.

For example, some of the rural areas, particularly and predominantly white, Sunday School kids, had the opportunity to touch me and feel that I was really a human being, and black people are indeed humans. Some kids even wondered and innocently asked me, 'why have you fallen, rolled and dipped (immersed) yourself in the dirty mud? Why didn't you wash before coming to church?'

Smiling I would reply, 'it is the colour of my skin. It is just a permanent suntan; it cannot be washed off. I got it, I inherited and just got it from my parents, great, great and very great grandad and grandma. That is how you got your skin too.

I come from Africa, the land of plenty of sunshine, the land where sunshine, is twelve hours every day throughout the year.' I reiterated, I am an African, I am a Kenyan, that is how I got the colour of my skin.' I therefore had wonderful opportunities to explain and teach a lot.... I shared a lot of African stories with a lot of moral teaching, related to the Christian Bible and faith.

When I lost my ministerial connexion with The Methodist Church in Kenya, in 1996, I found other places and opportunities to serve. I was requested to offer chaplaincy services to the diaspora people. As I was one of them, especially those from East Africa and the neighbouring countries, I grabbed the opportunity.

This led to another request of being appointed Pastor-in-Charge of an Ecumenical Swahili Service Congregation in London. This was under the auspices of The Lutheran Church in Great Britain (LCiGB), at St Anne's Lutheran Church, near St Paul's Cathedral, London, now moved elsewhere.

For sometimes, while I was a teacher, I gave up the ordained ministry and preaching. For that short period, I worshipped at St George's Church, Chesterton, Cambridge, where I thought, nobody would know me. Moreover, it was Church of England, leaning more towards the High Anglican, with Sung Eucharist and colourful vestments. 'A nice place to hide, mingle and remain incognito,' I thought.

Surprisingly, within no time, and within just a short period, the vicar spotted me. For unknown reason, she reckoned that I elegantly stood out like a beautiful giraffe. She approached me and said I feel, like you are an 'extraordinary member,' she continued, you look more like new to this parish.' I could no longer hide, I could no longer run, from whatever I was hiding and running from.

While I reflected on her remarks, she then asked me, 'are you resident in UK, in this parish?' Without hesitation, I answered, 'yes, I am'. That seemed to have ignited further interrogation, 'Can you lead a Bible Study Group, in your house? I thought and said to myself again, 'oh dear God, my hiding place is now completely gone, no more hiding, I can no longer run, I can no longer hide.'

While I was still contemplating about my blown off camouflage, the Vicar continued, 'I am short of one house group for the Lent Bible Study Group, I would appreciate, if you can lead one. Looking at you, I think you can manage.'

The Lent Passages include stories, such as the story of Jonah. Giggling and jokingly, she said, 'of course Jonah, is close to your name, perhaps etymologically, your namesake, or closer to it.'

Laughing, she remarked, 'I didn't do much Hebrew. I came in through the back door, 'female ordination.' I was among the first female priests to be ordained in the Church of England.' She continued, 'and my son is a Church Army Captain, an Evangelist.' As most Vicars and priests, she had a genuinely nice sense of humour.

The mention of the Jonah story touched me to the core. It was one of my childhood memorable stories. I recalled Ivonda School Sunday School and my mother's Indigenous Church Sunday School. All the two, taught me the story of Jonah, from a child's perspective.

Accordingly, Jonah was sent by His Father (God) on an errand to Nineveh but declined to go on His father's errand. His endeavour to run away, escape from his Father, and the appointed mission never materialised.

Subsequently, Jonah ended up in the belly of a big fish, a whale for that matter. As a child I just loved the story of Jonah and the whale, especially the way mum used to narrate it for me. Being illiterate, it was from her memory, yet almost, verbatim, word for word. She could draw from it several moral teachings for me.

'I will give you a booklet to help you, with weekly notes,' she said, trying to entice me and twist my arm into taking the challenge, that nobody was willing to snap. I was incredibly surprised and dumbfounded.

I had hoped to worship at St George's incognito, but now here I am! I have been found out, and singled out, among many. I could not hide any more. My camouflage was gone. I was exposed, I had to surrender, more so, it was church work, God's work.

I took the challenge and I took the 'plunge. It was 'back to the drawing table.' I agreed, without 'letting the cat out of the bag.' We had wonderful sessions. I was able to draw on my studies, especially, the New Testament Greek, to explore the New Testament passages at hand with my group. I had very encouraging feedbacks, in fact excellent feedbacks, from the Group.

At the end of the Lent Session and Season, the Group made an excellent presentation. Finally, the group bequeathed me a marble like gift. Simple but exceedingly valuable. I have used it in teaching and managing difficult groups in my teaching career. Wherever I used it, it worked magic. Using it has been and was always a worthy risk to take.

Through looking at it, then respectfully touching it, most of my learners, developed, appreciated the significance of taking turns and a respect and value for others. It helped the learners reflect, especially what other people value most, including respecting others' beliefs and what they themselves particularly, value most, believe, and hold dear to their hearts.

The Bourne Road, Cambridge, Lent Group, felt that I can make a good priest, pastor and preacher. Members of the group secretly approached the vicar and encouraged the Vicar to talk to me about possibilities of ministerial opportunity, in the Church of England.

The vicar did not hesitate to approach me. She just did that, just to discover, I was a Methodist Minister. However, I politely told her that, I had been removed from The Kenyan Methodist Church Full Connexion. In ordinary language, I had been fired, sacked, and I was hiding and taking refuge in her congregation, her church.

This did not deter her. She boldly approached me again, requesting to in co-operate me in her parish. As she was a vicar of action, like 'The Vicar of Dibley' sitcom, she wrote to the Diocesan Bishop, seeking dispensation. To my surprise, the Bishop was Prof Stephen Sykes, who had been my professor.

Prof Sykes taught me Contemporary Christian Thought i.e. Contemporary Theology. He had been a Lecturer and Regius Professor of Divinity, Cambridge University. The bishop gave me the necessary dispensation. Soon, I was back in the ministry, highly active again, with particularly good feedbacks.

Later, in view of my 'exemplar' contribution, I was recommended to Canon John Beer, Archdeacon of Huntingdon and Fellow of Fitzwilliam College, Cambridge

University, for ministerial conversion course, from Methodism, to Anglicanism (Church of England). I was enrolled on the East Anglian Ministerial Formation, in preparation for ordination in the Church of England.

In contrast, during my Ministerial Formation training, I was attached to St John's Church, Waterbeach, Cambridge. Having worked with Engineers Brigade in Kenya, I loved it to bits. It had some chaplaincy work to the Engineers Army Base and Barracks, at Waterbeach, which has now been closed and turned into a private housing.

With my extensive background, I had exemption that gave me significant edge, credits towards the course. This reduced my duration on the course. I therefore took just one year of the distance learning course and I was ready for ordination as Non-stipendiary Priest.

A few weeks to my ordination, my marriage to Margaret Mebo, was just about to collapse. It had broken down irretrievably. In view of the impending divorce, the Bishop declined to ordain me. I lost my imminent ordination. It was a double loss. I lost my marriage of over seventeen years and imminent ordination into the Church of England. Therefore, I never eventually became a priest in the Church of England. However, later in my life, I was ordained in the Anglican Church of Kenya (ACK), Katakwa Diocese.

While at Cambridge, in 1986, I visited Israel and Egypt. I went on a six weeks course at St George's College Jerusalem. I was sponsored by Fitzwilliam College and Cambridge University Travel Grants. I was impressed to meet my Summer Greek, Hebrew Languages and Old Testament lecturer in Jerusalem. He was a visiting scholar and lecturer at the College.

I visited various significant Biblical, geographical, historical and archaeological sites, including a trip across the Negev desert and Sinai Peninsula and wilderness. I had a glimpse of Lebanon, Syria and Jordan, especially the almost drying River Jordan, the Sea of Galilee, Dead Sea, Samaria, Nazareth and the Red Sea.

To my surprise, the Red Sea was not red as such. Moreover, it was a fantastic, beautiful clear blue water sea and gorgeous sandy beach. Unlike the Red Sea, the Dead Sea was slimy and dead. Surprisingly, I sat on the Dead Sea and I just floated; I did not sink.

I was mesmerised, to encounter The Great Rift Valley, whose features just made me feel at home. The visit to Old Jerusalem, particularly, the Western Wall, the Wailing Wall, Al Aqsa Mosque, brought home, a lot of mixed feelings. I just stood there in owe and wonder, after walking through a lot of old water tunnels underneath.

The visit to Bethlehem broke my heart even more. This was at the height of the bitter confrontations between Israel and the Palestinians, led by the late Yasar Arafat. It reminded and brought back to me a flash back feeling of the Mau Mau and British conflict, in my childhood.

St Catherine's Coptic Church Monastery visit, in the Sinai Peninsula, with Eucharist at Sunrise on the summit of Mt Sinai, two thousand, two hundred and eighty-five metres high (2,285 m), was just awesome and an amazing, indescribable experience. It is a pity I lost my diaries and daily detailed entries of the owe some experience. Overall, the whole trip was just very impressive, amazing and awe-inspiring!

When I returned to KDF, I was privileged and honoured to visit many places. My visit to USA East Coast in 1990 stands out. I had some leadership training and visited a lot of military academies and barracks from Fort Brag North Carolina, through Virginia, West Virginia, Annapolis, Naval College and Base, Maryland and The Capital, Washington, DC.

The visit to The Pentagon, The Capital Hill and Whitehouse, Washington DC, was the pinnacle of the trip. It culminated with an honourable, International Officers Prayer and Breakfast. This was in the presence of three Commander in Chiefs: President George Bush Senior, USA, President Hussain Muhammad Ershad, Bangladesh and President Daniel Arap Moi, Kenya.

In military terms, the experience of being in the same room and hall, saluting, mingling with and subsequently, shaking hands with Four Star Generals, from all over the world, and Commander in Chiefs, was just gobsmacking and indeed awesome.

I looked at myself, several times in the mirror, I asked myself, am I the boy nicknamed 'Foolish John?' I actually wondered and asked myself again, 'am the boy the apparent 1966 'failure,' from the Mud-hut of Ishanji Village? I was just thunder-stuck!

Two days later, I checked out of The Hilton five-star hotel. I was on the road again to Senior Officers Military Academy, Carlisle, Pennsylvania, visiting several military bases through Delaware, New Jersey, West Point elite US Military Academy, New York, Connecticut, up to the Naval Base in Rhode Island.

I had several lay-by days and stopovers at various military bases: Army, Navy, Air-force and Coast Guards, in each of these respective states. I immersed myself in leadership training at the various military institutions and services.

In New York, I could not help, but visit a few civilian areas of my interest. I could not exit New York City without a visit to the port, Twin Towers, Manhattan, China Town, the United Nations Headquarters and the Statue of Liberty. Those were some of the places that I had read about in my pursuits and interests. They were in my dreams, to visit in my lifetime.

I was privileged, to share, to serve and minister to God's people of all sorts and varied backgrounds. As a pastor, I always had mixed feelings: Feelings of being privileged, at the same time, feelings of being humbled.

I always felt honoured to experience and share in God's blessings to His people, and with His people, especially in significant events and turning points in people's lives and pilgrimage. These included, events like dedications, baptisms (christenings), confirmations, weddings, marriages, and other great celebrations. I was favoured to preside and partake in Eucharist, Holy Communion, fellowships, pastoral duties, visits, and even difficult times in people's lives, such as great loss, sorrow, death and bereavement.

On the other hand, I have always been humbled. I have often asked myself: Who am I to be blessed this much?' Furthermore, 'Who am I, to serve and minister to God's people?' Moreover, the minister and ministry carry, overwhelming weight.

For me, this was symbolised, by the weight of the hands, laid on my head, during my ordination at Kaaga, Meru County, Kenya, as a Methodist Minister, and later, at Amagoro, Busia County, Western Kenya, as an Anglican Priest in Katakwa Diocese. This has left a significant, overwhelming impact and an indelible mark on my life.

Chapter Thirty-Eight: Different Paths, Separate Ways

The question of using different ways and even separate ways whenever necessary, to get where you really want to get, has always baffled me, and yet it works. In most cases, as it is often not an easy walk or even easy to explore the most worthwhile, among the many routes to be explored. The most appropriate is only realised and confirmed retrospectively.

Regrettably, not by death, but just by geographical separation, in 1997, I lost my long-term best friend Stephen Ambani, without whom, I would not be who I am. I met Stephen at Chamakanga Primary School, Vihiga County. Stephen Ambani later took me in, when I had hit the rock bottom in Gatina Slum, Nairobi. I wore his moccasins, as a 'shamba boy in Nairobi.'

Later, I followed into Stephen's footsteps, at Lavington United Church, as a Caretaker. For me, Stephen was a friend indeed, even when in need, Stephen was there as a friend indeed. We often went through a lot together, we went through 'thick and thin,' together, so they say. Sometimes, we sometimes followed different paths. At other times, we followed and walked the same paths. Nevertheless, our paths often eventually crossed, and even crisscrossed each other.

In 1969, Stephen opted for an Evangelist route, and ended up at Church Army in East Africa Training College. Conversely, in 1970, I opted for the ordination route in The Methodist Church in Kenya. For a while, we went different and separate ways. Once again, as we went different ways, our paths did not cross for some time.

We met again many years later, to be specific, 1983 in the Kenya Defence Forces (KDF). By then, Stephen, as usual, had preceded me. He had joined KDF. By this time, he was a KDF Senior Sergeant stationed at Embakasi Garrison, Nairobi.

As a Church Army evangelist, my friend was commonly known as *Mwalimu*, teacher, Catechist, while by then, I was a Chaplain, a Padre, a Lieutenant, soon to rise to the rank of a Captain and later Major. It was disheartening for me to be regularly saluted by my friend Stephen.

Stephen was in the Other Ranks, in the Service Personnel, while I was an officer, in the Officers Corps, a Commissioned Officer. In the military, Other Ranks, including Non-Commissioned Officers (NCO), salute commissioned officers like my friend properly did. That is the military, the junior salutes or greets the senior first and the senior reciprocates.

However, my friend was a Senior Non-commissioned Officer. Other lower ranks just freeze for Senior NCOs as a sign of respect. Stephen was the man who built me, jerked me up, who made me to be who I was and I am. He gave room to excel, he gave me space, room for me to excel. Here he was in the military with me but viewed as my junior.

Stephen had always led, and I had always followed. I always followed the leader (Stephen), and his leadership. Now as a Senior Sergeant, he was supposed to follow my leadership. Tables had been turned around, in fact, one would say, upside down. That is that, that is how it is in the military. That is how it was with us, when our paths crossed again.

I vowed to myself, to do whatever it takes, and whatever I could within my means, to help my friend and other potential able NCOs to acquire relevant qualifications, necessary for subsequent commission as Chaplains and become officers. I knew Stephen very well; I knew him so well. I knew his capability and potential. I knew he was able and capable.

With my effort, Chaplaincy recruitment policies were reviewed. Soon, Stephen was shortlisted, to be recommended for this new adventure. But due to confidentiality, I could not divulge the 'strictly confidential' information, to him, about the forthcoming reviews and subsequent changes. I could not even share about his forthcoming, subsequent commission It was still confidential, furthermore, it was supposed to be a nice surprise.

One day, I heard Stephen was intending to leave the KDF. I, thereafter, immediately summoned him to my office. I begged Stephen to stay put in the KDF, even just for a few days, but he declined.

Stephen asked me, 'Afande, Sir, is it an order?' Stephen had exceptionally good sense of humour. With Stephen, you never knew when he was serious or just being funny, joking as usual. We had wonderful times together before the military service and in the military. We had wonderful jokes. Some of the jokes could 'crack our ribs,' with great laughter and even if there were any audience, they would be mesmerised.

There were times that we would giggle, laugh until we cried, shed literal serious 'tears of joy.' Whenever we met, we had a lot to reminiscent on and about. We could talk and laugh, talk and laugh until, suddenly it was sunrise. No sleep, no winking of the eye until morning, planned or unplanned. But this time, I felt that Stephen was serious.

As Stephen's questioned, I investigated, tried to read his lips, his face, and seriousness was written all over his face. He appeared to be in deep thought. Likewise, I therefore also reciprocated in accordance with the atmosphere of the time and place.

I genuinely replied, 'no, of course not, it is not an order *Mwalimu*.' He replied, 'thank you Sir, therefore, I am leaving the military soon. With a beaming face, as if doubtfully joking, with a smile on his face, he added, 'that is if all goes well and to plan.' Of course, he was not sure, if KDF will be willing to release him promptly. We all laughed.

Senior Sergeant Stephen Ambani had made up his mind. I had known Stephen to be decisive. Once he makes up his mind, and decide, he could not be easily convinced or swayed. He had to see it through. Therefore, Senior Sergeant Stephen Ambani, left KDF sooner than me, to be ordained an Anglican Priest by the late Bishop Kipsang Muge, Bishop of Eldoret Diocese, Uasin Gishu County, Kenya.

When I was about to complete my studies at Cambridge University, our paths met again. This time, our paths crossed each other's way, not in KDF, nor Kenya, but in UK. Stephen had come for a short course at St John's College, Nottingham, UK without his family. I encouraged him and assured him that it was possible to fund raise and bring at least his dear wife, to share the same experience and exposure, lest they become strangers, when he returns to Kenya.

Leaving in the flat plains of Cambridgeshire, I loved Wales. I loved the sound of its distinctive aspirate language, quite different from English and closer to my local Luhya language. I loved the scenic hills and the valleys of Wales.

I therefore recommended and encouraged Stephen to venture into University of Wales. Henceforth, I not only recommended, but I encouraged Stephen to pursue further studies in the University of Wales, at Lampeter, a beautiful scenic place, in the heartland of Wales. I knew Stephen had the potential. I believed and I was convinced that with his determination, Stephen could make it.

Without any hesitation, and as a man of action, I started fundraising for and with my friend in his newfound venture and adventure. We both used to joke that we thrived and thrive in crisis. Here we were not afraid of challenges, especially challenging environs.

To kick-start and jump-start his fundraising, I donated £20 towards the fund-raising efforts. A big sacrifice for me then, but not enough in view of what Stephen had done for me in the past. I could not ever repay him.

To cut the long story short, Stephen managed to raise funds, not only for his wife to join him, but his entire family of three sons and one daughter to come over to Wales. After completion of his degree course at Lampeter, Stephen returned to Eldoret, Kenya. He worked as The Diocesan Administrative Secretary and later as The Provost, St Mathews Pro-Cathedral, Eldoret. A gain our paths did not cross for a while. Thus, Stephen's story had a nice moral good ending

I personally knew, Bishop Muge, even before he was consecrated Bishop. No sooner had Stephen settled back in, Kenya, Bishop Muge sadly, died mysteriously in a road accident while traveling from Busia in Western Kenya to his Eldoret Diocese.

My dear friend, Rev Ambani, had no option, but to step in and take his demised Bishop's mantle. Like his deceased predecessor and Bishop, The Rev Stephen Ambani, was outspoken and critical of the Moi's regime. Furthermore, he did not spare the echelon of the church either, especially, the complacency of the church then.

Later, I heard Rev Ambani was fired and sacked by the Anglican Church of Kenya (ACK). He left Kenya and settled in Wales. He later became a curate and subsequently a Vicar in The Church in Wales, under the Bishopric of Dr Rowan Williams, before he became the Archbishop of Canterbury. Stephen has remained in Wales, until his retirement due to ill-health and settled in Wales. While Stephen has been in Wales, I in England, our paths have crossed again several times and have continued to cross since then, and whenever possible.

More so, our paths crossed again at Hengrave Hall, Suffolk, UK, at the wedding of my daughter Sagina, whose middle name, literally means, sweet oranges, and was my friend Stephen's mother's name. That shows how close we were. Even our children are remarkably close friends too.

Through my daughter's wedding on 4 June 2016, I eventually found Stephen, my dear friend, the friend I had lost.

To want something so badly and get it,

To look for something so dearly and find it,

Is the greatest achievement.

It is the greatest and superlative joy,

It is the most significant and greatest gratification.

Chapter Thirty-Nine: The End

My Life is a story of determination and hope against all odds. The story of my life affirms that determination and hope works! Shaped by the events of time, my background and subsequent varied experiences over the years, I am who I am now, because of where I came from, where I grew up, how I grew up, where I have been and finally what I have encountered. My life is a story built not only by myself, but by others, with others and even for others.

My story has inevitably and invariably been a result of encountering and counteracting a lot of events, fear, failure, obstacles and challenges. It is a story about falling and rising again, failing and subsequently succeeding later. It is a story of dreaming big dreams; turning impossibilities into possibilities; turning problems into opportunities; turning fear into great courage; apparent death, into new life and new beginnings.

Amidst all the challenges encountered in my life so far, in retrospect, I have constantly received support, encouragement by and from family, friends, several people, including charitable organisations, the church, other religious organisations and even secular organisations; above all abundant blessings and providence from the Ultimate Being - God.

I have heard voices of failure. Likewise, I have also heard voices of encouragement, from both verbal and the written word. Unexpectedly, I have heard voices even through and by actions of others. I have also heard voices of success, especially later in life.

I have grown to love learning, reading and listening, especially hearing others' voices. In fact, as I am mainly a self-made, self-taught student, in many ways, a self-educated person, I believe it is through hearing others' voices, reading others' stories, that one can transform one's own life.

> My story is therefore a voice for others to hear. It is an open story for others to read. It is a story for others to learn from, especially from my failures and be encouraged, be assured and overall be comforted.

For some, and even for me personally, my story is a reality check. It is more of a realisation for others, that in all the challenges and successes of life, you are not alone! It is a legacy for my grandchildren, even my great grandchildren. It is a story for generations to come.

It is also a legacy to generations of children of the universe, wherever they have been and wherever they may be. Undoubtedly, as a matter of fact, it is indeed a story for everyone, young and old alike, to read and to hear voices of hope.

This is a story about a life lived day by day; in most cases, a life being lived, not knowing how the next day will unfold, and not knowing what the next day will offer or usher in. It is a life lived one day at a time: seizing the καιρος – *kairos*, the moment or opportune time in ancient Greek.

In many ways, and on many occasions, close friends have commended that my life has so far been lived to the full. It has been lived with 'great expectations. It has been lived with a resolve and a resolute to press on regardless.

I have endeavoured to press on, no matter what; seizing the opportune moment, *KAIPON ΓNΩØI (kairon gnothi)*, know your opportunity.

This is another ancient Greek word, emphasising the great idea of knowing your opportunity. In other words, an endeavour to know the opportunity, the treasure coated, coded and hidden near you or in the horizon, then acting on the opportunity and grabbing the opportunity.

On several occasions, I am often asked, "What have you learnt from your life or existence so far?" The story of my life endeavours to answer this question. Undoubtedly, I have learnt so much. I have learnt to press on, meander through the winding plains and contours of the highlands of life. Retrospectively, I can confidently say that my faith gives me the impetus to go on, the encouragement to press on, regardless and no matter what.

I have also learnt to navigate my life towards my destiny and an inward contentment of life, a midst daily challenges and intermittent glimpses of hope. I have learnt there is no need to fear. I, therefore, view challenges or problems as opportunities. In fact, I always endeavour to turn each challenge I encounter, into an opportunity, rather than just sit there and mourn over the respective problem.

With good reading skills beyond basic literacy skills, I have been able to read into situations and see faces of hope and faces of opportunity. I have been able to rise. I have been able to 'rise and shine!' Therefore, we can all 'rise and shine' again and again.

I have seized the moment; I have seized the 'opportune moments, the opportunity' at hand. We can therefore all seize the *kairos* – the 'opportune time'. I have explored possibilities. I have identified opportunities of how to make sure, my dreams come true. I have turned my dreams and ambitions into reality.

Thus, my Incredible Journey has helped me to develop the ability to discern opportunities, to decide when to listen and when to speak; when to wait and when to act; when to be patient and when to be in haste; when to move and act promptly, and when to be still, wait and just be silent.

I have also made many, many mistakes, a long this Incredible Journey. Sometimes, I have made real blunders. There have been times when I have listened to myself, listened to my own voice so much, and shunned hearing others' voices, especially God's voice. At other times, I have listened to others voices and ignored God's voice and even ignored my own inner voice.

All these have impacted me greatly, with a variety of consequences, outcomes and ramifications. All in all, thank God I have had opportunities to learn from. I have had opportunities to hear my own inner voice and to hear others' voices. I have learnt, the secret to success is learning from your own mistakes, over and over and learning from others' mistakes as well.

As I have made a lot of mistakes and a lot of blunders in my life, I have therefore learned a lot more. As I continue, and go on walking on the path of learning, I am also proceeding forth and continuing to learn a great deal. Mistakes and blunders I have made, have become signposts to greater adventures, greater opportunities, higher and bigger dreams.

All said and done, it was not by might, but by God's grace that I am, who I am. Without God's graciousness, all my efforts and determination would have been but all in vain.

In the beginning was the λογος - *logos*, the word (God) and God is, will be there at the END.

More things you might like

If you enjoyed this, you might also like:

Being a poet, being an Archbishop, being human, Rowan Williams, writer, poet, theologian

Into war games, into community, into the army, Christophe Finnegan, retired Army Corporal

Time for the world to learn from Africa, Ruth Finnegan, anthropologist

The story of a life, Helen Keller, writer

Questions for discussion, reflection or action

Does this account have any relevance for your own life? Or that of any of your friends or acquaintances? If so, what?

Do you think the pictures add anything to the account? Or illustrations generally? If so, what? (do you, or would you like to, add illustrations to any of your own writing? if so why or how?)

Does it matter? Or, put another way, do you think the reader will learn anything deep from this account? What}

Would you recommend this book to others? Why or why not?

The author says he has made 'mistakes' in his life. What were they, in your opinion and did they matter? Did he also make non-mistakes? Which were more important in the end?

Have *you* made mistakes? How much do they matter?

What most surprised you in this account?

HEARING OTHERS' VOICES

A series for general readers, and especially for idealistic young adults, edited by anthropologist Ruth Finnegan and physicist Roh-Suan Tung,

https://www.balestier.com/category/hearing-others-voices/

The series logo was designed by Rob Janoff, creator of the famous Apple logo

Published 2018-20

(available from lulu.com online bookshop, Barnes and Noble, and/or amazon)

Taking a bite from the apple, Rob Janoff, creator of the Apple logo

Time for the world to learn from Africa, Ruth Finnegan FBA, anthropologist

Voices from the Christian west, Arthur Hawes, theologian, Emeritus Archdeacon

From blank canvas to garment: a creative journey of discovery, Marella Campagna, fashion designer

Listen world! Evelyn Glennie, the world's premier solo percussionist

Native American knowledge systems, Clara Sue Kidsell, historian of science

Façonner la parole en Afrique de l'Ouest / Voices of West Africa, Cecile Luguy, Africanist

For peace: Voices of protest and aspiration, an anthology, edited by Ruth Finnegan, anthropologist

Decisions, decisions, decisions, with compassion and love: voice from the headteacher's study, Neil James, headteacher

Being a poet, being an Archbishop, being human, Rowan Williams FBA, writer, poet, theologian

Hunter-gatherers: something to learn, Alan Barnard FBA, anthropologist

Grass Miracle from the earth, David Campbell Callender, naturalist

Einstein's theory of relativity, simple guide by an expert, H.A.Lorentz, close colleague of Einstein's

Our amazing world, seen by a scientist, a thinker, an Astronomer Royal, Martin Rees, FRS, cosmologist

Mind how you go: mind, body or spirit? Arthur Hawes, theologian and mental health worker

An *artist-priest: is it possible?* Rev Ernesto Lozada Uzuriaga, painter and church minster

A refugee, a doctor, a singer - and a Lieutenant Colonel, Thao Nguyen, General Practitioner

Being a pastry cook, a restaurant owner, an immigrant, and more, Stefan Rinke, chef

From youth offender to tattoo'd charity worker, educator and visionary, David Tissington, volunteer

The hidden ordinary, and the extraordinary in it, Ruth Finnegan, anthropologist

The horse in history, an amazing adventure, Basil Tozer, historian

Shucking capers, Small stories from a big island, Maria Teresa Agozzino

"Listen to this": the astounding ups and downs of quotation marks, Ruth Finnegan, writer

How do we know it's really true? Philosophy might help, Bertrand Russell, philosopher

Will we survive? The transantarctic expedition of 1914-17, Ernest Shackleton, explorer

The story of a life, Helen Keller, writer

Meet the Sun, Ruth Finnegan and Claudio Vita-Finzi, heliogeologist

Life's journey cartographic meanderings, John Hunt, cartographer

Into war games, into community, into the army, Christophe Finnegan, retired Army Corporal

Coming soon

Your amazing body, Ani Vardanian. physiotherapist

Time for the world to learn from China, Yunxia Wu, anthropologist

Being a street kid, being a street watcher, being there, Marcus Hurcombe, Youth worker

Hear the universe begin, Roh-Suan Tung, physicist

Being a software engineer and its magic! Ian Trimnell, engineer

Storms, their amazing life, Tom Schofield, sea captain

Get your teeth into it. Dentistry through my eyes, Jesal Pankhania, dentist

Being on the inside as an outsider: or doing thinking about thinking doing, Raymond Apthorpe, anthropologist

Gypsy voices, edited by Judith Okely, anthropologist

Administrating, Master-Minding and such, a fun life, Ken Edmond, administrator

Donkeys, wonders of the humblest, David Campbell Callender, naturalist

Join us!

https://m.facebook.com/HearingOthers?_rdr

Welcome from us all, specially the series editors Ruth and Roh.

We look forward to your ideas and questions and arguments and (seriously!) criticisms and challenges. It would be specially interesting for your colleagues across the world to have your (honest) reactions to any of the discussion questions.

Photos and videos too, images, and links to lots of music and poetry and thoughts please, your own and others'. The series, after all, is 'Hearing Others' Voices' - yours very much included - so that's what it's all about.

Printed in Great Britain
by Amazon